MARK WAID PETE WOODS

ARCHIE

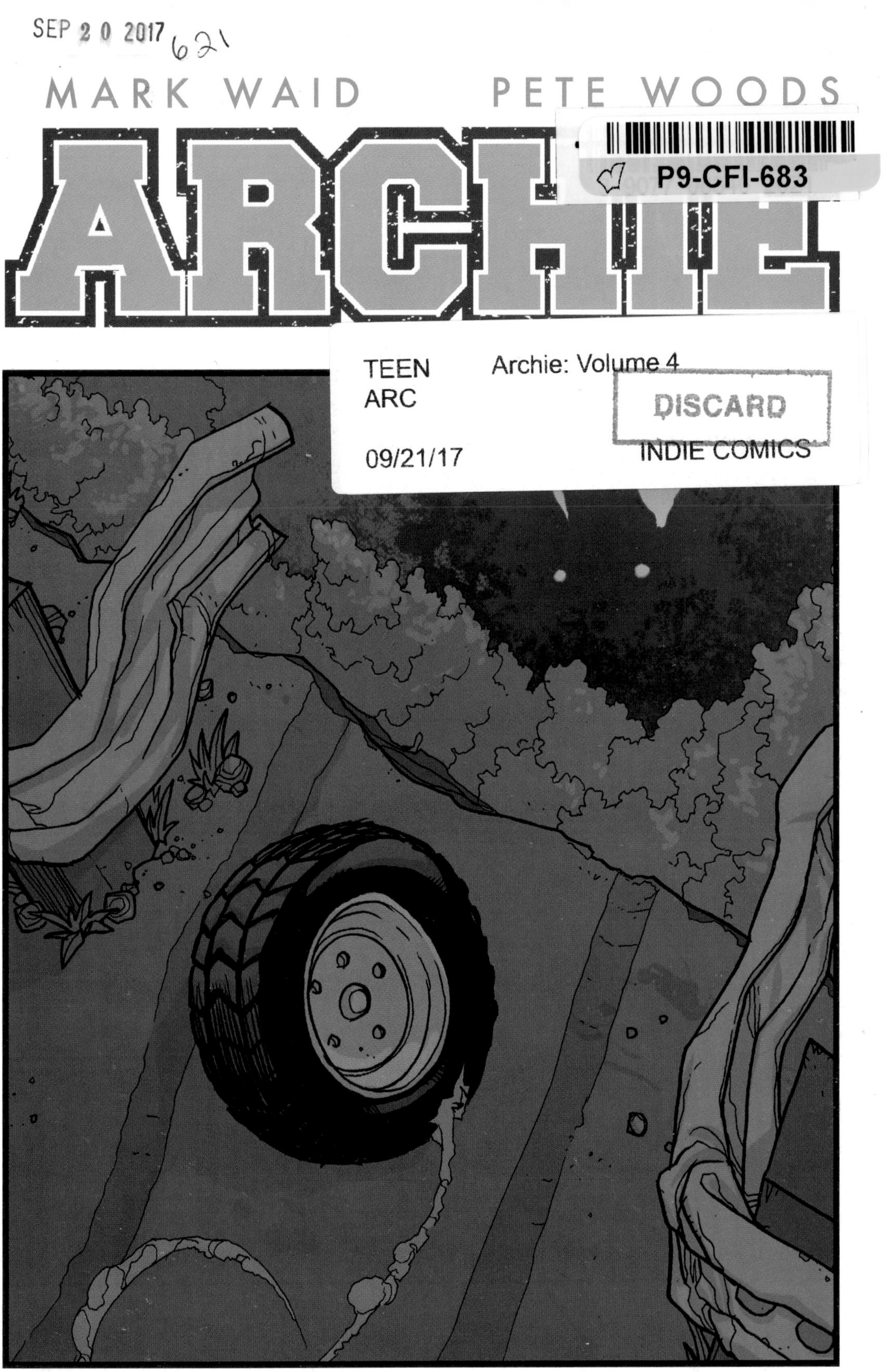

OVER THE EDGE

STORY BY
MARK WAID

ART BY
PETE WOODS

LETTERING BY
JACK MORELLI

COVER ART BY
ROBERT HACK

EDITORS
MIKE PELLERITO &
VINCENT LOVALLO

ASSOCIATE EDITOR
STEPHEN OSWALD

ASSISTANT EDITOR
JAMIE LEE ROTANTE

EDITOR-IN-CHIEF
VICTOR GORELICK

GRAPHIC DESIGN BY
KARI McLACHLAN

PUBLISHER
JON GOLDWATER

EVERYTHING CHANGES

ARCHIE®

by MIKE PELLERITO

This volume of *Archie* contains some of the most pivotal and ground-breaking stories that have appeared in this comic so far. As you have seen in The CW *Riverdale* TV series, the characters are versatile, strong-willed, likable and enthralling—and the same can be said for the cast and stories that appear in our comics.

When it comes to passion, intrigue and emotion—*Archie Vol. 4* has it all. Veronica returns from her exile in a far-off place and the separation puts her and Archie's relationship to the test—and that's only the start. A newly-kindled romance blooms between Dilton and Betty (that also foreshadows a crucial moment for Riverdale's perennial sweetheart), the Blossoms' backstory becomes even more complex and shrouded in secrecy, and, finally, a feud that's been 75 years in the making comes to a head—Archie Andrews and Reggie Mantle face off in an emotionally-packed story that shows how even the most petty, ego-based battles can end with the people who don't deserve it getting hurt the most.

When we discussed the idea for this story arc, we knew Mark Waid's brilliant writing would be able to craft a tale that perfectly balances humor and tragedy, from a hilarious scene featuring a group of waiters plotting Archie's demise to an ending that would make even the hardest of hearts cry. Couple that with Pete Woods' artistic ability to convey the wide range of emotions displayed in this story and you've got something that's bound to stick with readers forever. And man, does Pete draw great cars!

It's obvious by the end of this volume how important these characters are to each other and to the readers. And, as we approach the next story line for Archie and his friends, it will also be clear who the heart of Riverdale really is.

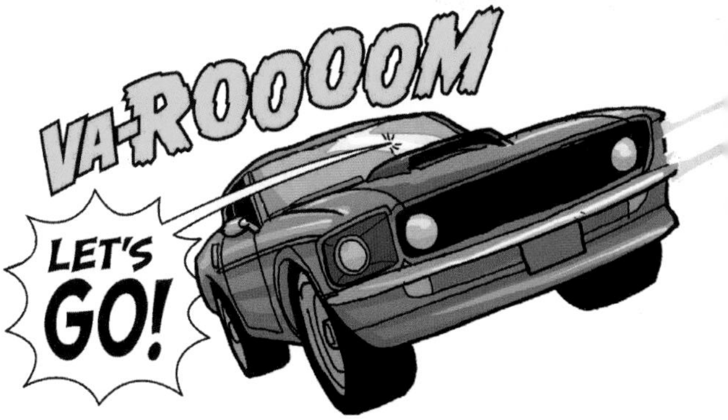
VA-ROOOOOM
LET'S GO!

ISSUE EIGHTEEN

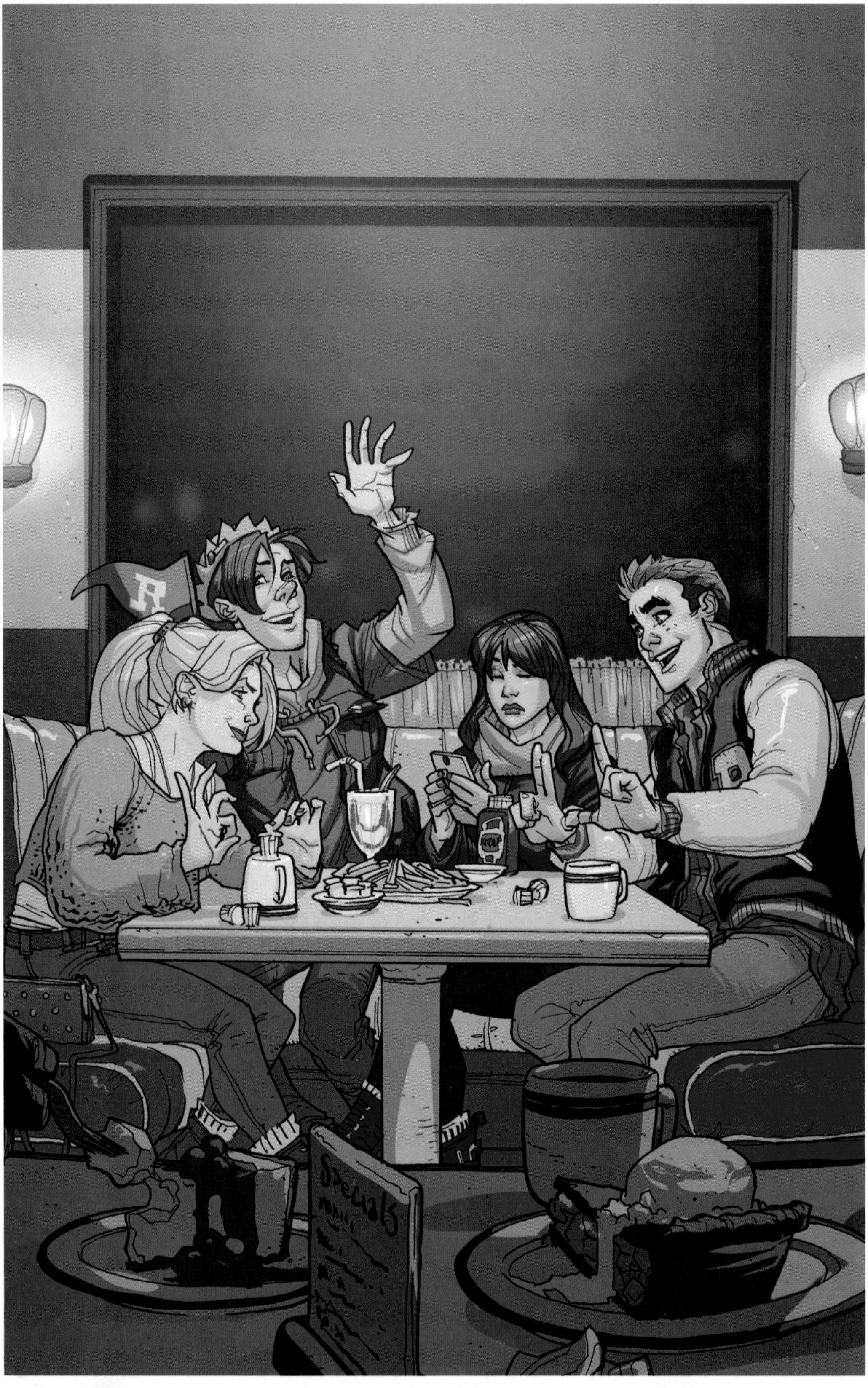
Specials

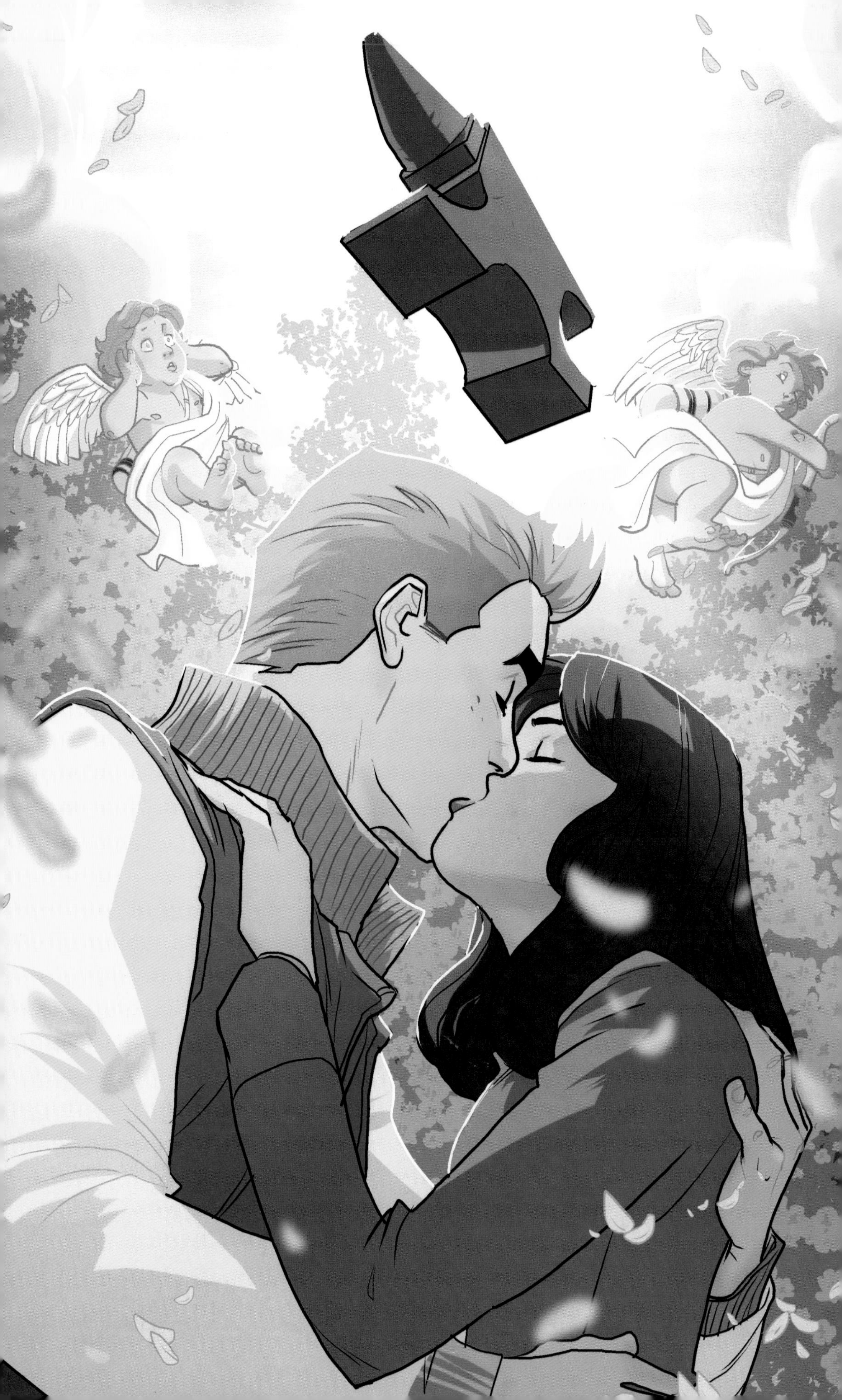

CHAPTER ONE: NO REASON

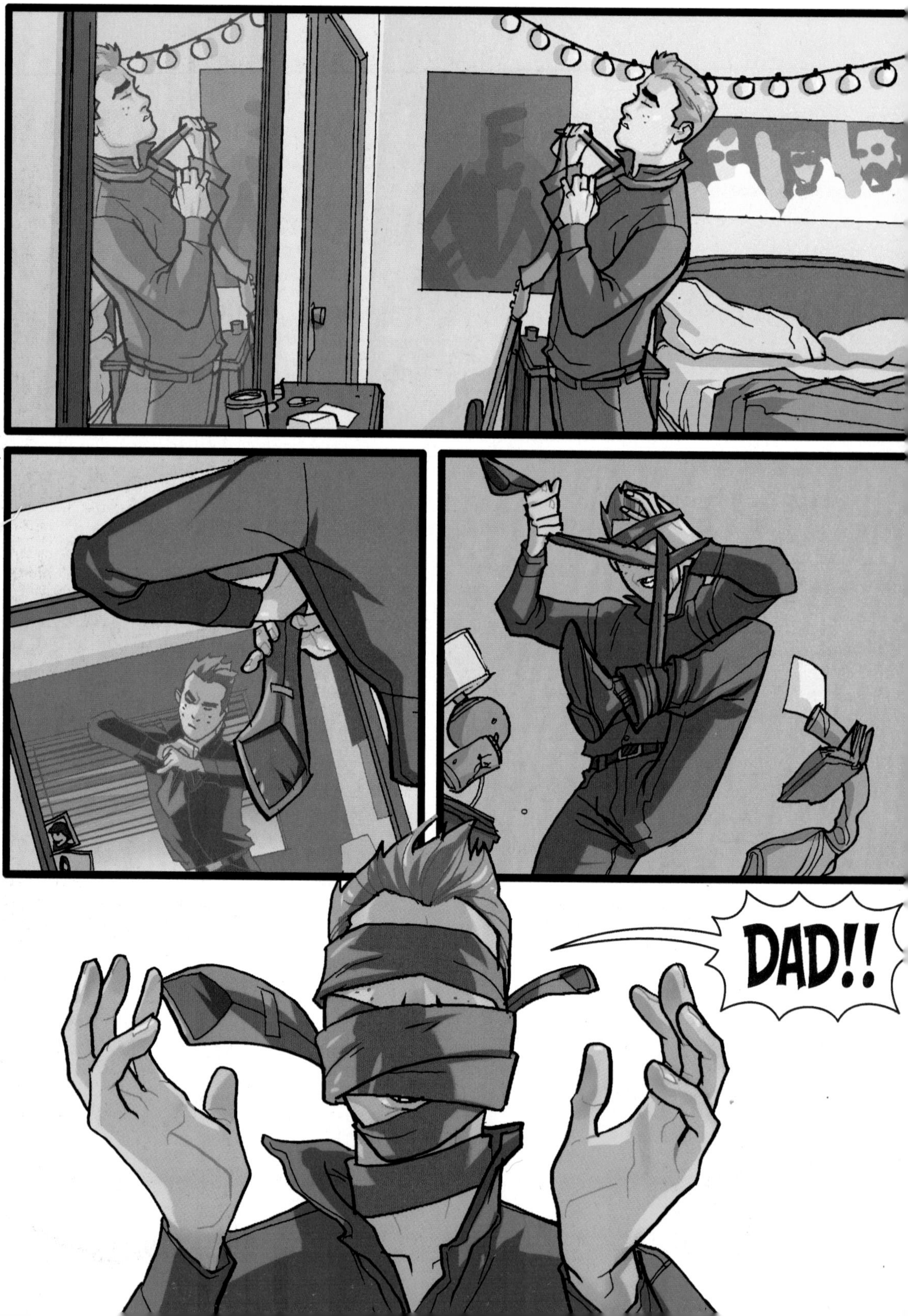
DAD!!

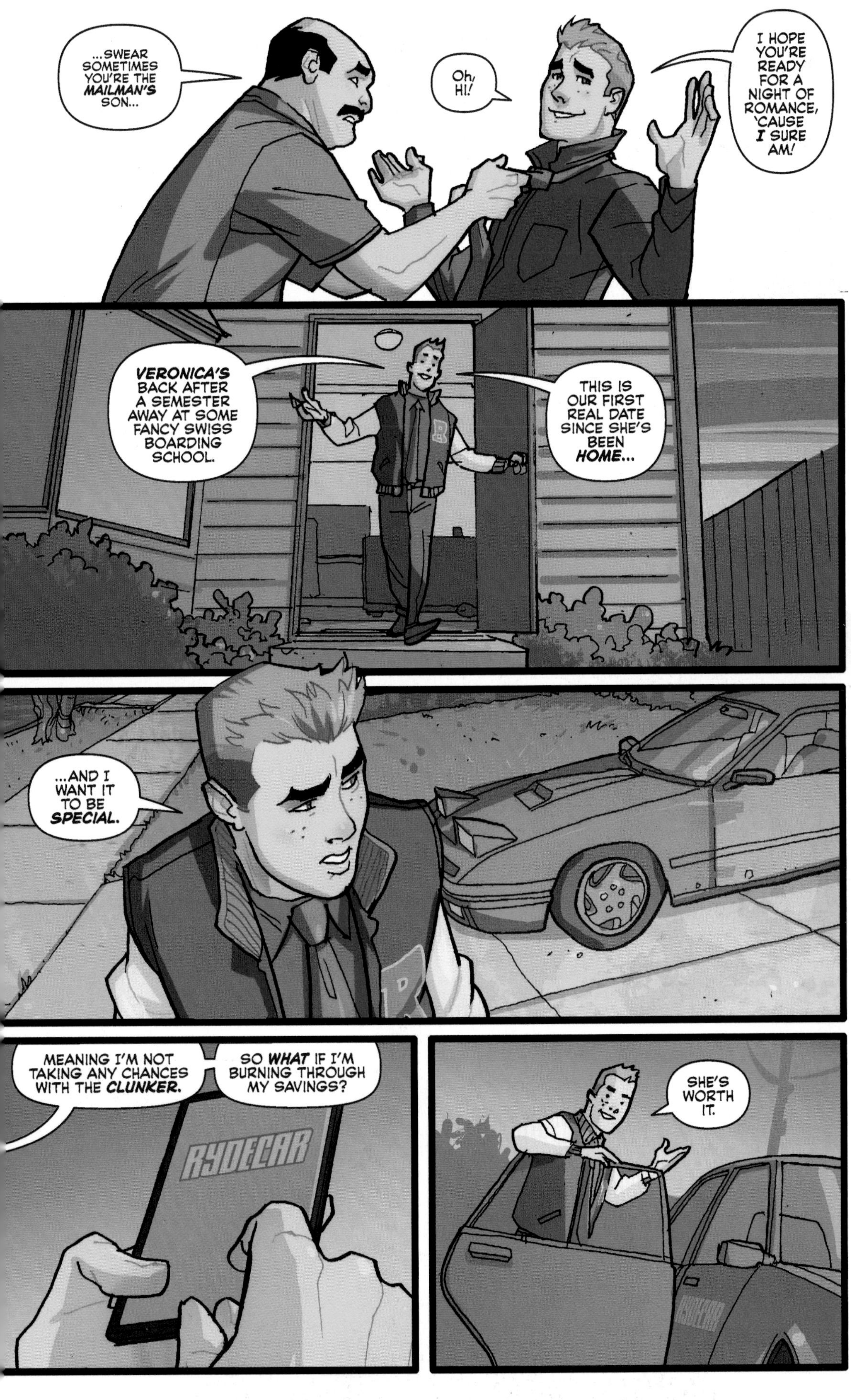
...SWEAR SOMETIMES YOU'RE THE MAILMAN'S SON...
Oh, HI!
I HOPE YOU'RE READY FOR A NIGHT OF ROMANCE, 'CAUSE I SURE AM!
VERONICA'S BACK AFTER A SEMESTER AWAY AT SOME FANCY SWISS BOARDING SCHOOL.
THIS IS OUR FIRST REAL DATE SINCE SHE'S BEEN HOME...
...AND I WANT IT TO BE SPECIAL.
MEANING I'M NOT TAKING ANY CHANCES WITH THE CLUNKER.
SO WHAT IF I'M BURNING THROUGH MY SAVINGS?
RYDECAR
SHE'S WORTH IT.
RYDECAR

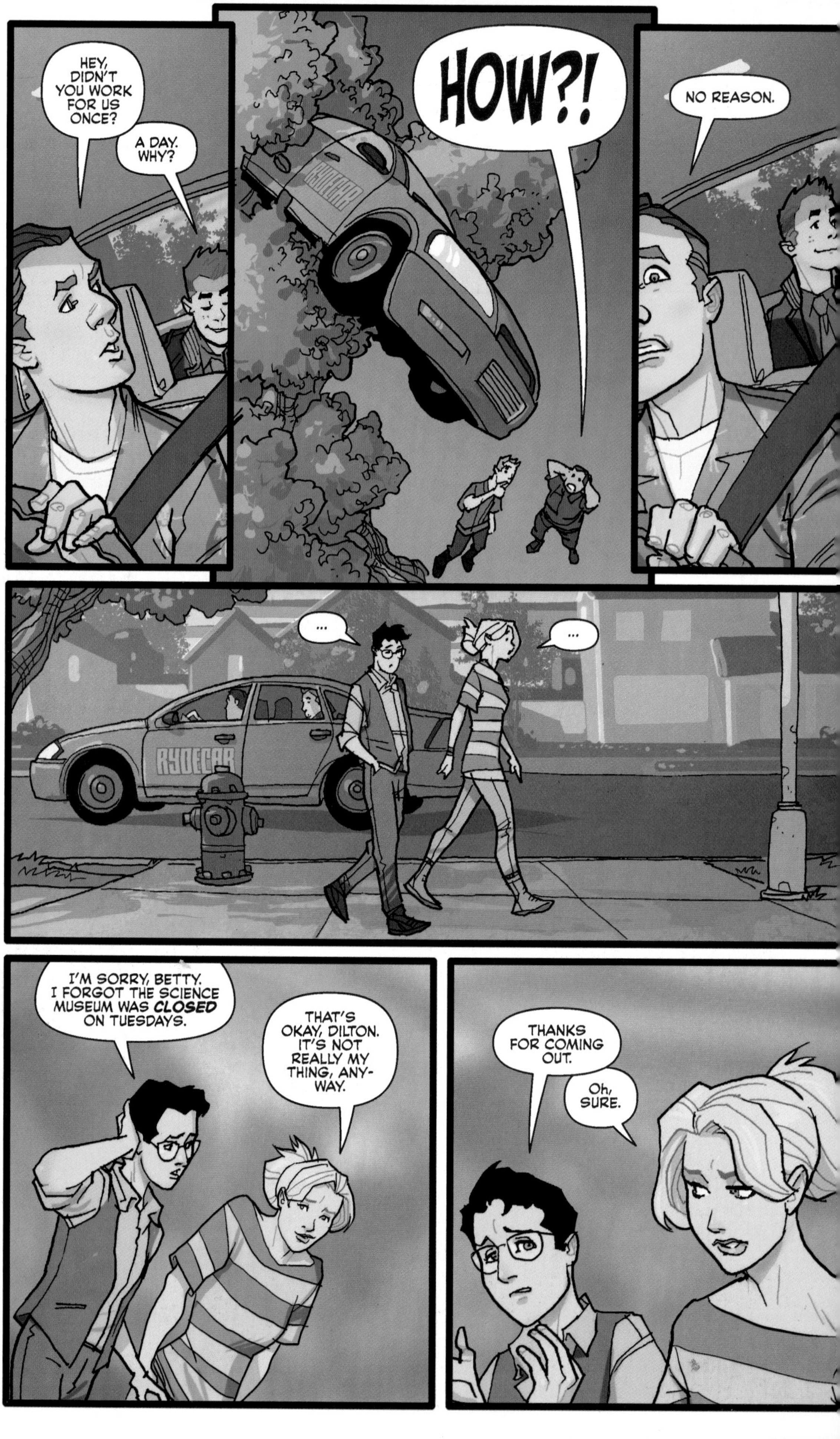
HEY, DIDN'T YOU WORK FOR US ONCE?
A DAY. WHY?
HOW?!
NO REASON.
...
...
I'M SORRY, BETTY. I FORGOT THE SCIENCE MUSEUM WAS *CLOSED* ON TUESDAYS.
THAT'S OKAY, DILTON. IT'S NOT REALLY MY THING, ANY-WAY.
THANKS FOR COMING OUT.
Oh, SURE.

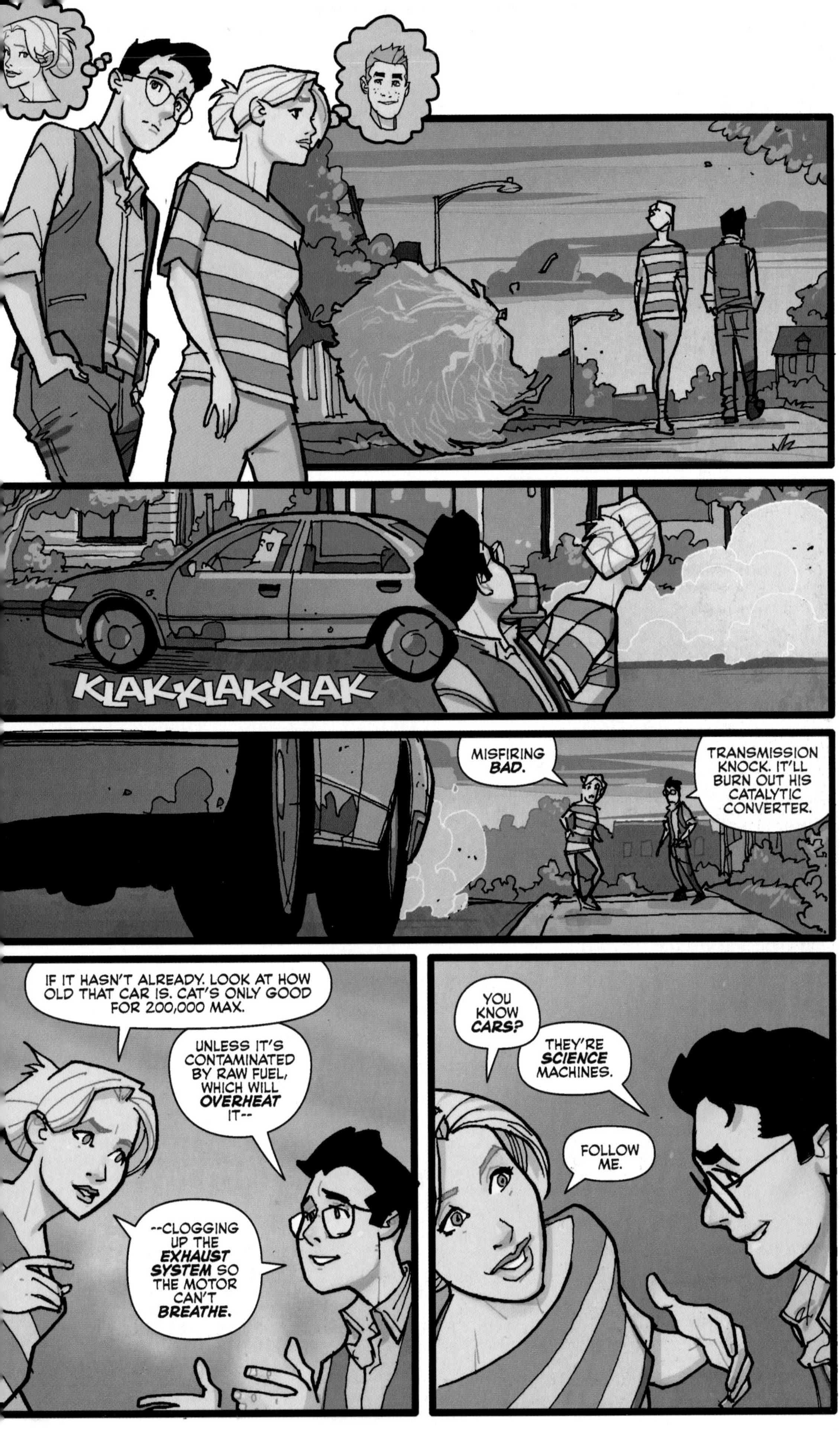
KLAKKLAKKLAK
MISFIRING BAD.
TRANSMISSION KNOCK. IT'LL BURN OUT HIS CATALYTIC CONVERTER.
IF IT HASN'T ALREADY. LOOK AT HOW OLD THAT CAR IS. CAT'S ONLY GOOD FOR 200,000 MAX.
UNLESS IT'S CONTAMINATED BY RAW FUEL, WHICH WILL OVERHEAT IT--
--CLOGGING UP THE EXHAUST SYSTEM SO THE MOTOR CAN'T BREATHE.
YOU KNOW CARS?
THEY'RE SCIENCE MACHINES.
FOLLOW ME.

CHAPTER TWO: Detective Jughead Jones

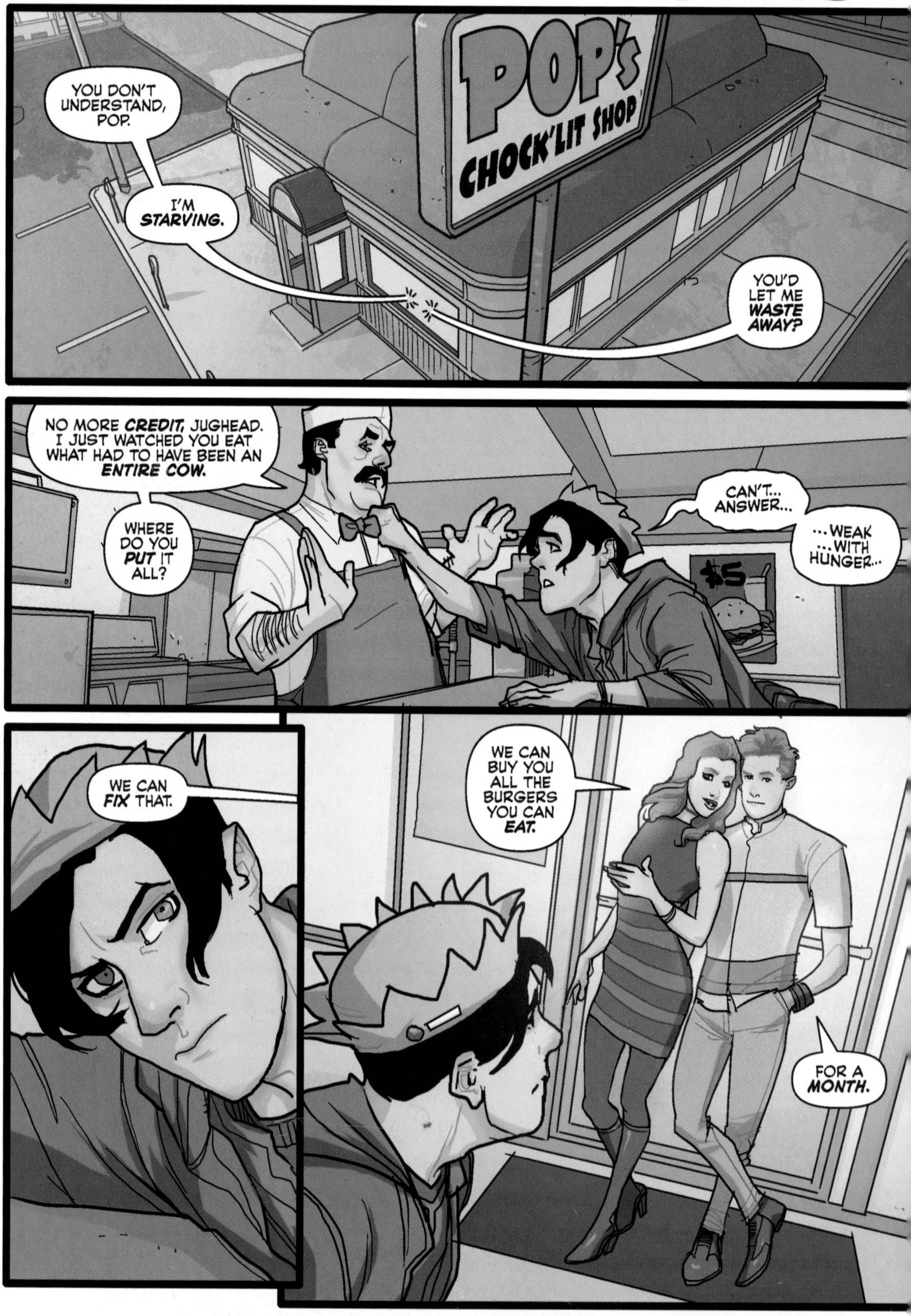

POP'S CHOCK'LIT SHOP
YOU DON'T UNDERSTAND, POP.
I'M STARVING.
YOU'D LET ME WASTE AWAY?
NO MORE CREDIT, JUGHEAD. I JUST WATCHED YOU EAT WHAT HAD TO HAVE BEEN AN ENTIRE COW.
WHERE DO YOU PUT IT ALL?
CAN'T... ANSWER...
...WEAK ...WITH HUNGER...
$5
WE CAN BUY YOU ALL THE BURGERS YOU CAN EAT.
WE CAN FIX THAT.
FOR A MONTH.

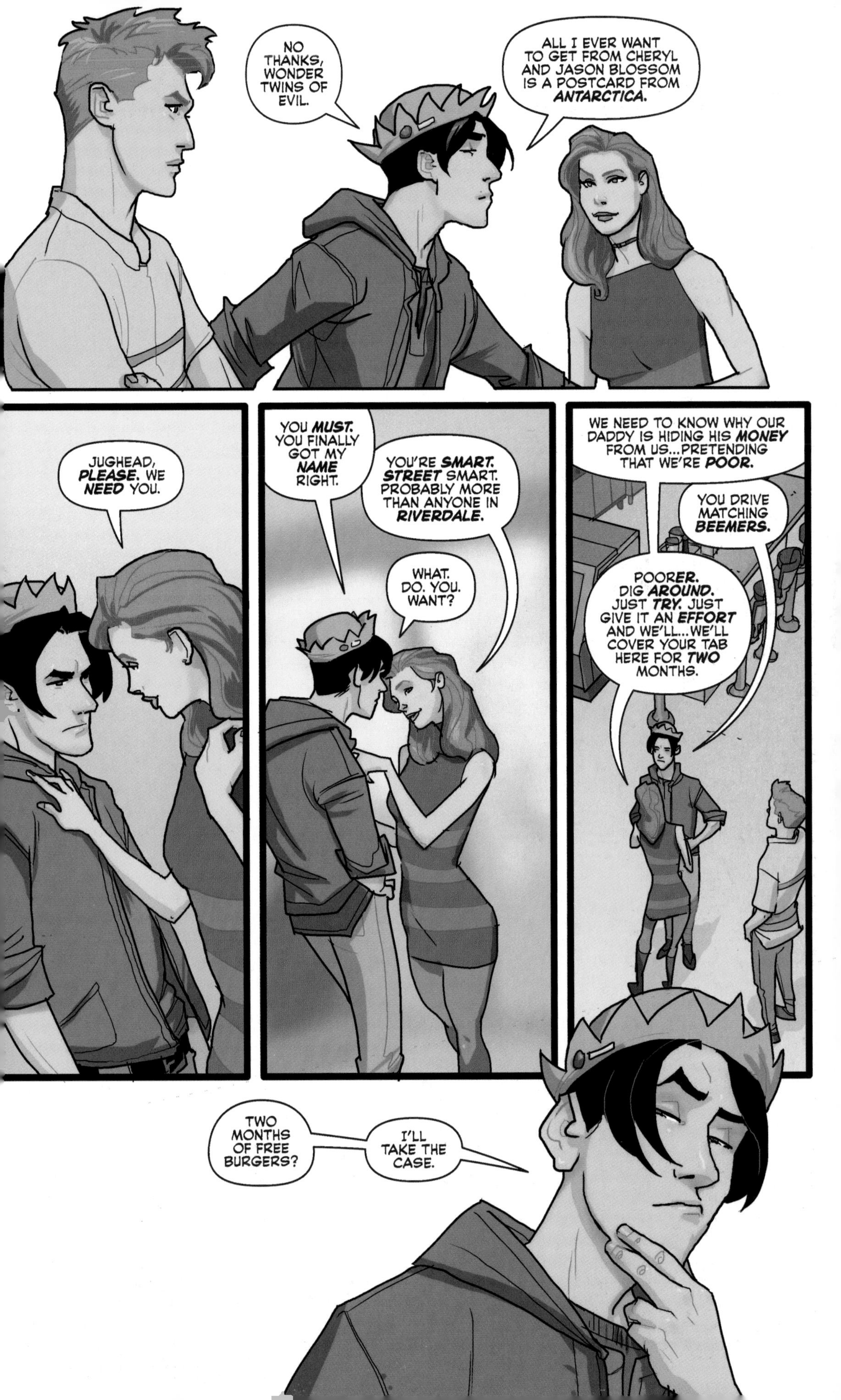
NO THANKS, WONDER TWINS OF EVIL.
ALL I EVER WANT TO GET FROM CHERYL AND JASON BLOSSOM IS A POSTCARD FROM ***ANTARCTICA.***
JUGHEAD, ***PLEASE.*** WE ***NEED*** YOU.
YOU ***MUST.*** YOU FINALLY GOT MY ***NAME*** RIGHT.
YOU'RE ***SMART. STREET*** SMART. PROBABLY MORE THAN ANYONE IN ***RIVERDALE.***
WHAT. DO. YOU. WANT?
WE NEED TO KNOW WHY OUR DADDY IS HIDING HIS ***MONEY*** FROM US...PRETENDING THAT WE'RE ***POOR.***
YOU DRIVE MATCHING ***BEEMERS.***
POOR***ER.*** DIG ***AROUND.*** JUST ***TRY.*** JUST GIVE IT AN ***EFFORT*** AND WE'LL...WE'LL COVER YOUR TAB HERE FOR ***TWO*** MONTHS.
TWO MONTHS OF FREE BURGERS?
I'LL TAKE THE CASE.

CHAPTER THREE: DOUBLE DATE

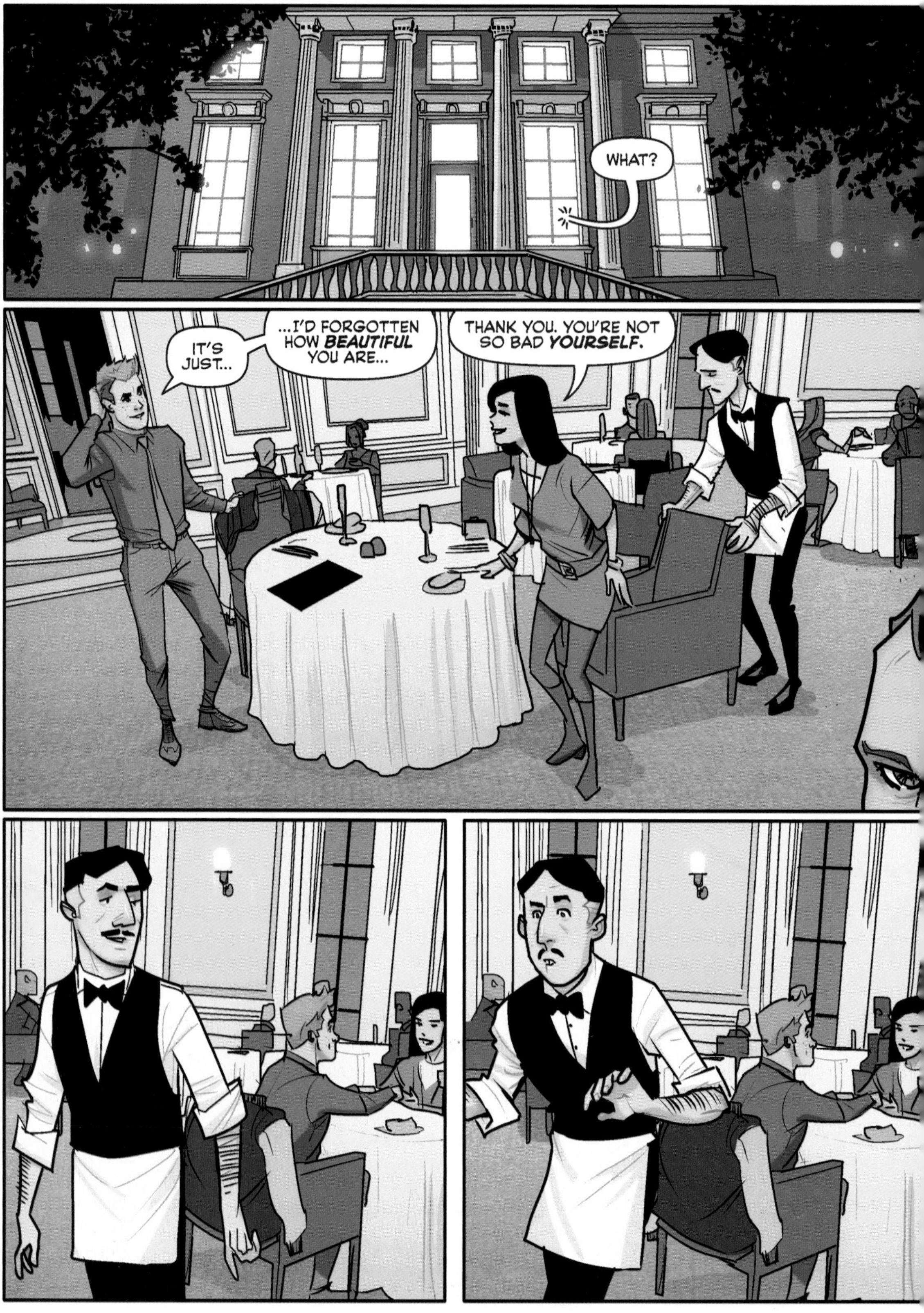
WHAT?
IT'S JUST...
...I'D FORGOTTEN HOW BEAUTIFUL YOU ARE...
THANK YOU. YOU'RE NOT SO BAD YOURSELF.

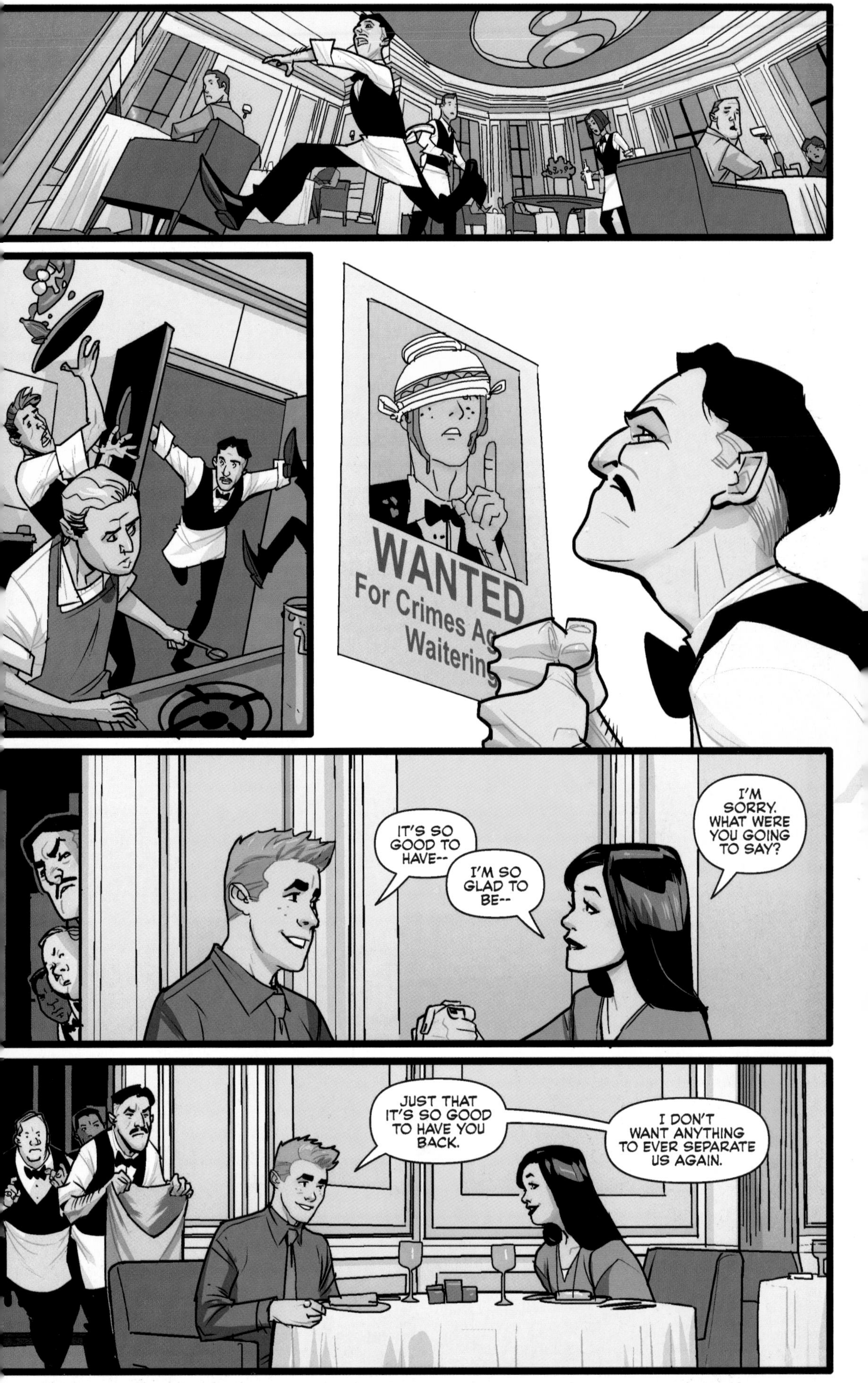
WANTED
For Crimes Ag
Waitering
IT'S SO GOOD TO HAVE--
I'M SO GLAD TO BE--
I'M SORRY. WHAT WERE YOU GOING TO SAY?
JUST THAT IT'S SO GOOD TO HAVE YOU BACK.
I DON'T WANT ANYTHING TO EVER SEPARATE US AGAIN.

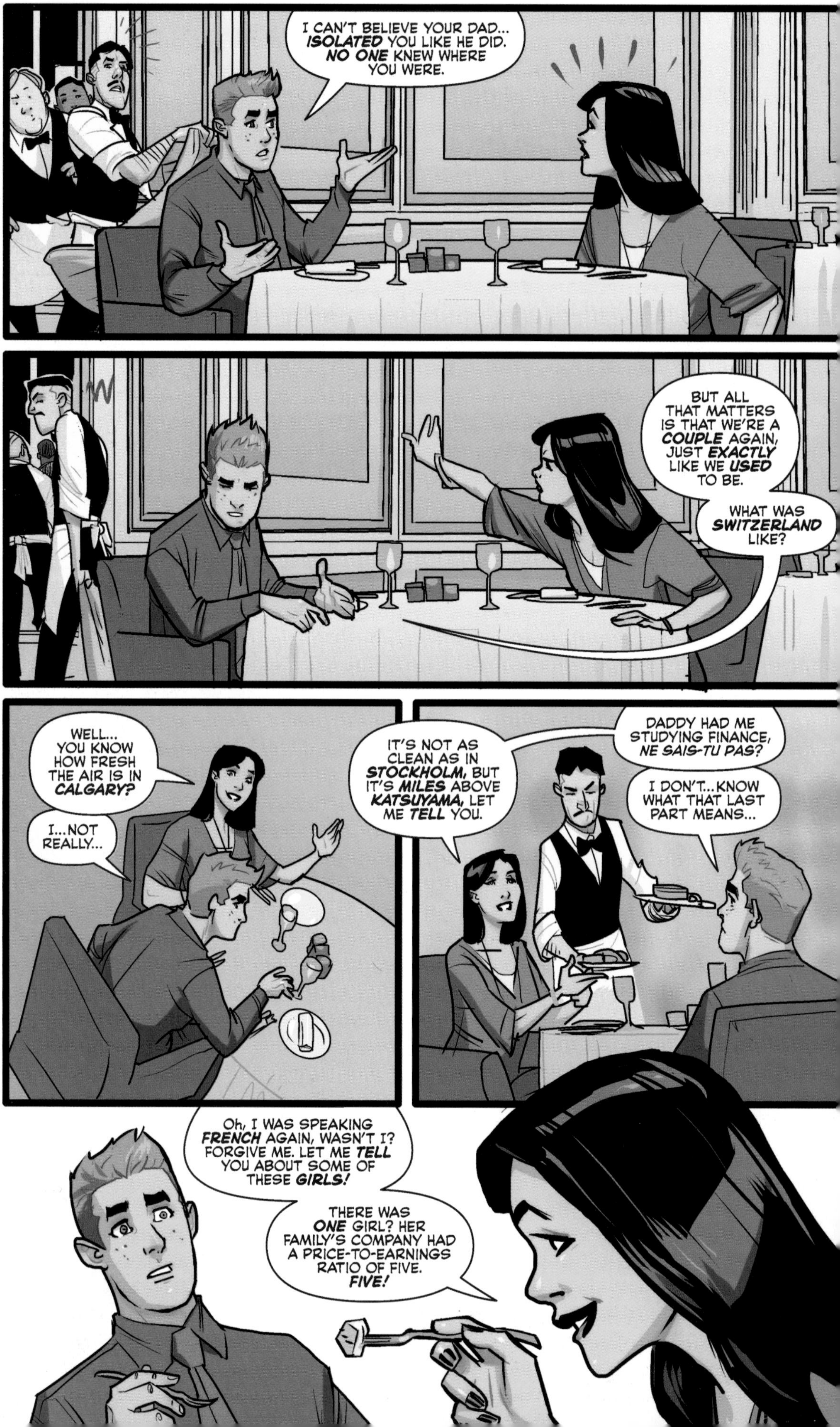
I CAN'T BELIEVE YOUR DAD... ISOLATED YOU LIKE HE DID. NO ONE KNEW WHERE YOU WERE.
BUT ALL THAT MATTERS IS THAT WE'RE A COUPLE AGAIN, JUST EXACTLY LIKE WE USED TO BE.
WHAT WAS SWITZERLAND LIKE?
WELL... YOU KNOW HOW FRESH THE AIR IS IN CALGARY?
I...NOT REALLY...
IT'S NOT AS CLEAN AS IN STOCKHOLM, BUT IT'S MILES ABOVE KATSUYAMA, LET ME TELL YOU.
DADDY HAD ME STUDYING FINANCE, NE SAIS-TU PAS?
I DON'T...KNOW WHAT THAT LAST PART MEANS...
Oh, I WAS SPEAKING FRENCH AGAIN, WASN'T I? FORGIVE ME. LET ME TELL YOU ABOUT SOME OF THESE GIRLS!
THERE WAS ONE GIRL? HER FAMILY'S COMPANY HAD A PRICE-TO-EARNINGS RATIO OF FIVE. FIVE!

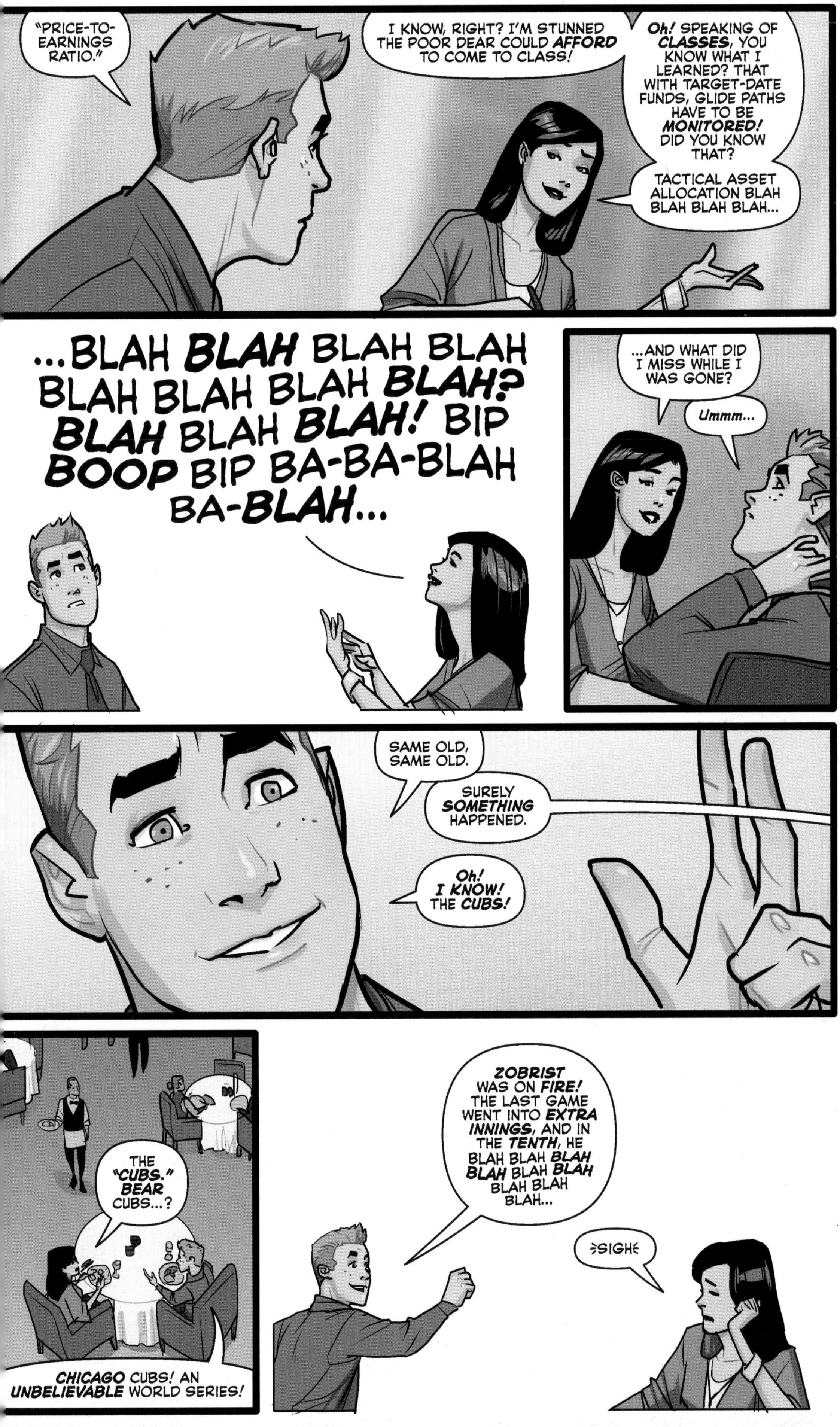
"PRICE-TO-EARNINGS RATIO."
I KNOW, RIGHT? I'M STUNNED THE POOR DEAR COULD AFFORD TO COME TO CLASS!
Oh! SPEAKING OF CLASSES, YOU KNOW WHAT I LEARNED? THAT WITH TARGET-DATE FUNDS, GLIDE PATHS HAVE TO BE MONITORED! DID YOU KNOW THAT?
TACTICAL ASSET ALLOCATION BLAH BLAH BLAH BLAH...
...BLAH BLAH BLAH BLAH BLAH BLAH BLAH BLAH? BLAH BLAH BLAH! BIP BOOP BIP BA-BA-BLAH BA-BLAH...
...AND WHAT DID I MISS WHILE I WAS GONE?
Ummm...
SAME OLD, SAME OLD.
SURELY SOMETHING HAPPENED.
Oh! I KNOW! THE CUBS!
THE "CUBS." BEAR CUBS...?
CHICAGO CUBS! AN UNBELIEVABLE WORLD SERIES!
ZOBRIST WAS ON FIRE! THE LAST GAME WENT INTO EXTRA INNINGS, AND IN THE TENTH, HE BLAH BLAH BLAH BLAH BLAH BLAH BLAH BLAH BLAH...
SIGH

CHAPTER FOUR: The TEMPTATION of Dilton Doiley

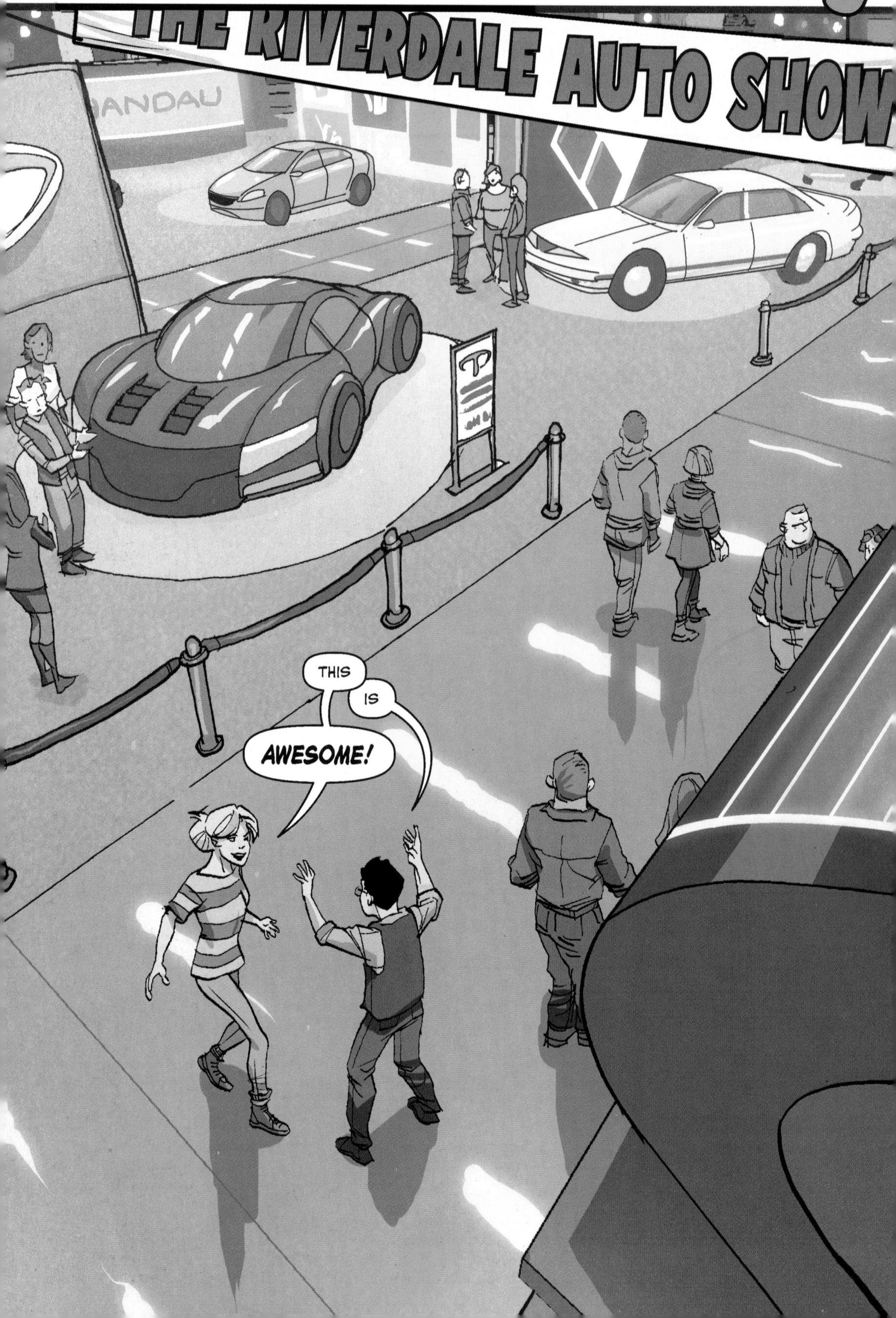

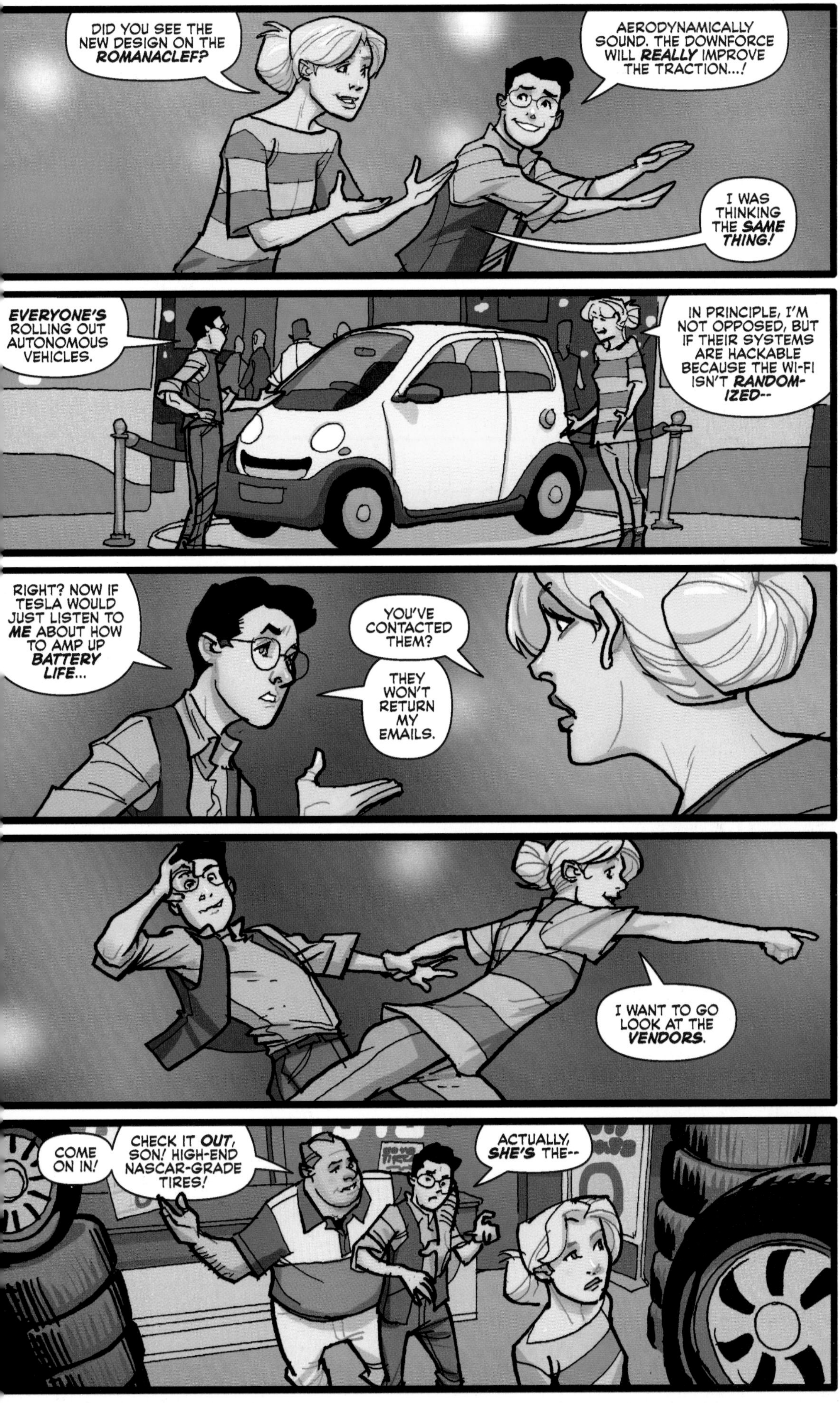

DID YOU SEE THE NEW DESIGN ON THE *ROMANACLEF?*
AERODYNAMICALLY SOUND. THE DOWNFORCE WILL *REALLY* IMPROVE THE TRACTION...!
I WAS THINKING THE *SAME THING!*
EVERYONE'S ROLLING OUT AUTONOMOUS VEHICLES.
IN PRINCIPLE, I'M NOT OPPOSED, BUT IF THEIR SYSTEMS ARE HACKABLE BECAUSE THE WI-FI ISN'T *RANDOM-IZED--*
RIGHT? NOW IF TESLA WOULD JUST LISTEN TO *ME* ABOUT HOW TO AMP UP *BATTERY LIFE*...
YOU'VE CONTACTED THEM?
THEY WON'T RETURN MY EMAILS.
I WANT TO GO LOOK AT THE *VENDORS*.
COME ON IN!
CHECK IT *OUT*, SON! HIGH-END NASCAR-GRADE TIRES!
ACTUALLY, *SHE'S* THE--

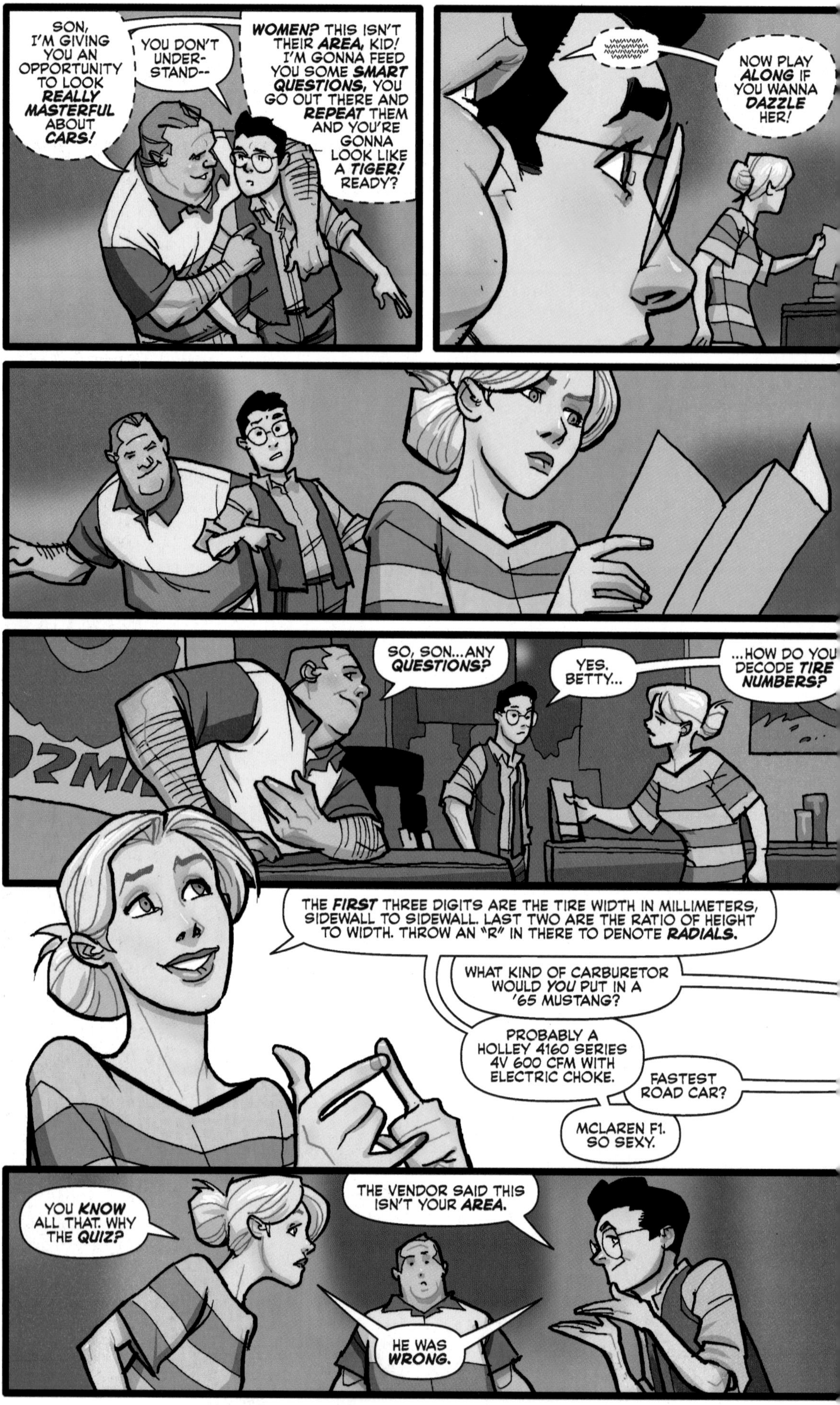
SON, I'M GIVING YOU AN OPPORTUNITY TO LOOK REALLY MASTERFUL ABOUT CARS!
YOU DON'T UNDER-STAND--
WOMEN? THIS ISN'T THEIR AREA, KID! I'M GONNA FEED YOU SOME SMART QUESTIONS, YOU GO OUT THERE AND REPEAT THEM AND YOU'RE GONNA LOOK LIKE A TIGER! READY?
NOW PLAY ALONG IF YOU WANNA DAZZLE HER!
SO, SON...ANY QUESTIONS?
YES. BETTY...
...HOW DO YOU DECODE TIRE NUMBERS?
THE FIRST THREE DIGITS ARE THE TIRE WIDTH IN MILLIMETERS, SIDEWALL TO SIDEWALL. LAST TWO ARE THE RATIO OF HEIGHT TO WIDTH. THROW AN "R" IN THERE TO DENOTE RADIALS.
WHAT KIND OF CARBURETOR WOULD YOU PUT IN A '65 MUSTANG?
PROBABLY A HOLLEY 4160 SERIES 4V 600 CFM WITH ELECTRIC CHOKE.
FASTEST ROAD CAR?
MCLAREN F1. SO SEXY.
YOU KNOW ALL THAT. WHY THE QUIZ?
THE VENDOR SAID THIS ISN'T YOUR AREA.
HE WAS WRONG.

CHAPTER FIVE: Jughead Jones Gumshoe

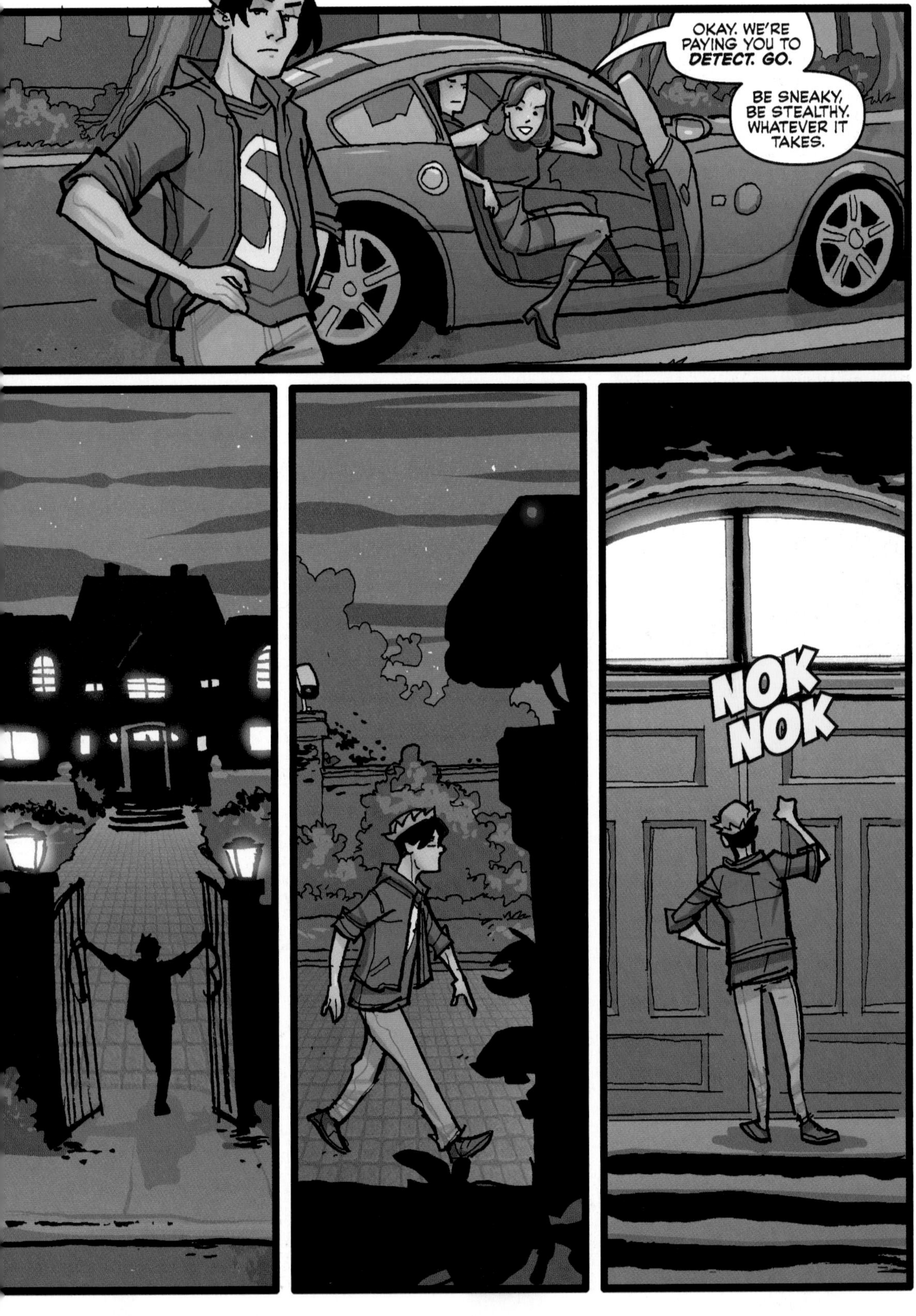

OKAY. WE'RE PAYING YOU TO DETECT. GO.
BE SNEAKY, BE STEALTHY. WHATEVER IT TAKES.
NOK NOK

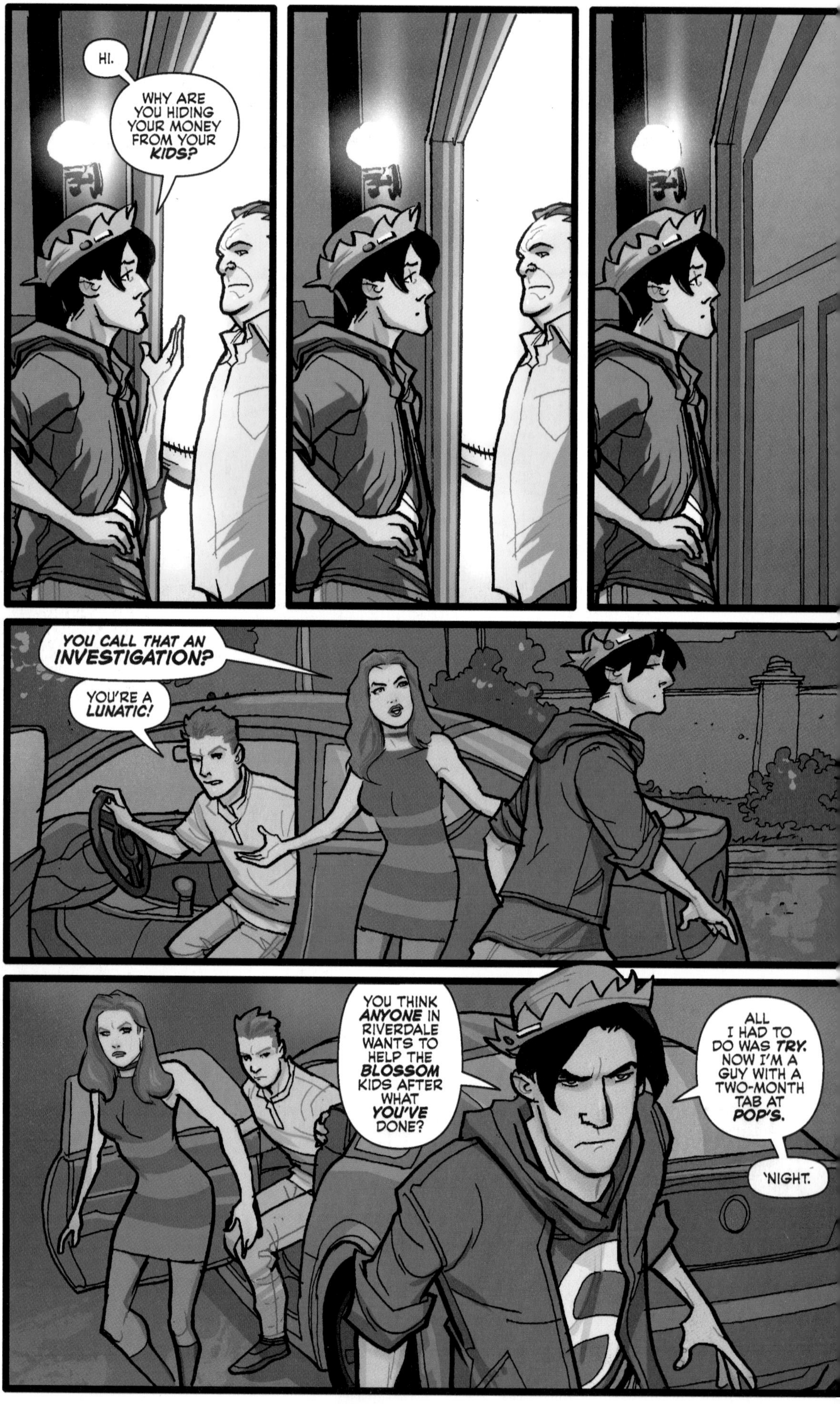
HI.
WHY ARE YOU HIDING YOUR MONEY FROM YOUR KIDS?
YOU CALL THAT AN INVESTIGATION?
YOU'RE A LUNATIC!
YOU THINK ANYONE IN RIVERDALE WANTS TO HELP THE BLOSSOM KIDS AFTER WHAT YOU'VE DONE?
ALL I HAD TO DO WAS TRY. NOW I'M A GUY WITH A TWO-MONTH TAB AT POP'S.
'NIGHT.

CHAPTER SIX: COIL PACK?

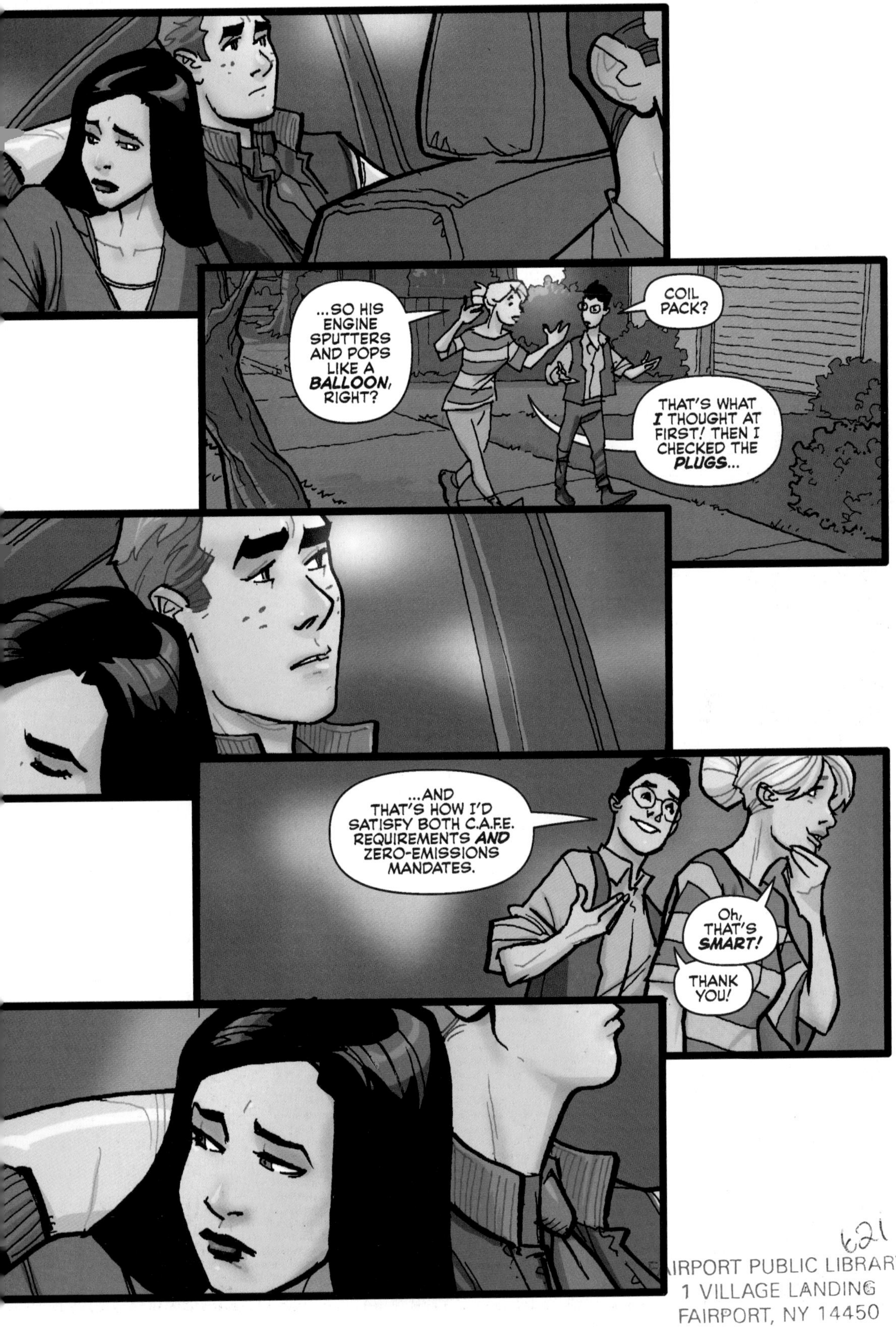
...SO HIS ENGINE SPUTTERS AND POPS LIKE A BALLOON, RIGHT?
COIL PACK?
THAT'S WHAT I THOUGHT AT FIRST! THEN I CHECKED THE PLUGS...
...AND THAT'S HOW I'D SATISFY BOTH C.A.F.E. REQUIREMENTS AND ZERO-EMISSIONS MANDATES.
Oh, THAT'S SMART!
THANK YOU!

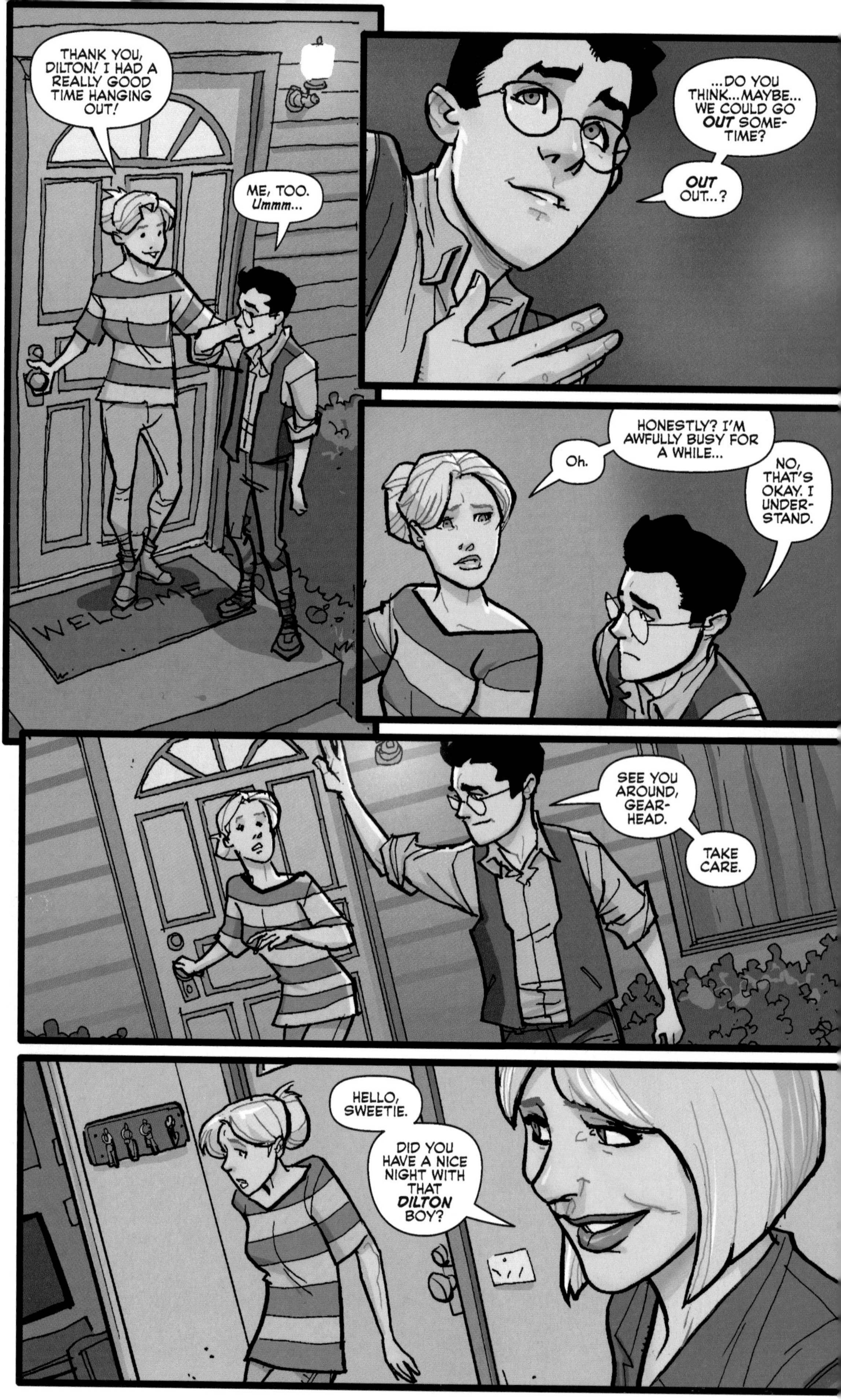
THANK YOU, DILTON! I HAD A REALLY GOOD TIME HANGING OUT!
ME, TOO. *Ummm...*
...DO YOU THINK...MAYBE... WE COULD GO ***OUT*** SOME-TIME?
OUT OUT...?
Oh.
HONESTLY? I'M AWFULLY BUSY FOR A WHILE...
NO, THAT'S OKAY. I UNDER-STAND.
SEE YOU AROUND, GEAR-HEAD.
TAKE CARE.
HELLO, SWEETIE.
DID YOU HAVE A NICE NIGHT WITH THAT ***DILTON*** BOY?
WELCOME

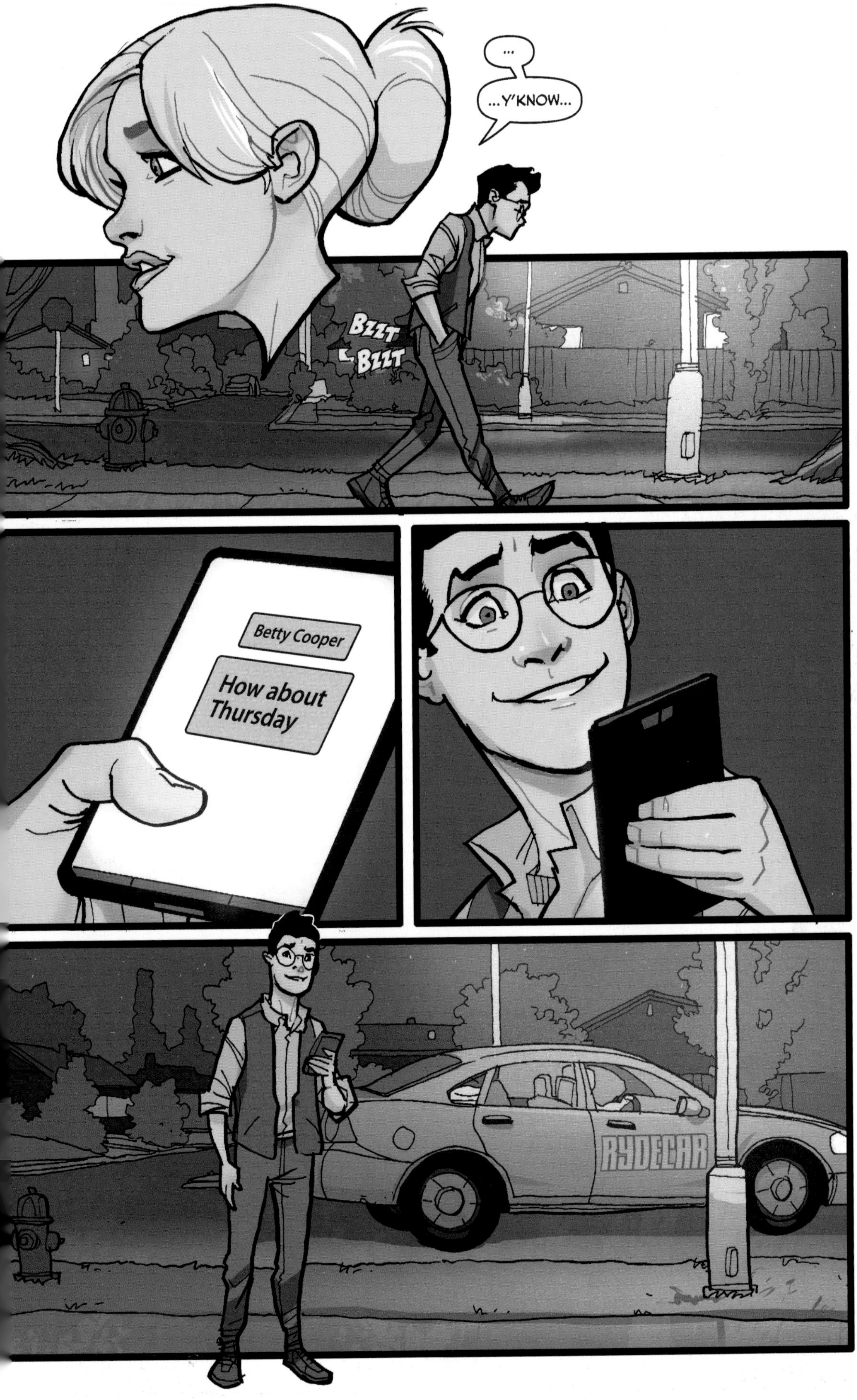
...
...Y'KNOW...
BZZT
BZZT
Betty Cooper
How about Thursday
RYDECAR

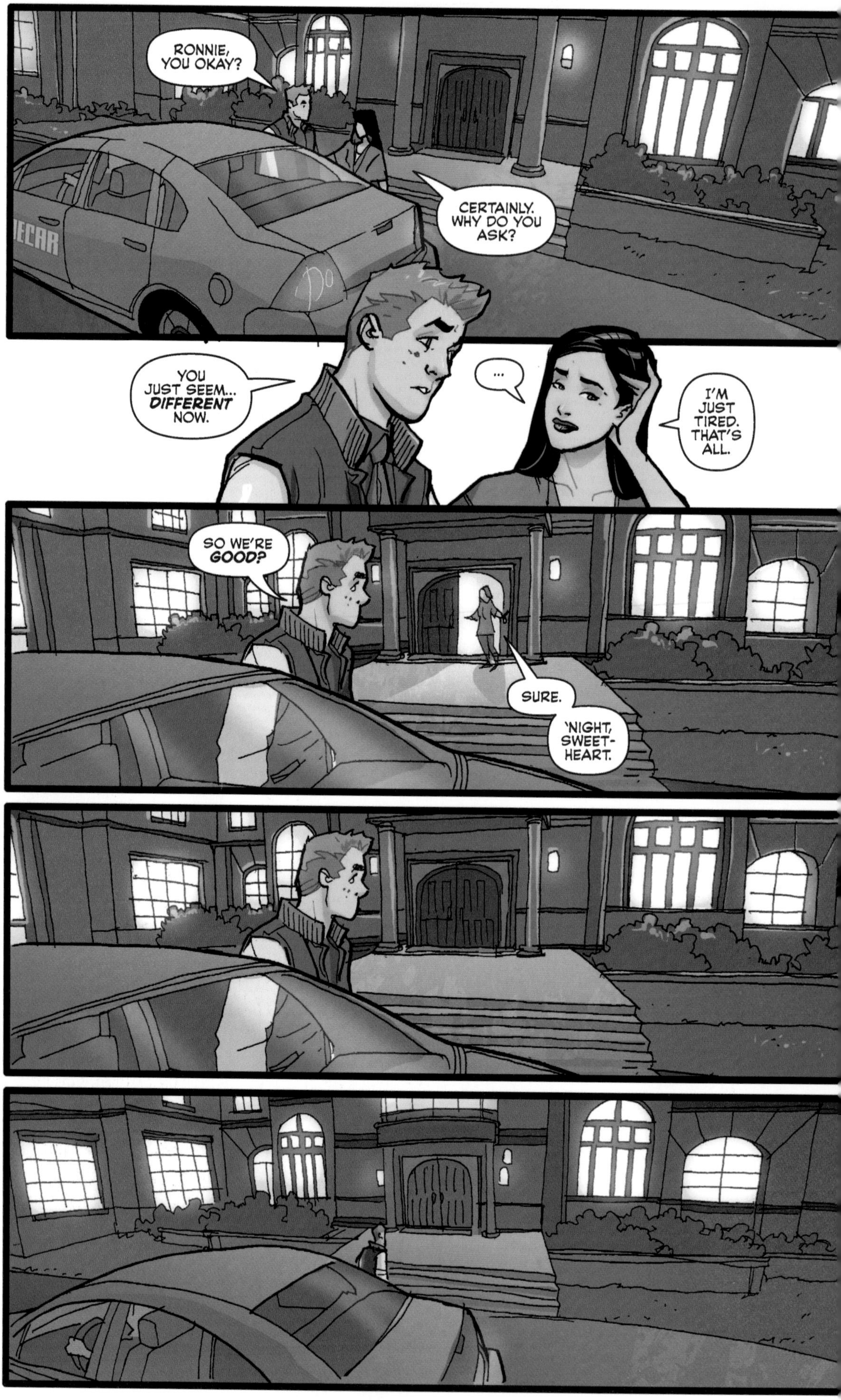
RONNIE, YOU OKAY?
CERTAINLY. WHY DO YOU ASK?
YOU JUST SEEM... **DIFFERENT** NOW.
...
I'M JUST TIRED. THAT'S ALL.
SO WE'RE **GOOD?**
SURE.
'NIGHT, SWEET-HEART.

TO BE CONTINUED...

ISSUE NINETEEN

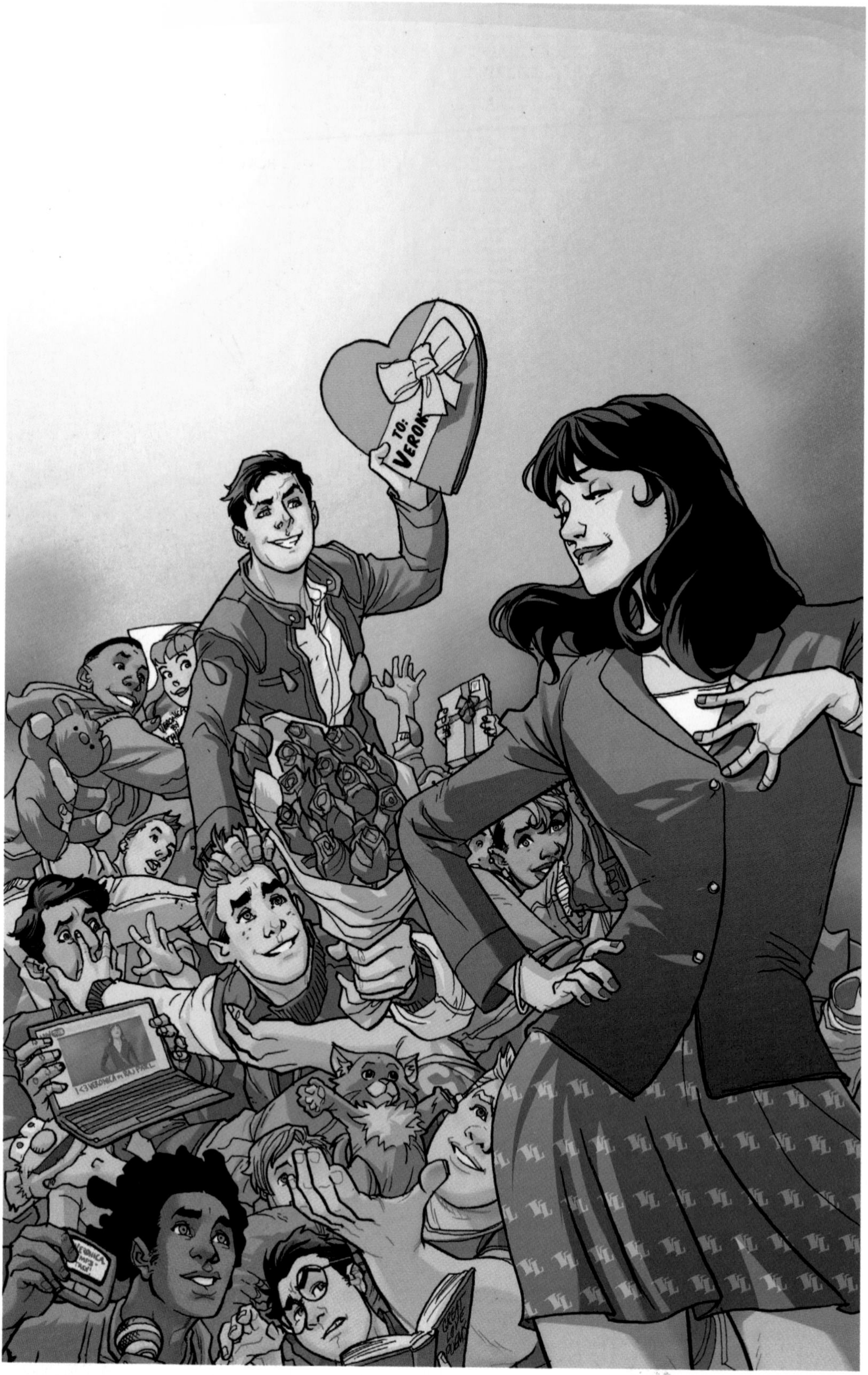
TO:
VERON

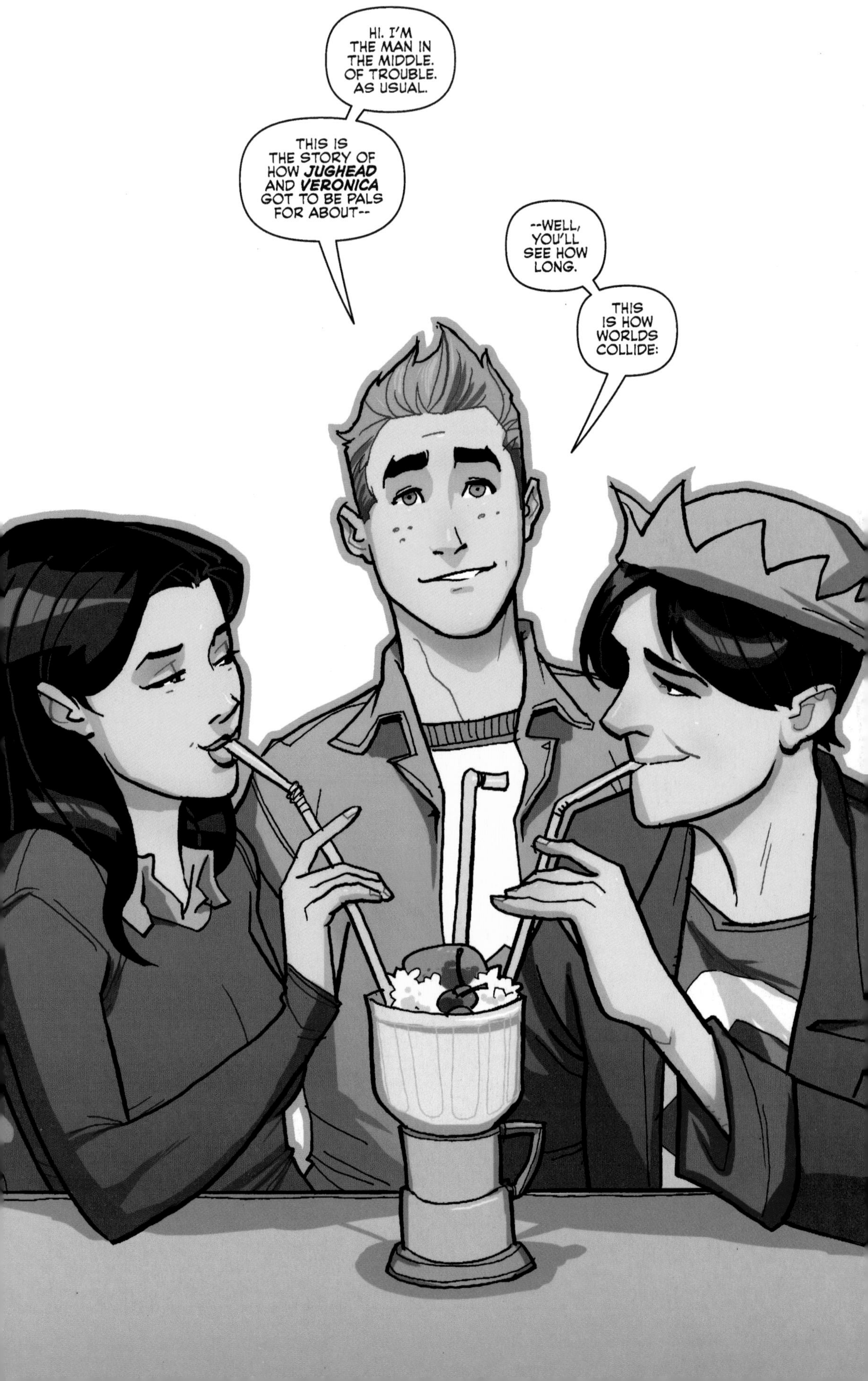
HI. I'M THE MAN IN THE MIDDLE. OF TROUBLE. AS USUAL.
THIS IS THE STORY OF HOW *JUGHEAD* AND *VERONICA* GOT TO BE PALS FOR ABOUT--
--WELL, YOU'LL SEE HOW LONG.
THIS IS HOW WORLDS COLLIDE:

CHAPTER ONE: When All is Sad and Done

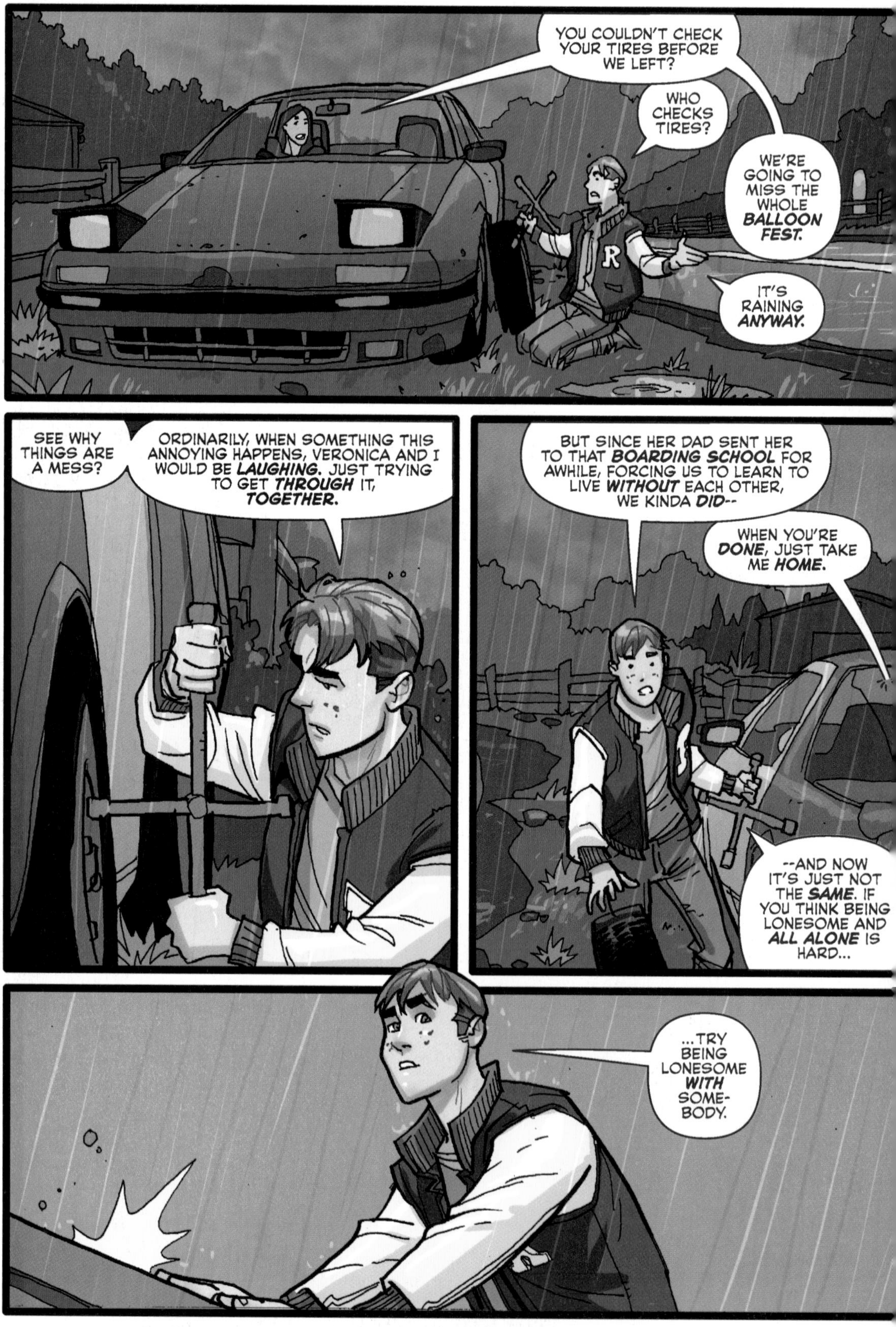
YOU COULDN'T CHECK YOUR TIRES BEFORE WE LEFT?
WHO CHECKS TIRES?
WE'RE GOING TO MISS THE WHOLE BALLOON FEST.
IT'S RAINING ANYWAY.
SEE WHY THINGS ARE A MESS?
ORDINARILY, WHEN SOMETHING THIS ANNOYING HAPPENS, VERONICA AND I WOULD BE LAUGHING. JUST TRYING TO GET THROUGH IT, TOGETHER.
BUT SINCE HER DAD SENT HER TO THAT BOARDING SCHOOL FOR AWHILE, FORCING US TO LEARN TO LIVE WITHOUT EACH OTHER, WE KINDA DID--
WHEN YOU'RE DONE, JUST TAKE ME HOME.
--AND NOW IT'S JUST NOT THE SAME. IF YOU THINK BEING LONESOME AND ALL ALONE IS HARD...
...TRY BEING LONESOME WITH SOME-BODY.

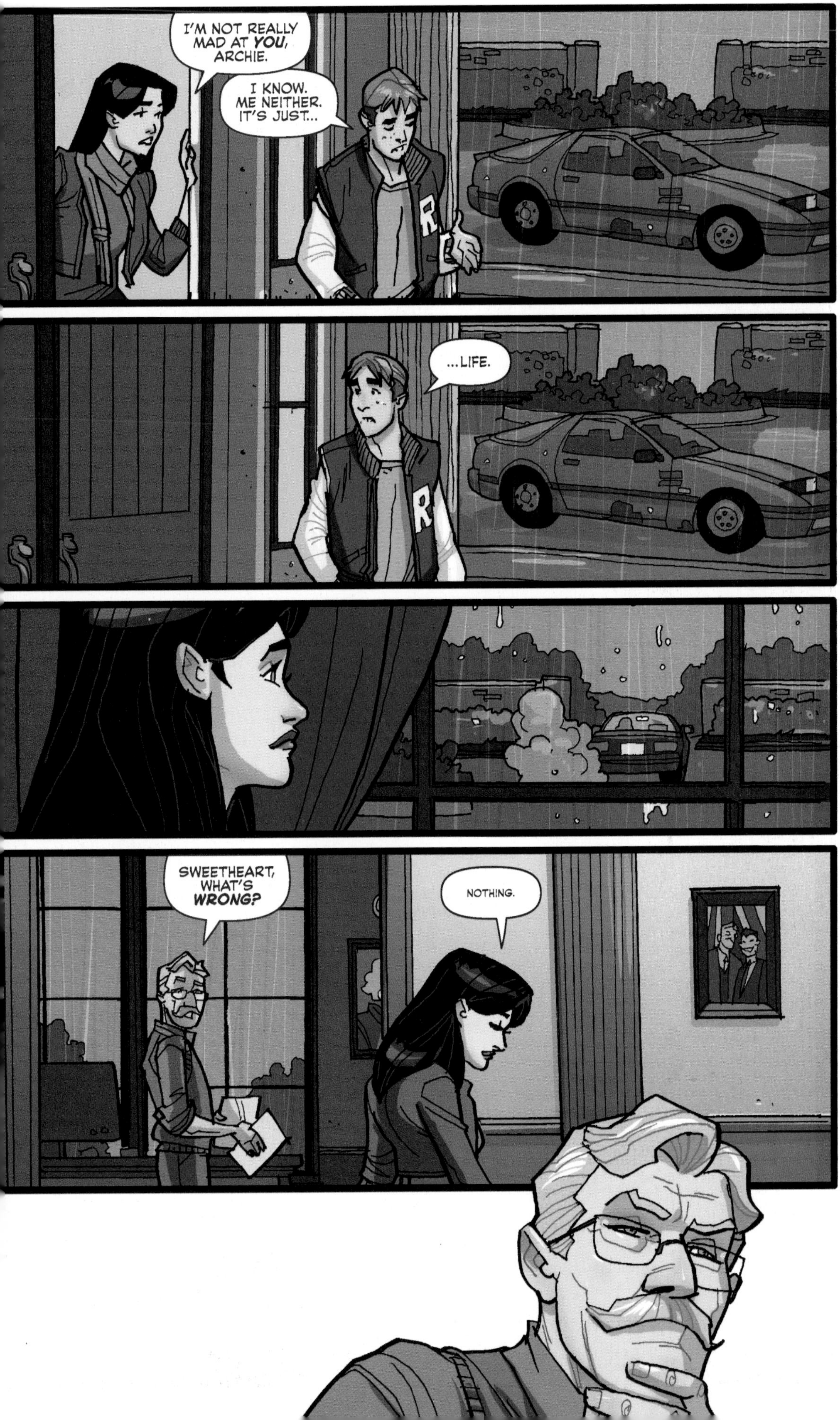
I'M NOT REALLY MAD AT YOU, ARCHIE.
I KNOW. ME NEITHER. IT'S JUST...
...LIFE.
SWEETHEART, WHAT'S WRONG?
NOTHING.

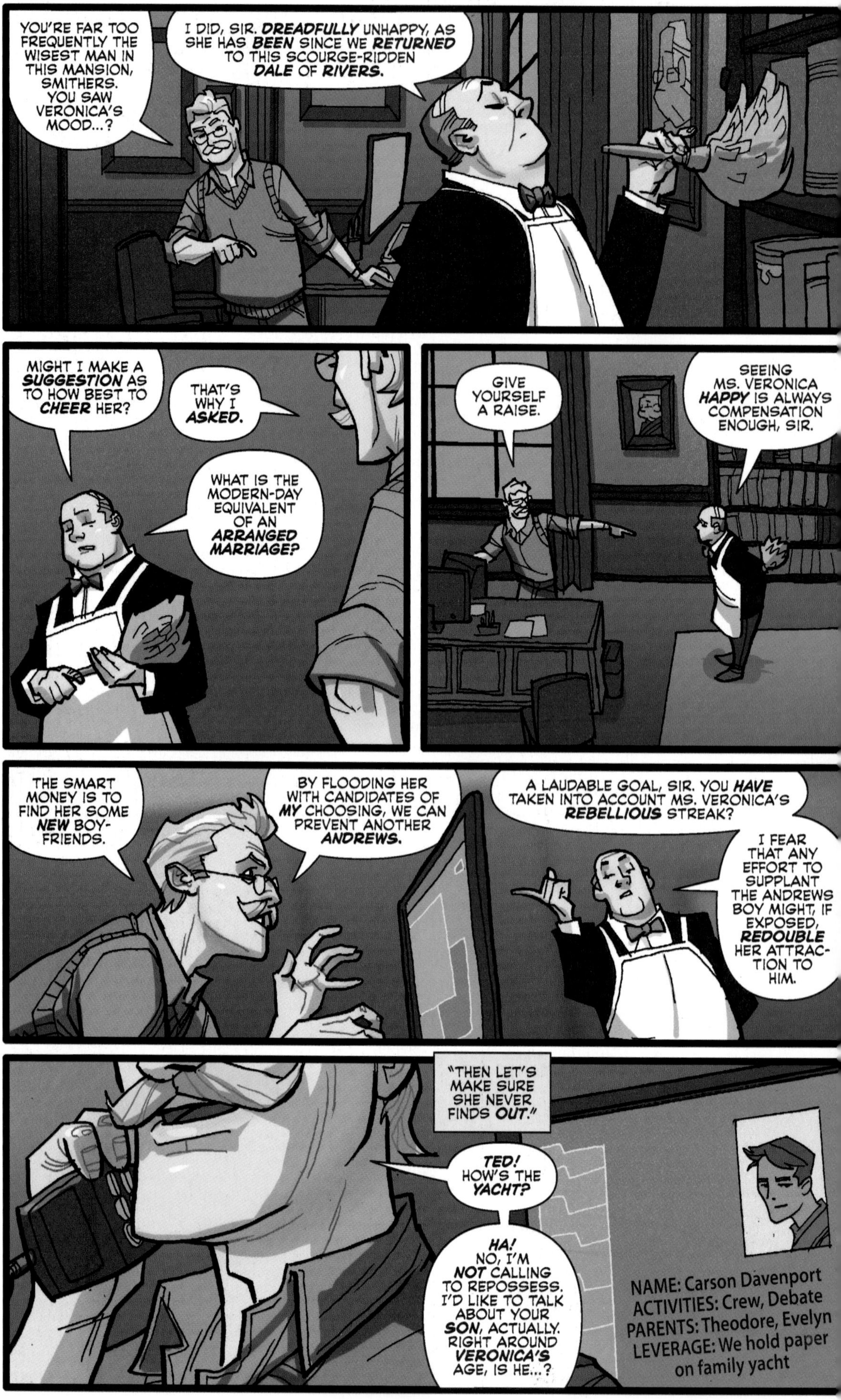

YOU'RE FAR TOO FREQUENTLY THE WISEST MAN IN THIS MANSION, SMITHERS. YOU SAW VERONICA'S MOOD...?
I DID, SIR. DREADFULLY UNHAPPY, AS SHE HAS BEEN SINCE WE RETURNED TO THIS SCOURGE-RIDDEN DALE OF RIVERS.
MIGHT I MAKE A SUGGESTION AS TO HOW BEST TO CHEER HER?
THAT'S WHY I ASKED.
WHAT IS THE MODERN-DAY EQUIVALENT OF AN ARRANGED MARRIAGE?
GIVE YOURSELF A RAISE.
SEEING MS. VERONICA HAPPY IS ALWAYS COMPENSATION ENOUGH, SIR.
THE SMART MONEY IS TO FIND HER SOME NEW BOY-FRIENDS.
BY FLOODING HER WITH CANDIDATES OF MY CHOOSING, WE CAN PREVENT ANOTHER ANDREWS.
A LAUDABLE GOAL, SIR. YOU HAVE TAKEN INTO ACCOUNT MS. VERONICA'S REBELLIOUS STREAK?
I FEAR THAT ANY EFFORT TO SUPPLANT THE ANDREWS BOY MIGHT, IF EXPOSED, REDOUBLE HER ATTRAC-TION TO HIM.
"THEN LET'S MAKE SURE SHE NEVER FINDS OUT."
TED! HOW'S THE YACHT?
HA! NO, I'M NOT CALLING TO REPOSSESS. I'D LIKE TO TALK ABOUT YOUR SON, ACTUALLY. RIGHT AROUND VERONICA'S AGE, IS HE...?
NAME: Carson Davenport
ACTIVITIES: Crew, Debate
PARENTS: Theodore, Evelyn
LEVERAGE: We hold paper on family yacht

CHAPTER TWO: P-TOO!

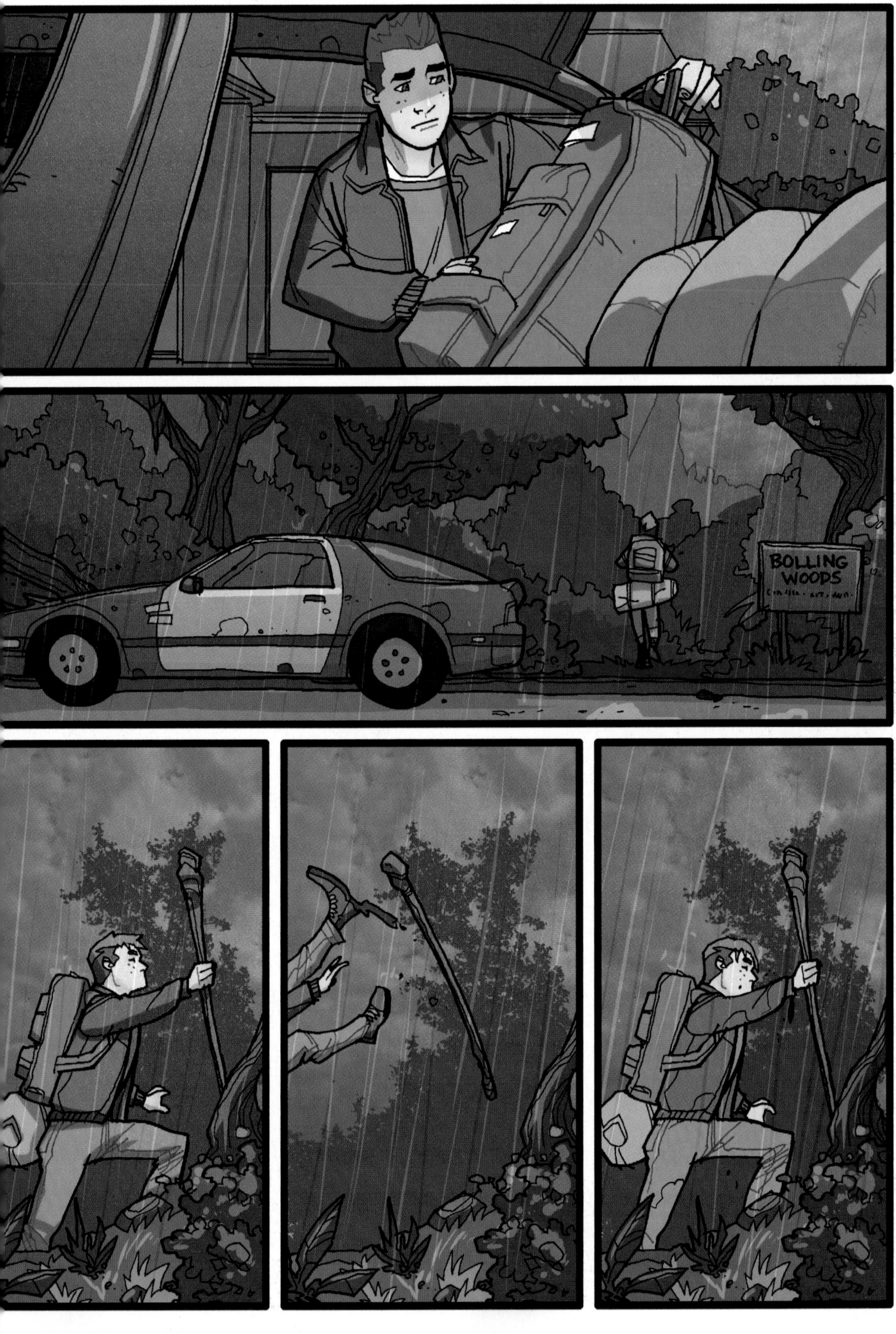
BOLLING WOODS

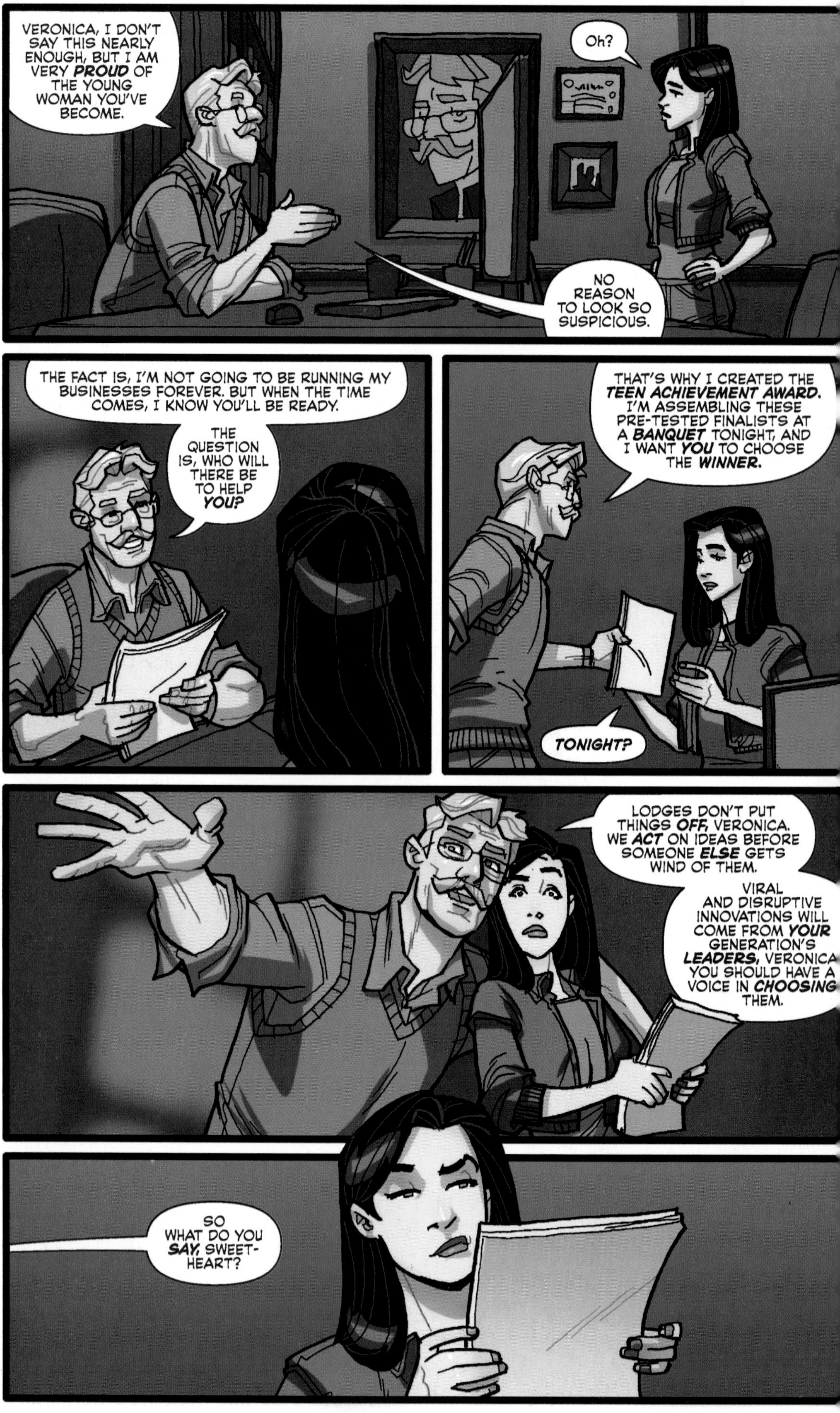

VERONICA, I DON'T SAY THIS NEARLY ENOUGH, BUT I AM VERY **PROUD** OF THE YOUNG WOMAN YOU'VE BECOME.
Oh?
NO REASON TO LOOK SO SUSPICIOUS.
THE FACT IS, I'M NOT GOING TO BE RUNNING MY BUSINESSES FOREVER. BUT WHEN THE TIME COMES, I KNOW YOU'LL BE READY.
THE QUESTION IS, WHO WILL THERE BE TO HELP **YOU?**
THAT'S WHY I CREATED THE **TEEN ACHIEVEMENT AWARD.** I'M ASSEMBLING THESE PRE-TESTED FINALISTS AT A **BANQUET** TONIGHT, AND I WANT **YOU** TO CHOOSE THE **WINNER.**
TONIGHT?
LODGES DON'T PUT THINGS **OFF,** VERONICA. WE **ACT** ON IDEAS BEFORE SOMEONE **ELSE** GETS WIND OF THEM.
VIRAL AND DISRUPTIVE INNOVATIONS WILL COME FROM **YOUR** GENERATION'S **LEADERS,** VERONICA. YOU SHOULD HAVE A VOICE IN **CHOOSING** THEM.
SO WHAT DO YOU **SAY,** SWEET-HEART?

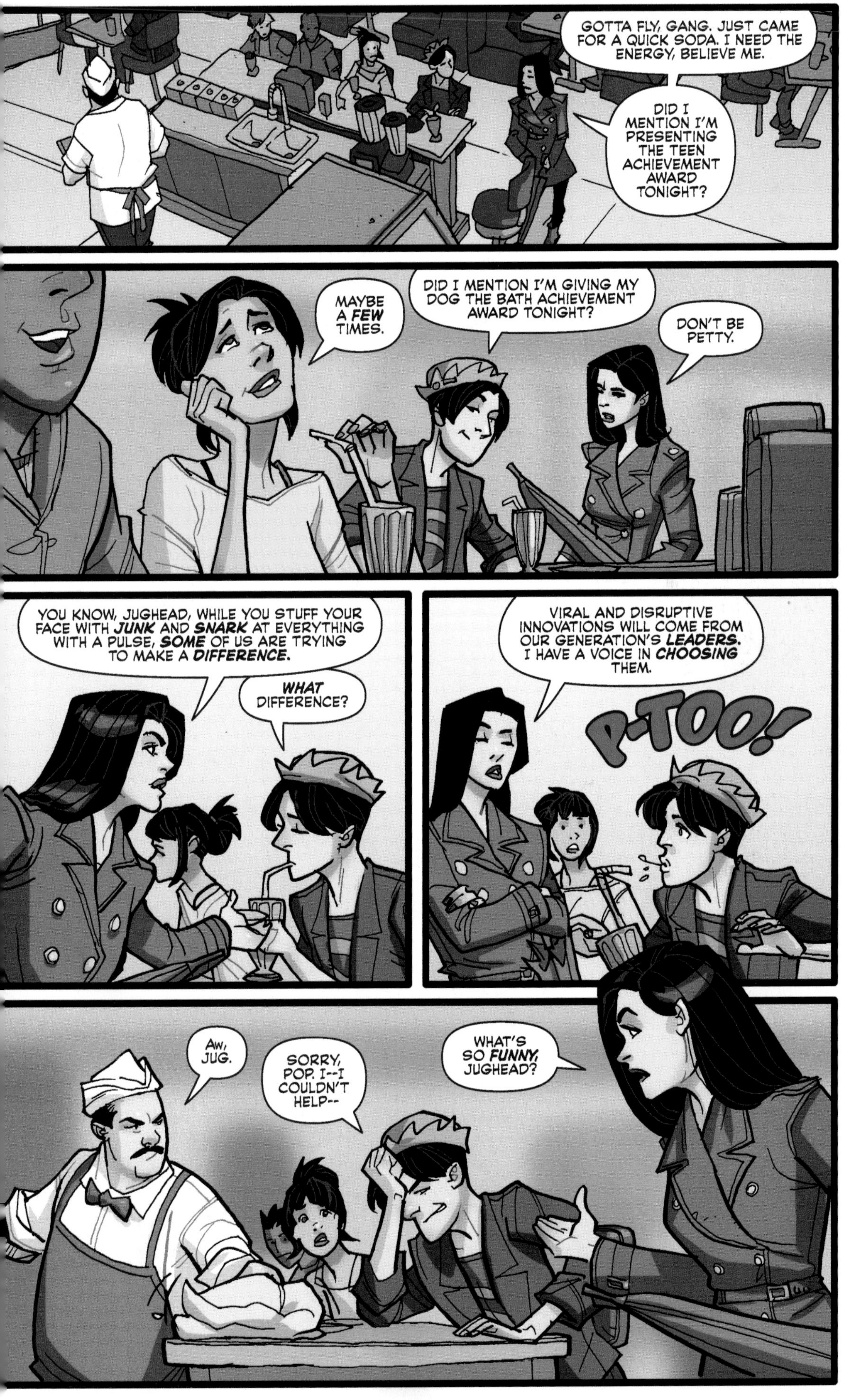
GOTTA FLY, GANG. JUST CAME FOR A QUICK SODA. I NEED THE ENERGY, BELIEVE ME.
DID I MENTION I'M PRESENTING THE TEEN ACHIEVEMENT AWARD TONIGHT?
MAYBE A *FEW* TIMES.
DID I MENTION I'M GIVING MY DOG THE BATH ACHIEVEMENT AWARD TONIGHT?
DON'T BE PETTY.
YOU KNOW, JUGHEAD, WHILE YOU STUFF YOUR FACE WITH *JUNK* AND *SNARK* AT EVERYTHING WITH A PULSE, *SOME* OF US ARE TRYING TO MAKE A *DIFFERENCE.*
WHAT DIFFERENCE?
VIRAL AND DISRUPTIVE INNOVATIONS WILL COME FROM OUR GENERATION'S *LEADERS.* I HAVE A VOICE IN *CHOOSING* THEM.
P-TOO!
AW, JUG.
SORRY, POP. I--I COULDN'T HELP--
WHAT'S SO *FUNNY,* JUGHEAD?

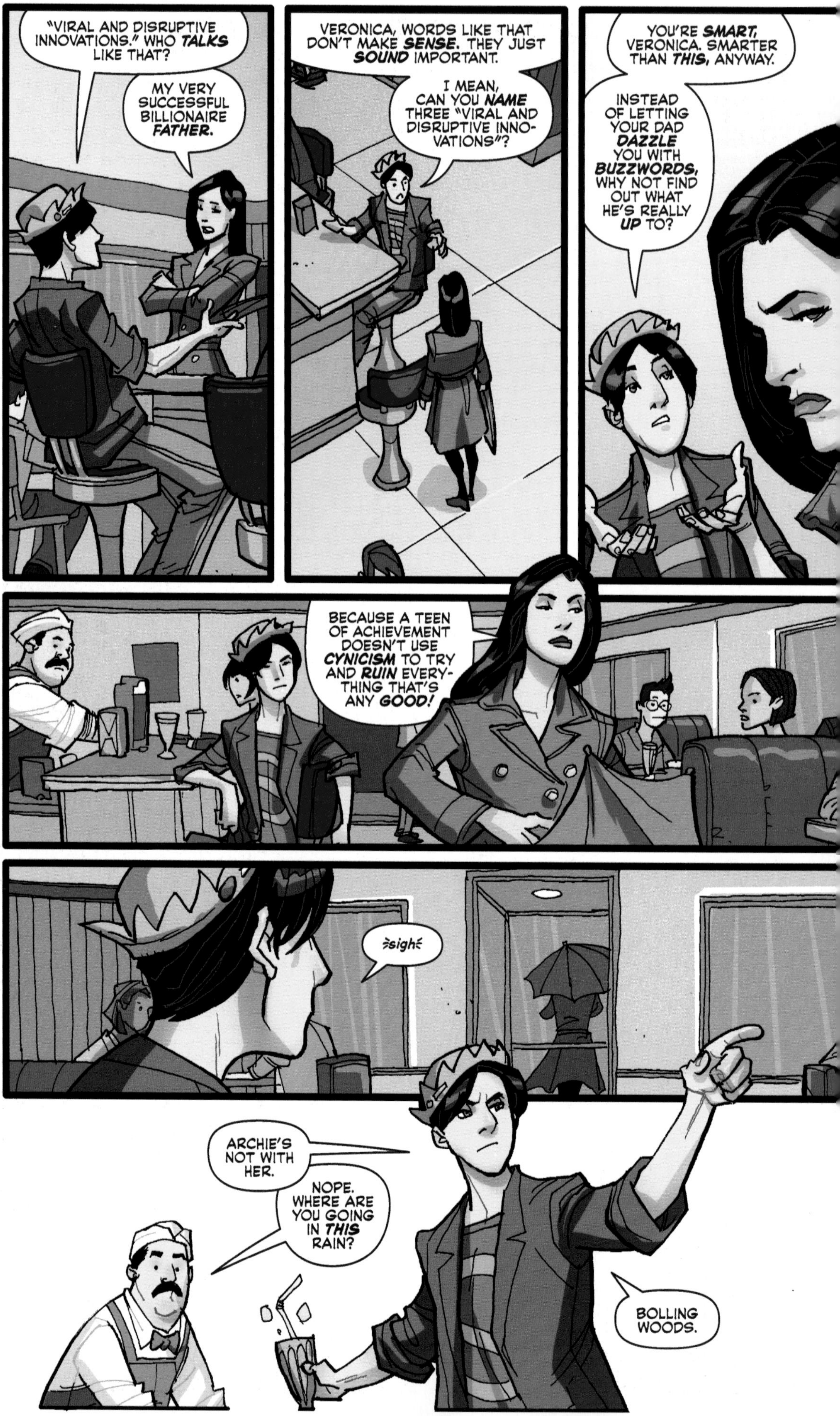

"VIRAL AND DISRUPTIVE INNOVATIONS." WHO TALKS LIKE THAT?
MY VERY SUCCESSFUL BILLIONAIRE FATHER.
VERONICA, WORDS LIKE THAT DON'T MAKE SENSE. THEY JUST SOUND IMPORTANT.
I MEAN, CAN YOU NAME THREE "VIRAL AND DISRUPTIVE INNO-VATIONS"?
YOU'RE SMART, VERONICA. SMARTER THAN THIS, ANYWAY.
INSTEAD OF LETTING YOUR DAD DAZZLE YOU WITH BUZZWORDS, WHY NOT FIND OUT WHAT HE'S REALLY UP TO?
BECAUSE A TEEN OF ACHIEVEMENT DOESN'T USE CYNICISM TO TRY AND RUIN EVERY-THING THAT'S ANY GOOD!
sigh
ARCHIE'S NOT WITH HER.
NOPE. WHERE ARE YOU GOING IN THIS RAIN?
BOLLING WOODS.

CHAPTER THREE: PEOPLE ARE VAMPIRES

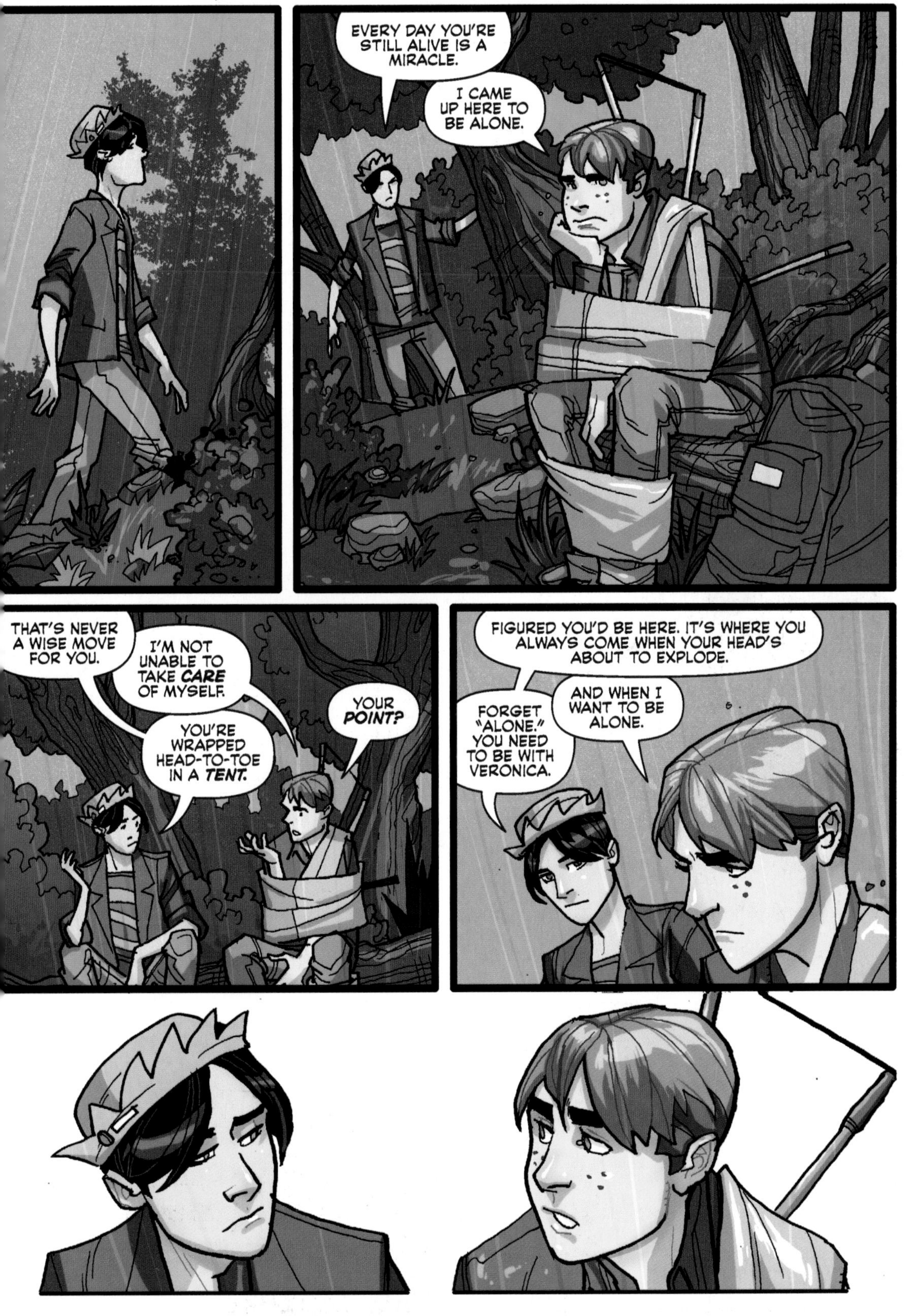
EVERY DAY YOU'RE STILL ALIVE IS A MIRACLE.
I CAME UP HERE TO BE ALONE.
THAT'S NEVER A WISE MOVE FOR YOU.
I'M NOT UNABLE TO TAKE *CARE* OF MYSELF.
YOU'RE WRAPPED HEAD-TO-TOE IN A *TENT.*
YOUR *POINT?*
FIGURED YOU'D BE HERE. IT'S WHERE YOU ALWAYS COME WHEN YOUR HEAD'S ABOUT TO EXPLODE.
AND WHEN I WANT TO BE ALONE.
FORGET "ALONE." YOU NEED TO BE WITH VERONICA.

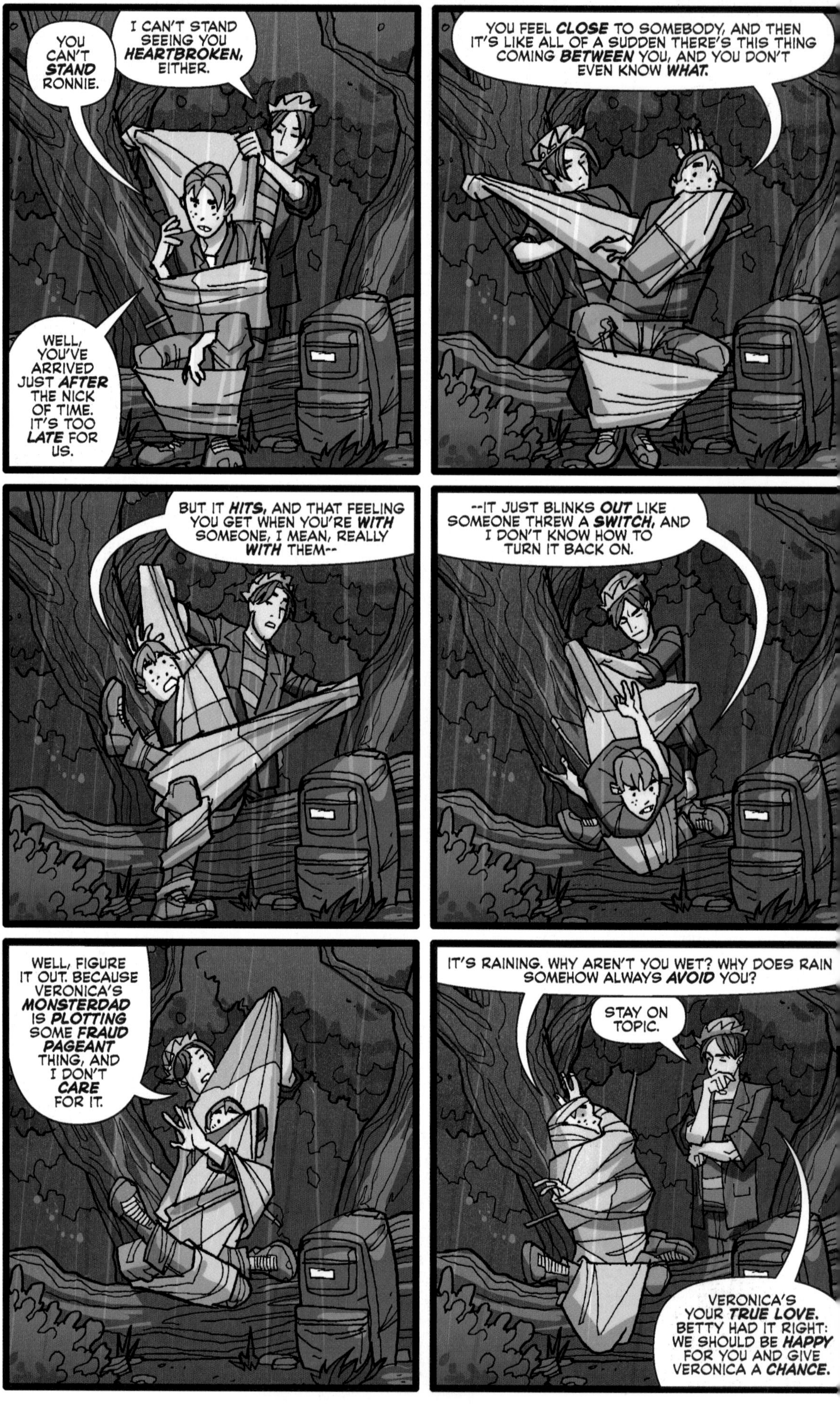
YOU CAN'T STAND RONNIE.
I CAN'T STAND SEEING YOU HEARTBROKEN, EITHER.
WELL, YOU'VE ARRIVED JUST AFTER THE NICK OF TIME. IT'S TOO LATE FOR US.
YOU FEEL CLOSE TO SOMEBODY, AND THEN IT'S LIKE ALL OF A SUDDEN THERE'S THIS THING COMING BETWEEN YOU, AND YOU DON'T EVEN KNOW WHAT.
BUT IT HITS, AND THAT FEELING YOU GET WHEN YOU'RE WITH SOMEONE, I MEAN, REALLY WITH THEM--
--IT JUST BLINKS OUT LIKE SOMEONE THREW A SWITCH, AND I DON'T KNOW HOW TO TURN IT BACK ON.
WELL, FIGURE IT OUT. BECAUSE VERONICA'S MONSTERDAD IS PLOTTING SOME FRAUD PAGEANT THING, AND I DON'T CARE FOR IT.
IT'S RAINING. WHY AREN'T YOU WET? WHY DOES RAIN SOMEHOW ALWAYS AVOID YOU?
STAY ON TOPIC.
VERONICA'S YOUR TRUE LOVE. BETTY HAD IT RIGHT: WE SHOULD BE HAPPY FOR YOU AND GIVE VERONICA A CHANCE.

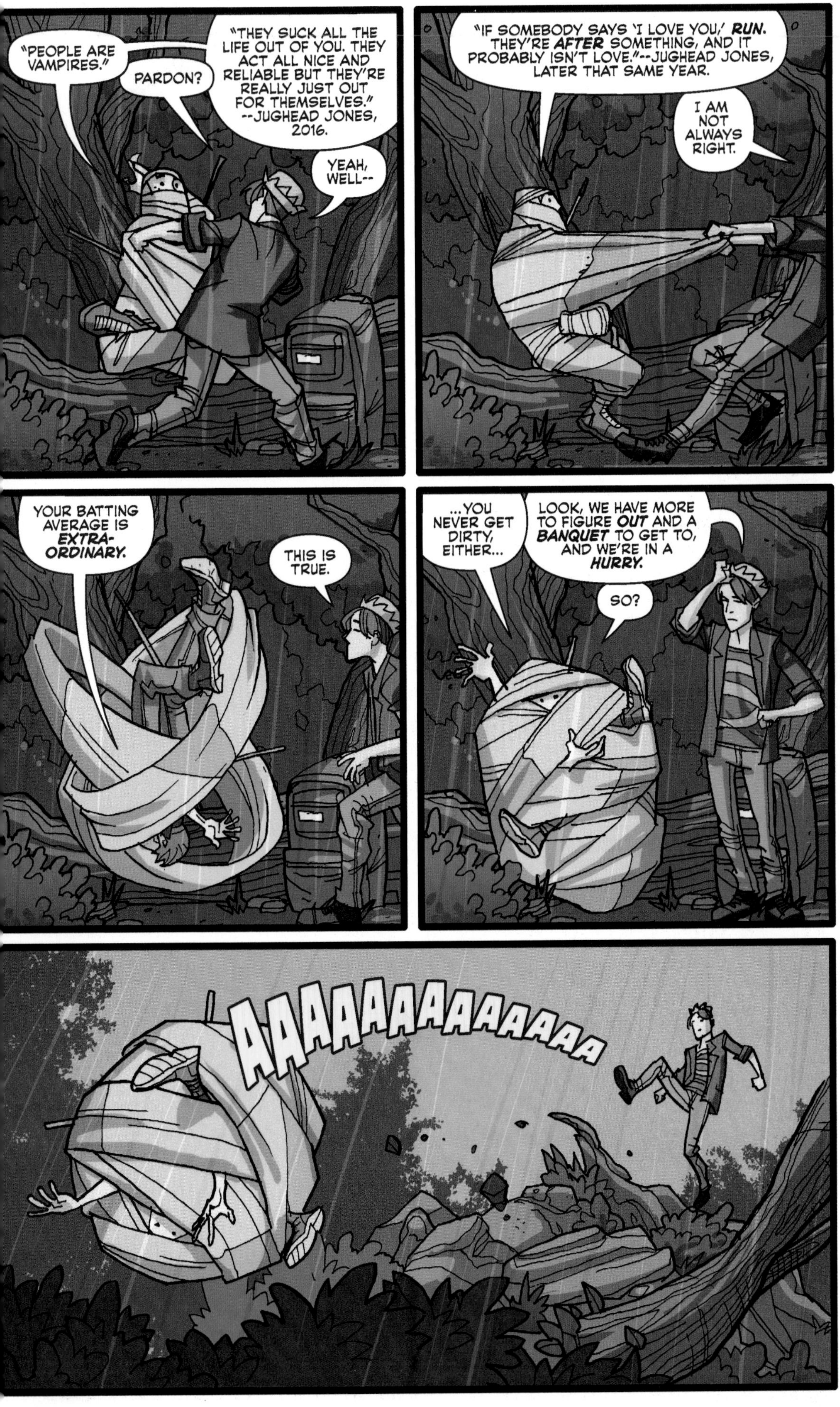
"PEOPLE ARE VAMPIRES."
PARDON?
"THEY SUCK ALL THE LIFE OUT OF YOU. THEY ACT ALL NICE AND RELIABLE BUT THEY'RE REALLY JUST OUT FOR THEMSELVES." --JUGHEAD JONES, 2016.
YEAH, WELL--
"IF SOMEBODY SAYS 'I LOVE YOU,' RUN. THEY'RE AFTER SOMETHING, AND IT PROBABLY ISN'T LOVE."--JUGHEAD JONES, LATER THAT SAME YEAR.
I AM NOT ALWAYS RIGHT.
YOUR BATTING AVERAGE IS EXTRA-ORDINARY.
THIS IS TRUE.
...YOU NEVER GET DIRTY, EITHER...
LOOK, WE HAVE MORE TO FIGURE OUT AND A BANQUET TO GET TO, AND WE'RE IN A HURRY.
SO?
AAAAAAAAAAAAAA

CHAPTER FOUR: Bartók

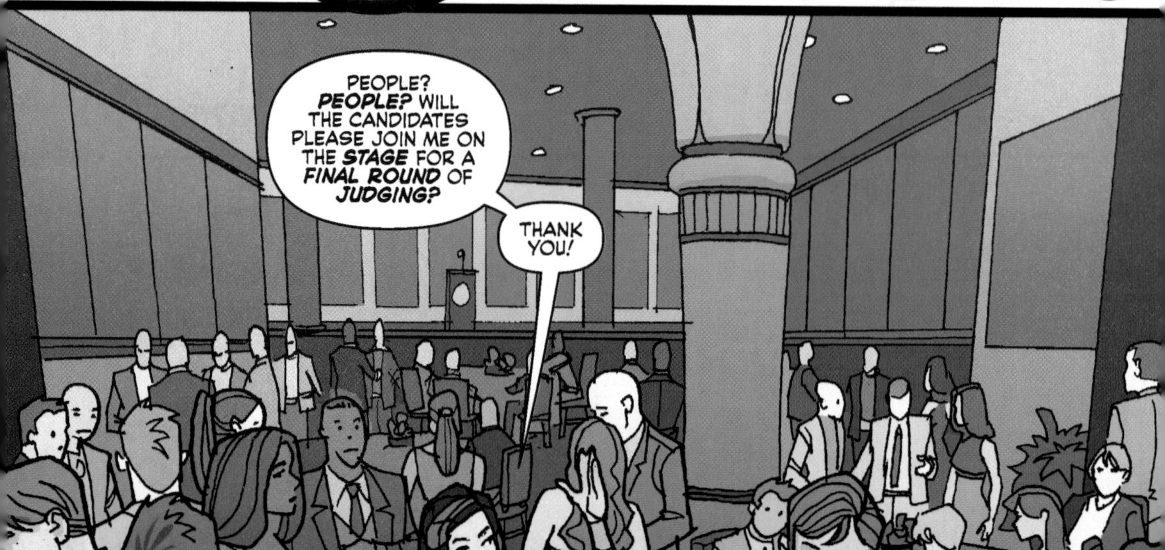

PEOPLE? **PEOPLE?** WILL THE CANDIDATES PLEASE JOIN ME ON THE **STAGE** FOR A **FINAL ROUND** OF **JUDGING?**
THANK YOU!

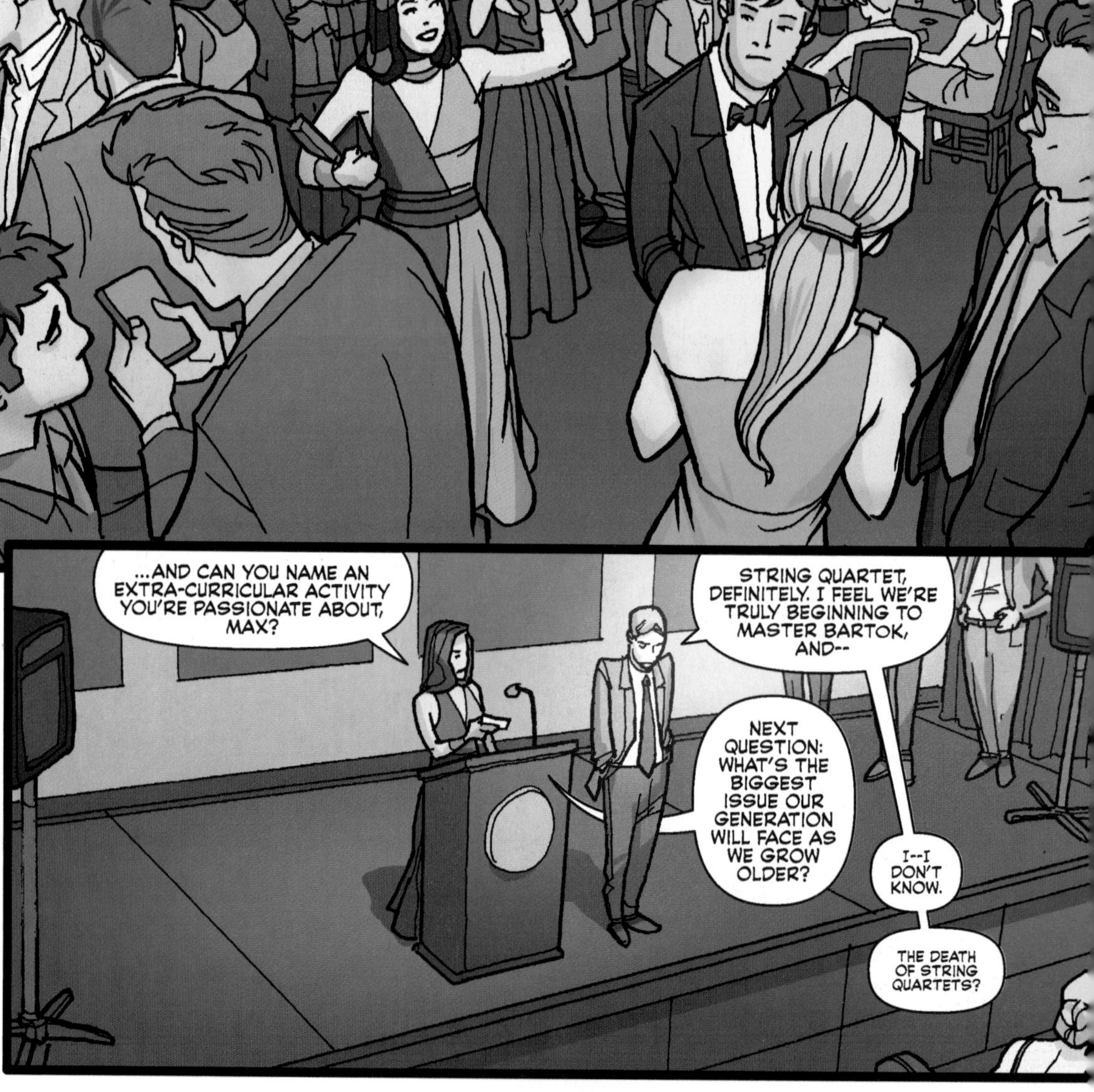

...AND CAN YOU NAME AN EXTRA-CURRICULAR ACTIVITY YOU'RE PASSIONATE ABOUT, MAX?
STRING QUARTET, DEFINITELY. I FEEL WE'RE TRULY BEGINNING TO MASTER BARTOK, AND--
NEXT QUESTION: WHAT'S THE BIGGEST ISSUE OUR GENERATION WILL FACE AS WE GROW OLDER?
I--I DON'T KNOW.
THE DEATH OF STRING QUARTETS?

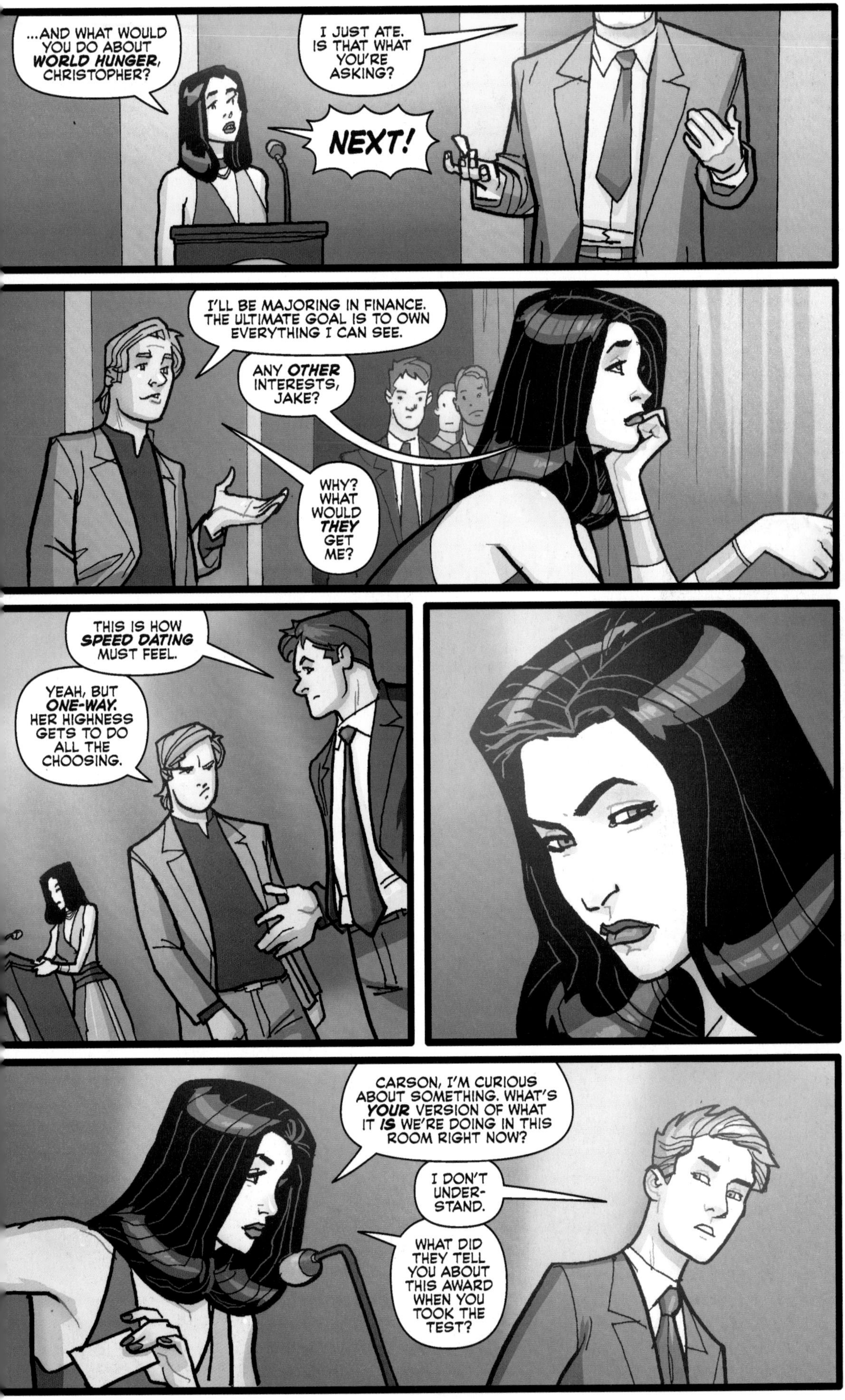
...AND WHAT WOULD YOU DO ABOUT WORLD HUNGER, CHRISTOPHER?
I JUST ATE. IS THAT WHAT YOU'RE ASKING?
NEXT!
I'LL BE MAJORING IN FINANCE. THE ULTIMATE GOAL IS TO OWN EVERYTHING I CAN SEE.
ANY OTHER INTERESTS, JAKE?
WHY? WHAT WOULD THEY GET ME?
THIS IS HOW SPEED DATING MUST FEEL.
YEAH, BUT ONE-WAY. HER HIGHNESS GETS TO DO ALL THE CHOOSING.
CARSON, I'M CURIOUS ABOUT SOMETHING. WHAT'S YOUR VERSION OF WHAT IT IS WE'RE DOING IN THIS ROOM RIGHT NOW?
I DON'T UNDER-STAND.
WHAT DID THEY TELL YOU ABOUT THIS AWARD WHEN YOU TOOK THE TEST?

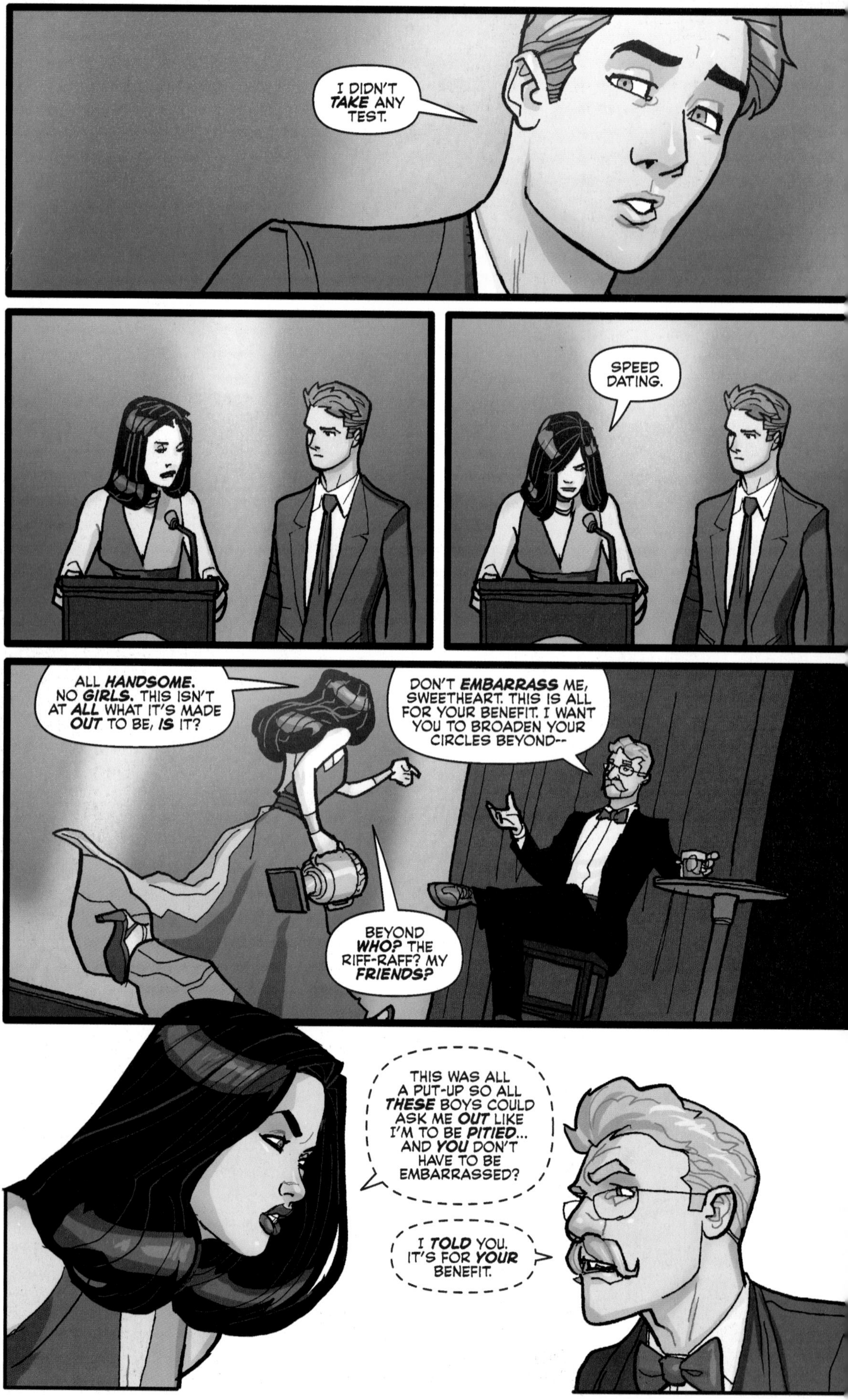
I DIDN'T TAKE ANY TEST.
SPEED DATING.
ALL HANDSOME. NO GIRLS. THIS ISN'T AT ALL WHAT IT'S MADE OUT TO BE, IS IT?
DON'T EMBARRASS ME, SWEETHEART. THIS IS ALL FOR YOUR BENEFIT. I WANT YOU TO BROADEN YOUR CIRCLES BEYOND--
BEYOND WHO? THE RIFF-RAFF? MY FRIENDS?
THIS WAS ALL A PUT-UP SO ALL THESE BOYS COULD ASK ME OUT LIKE I'M TO BE PITIED... AND YOU DON'T HAVE TO BE EMBARRASSED?
I TOLD YOU. IT'S FOR YOUR BENEFIT.

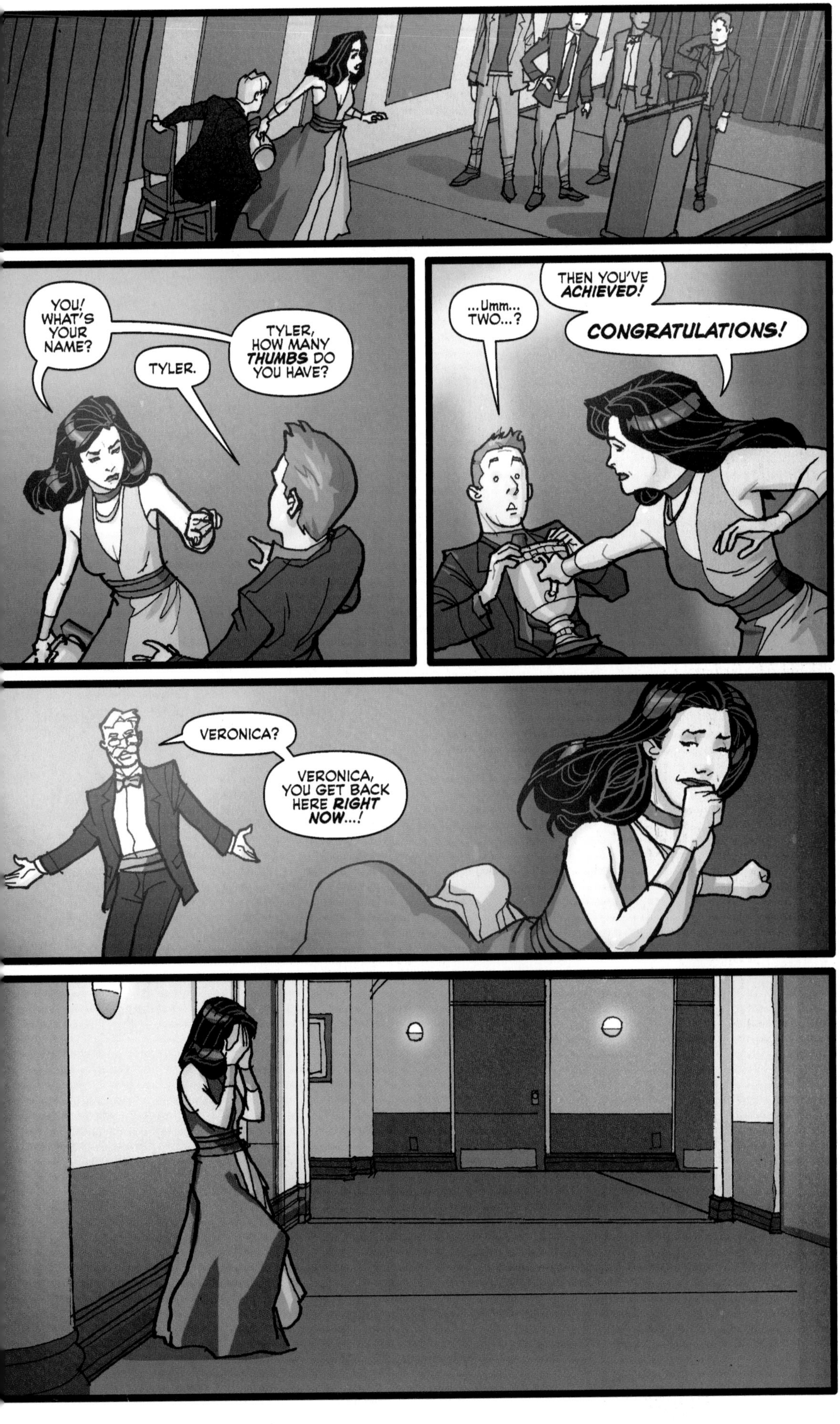
YOU! WHAT'S YOUR NAME?
TYLER.
TYLER, HOW MANY THUMBS DO YOU HAVE?
...Umm... TWO...?
THEN YOU'VE ACHIEVED!
CONGRATULATIONS!
VERONICA?
VERONICA, YOU GET BACK HERE RIGHT NOW...!

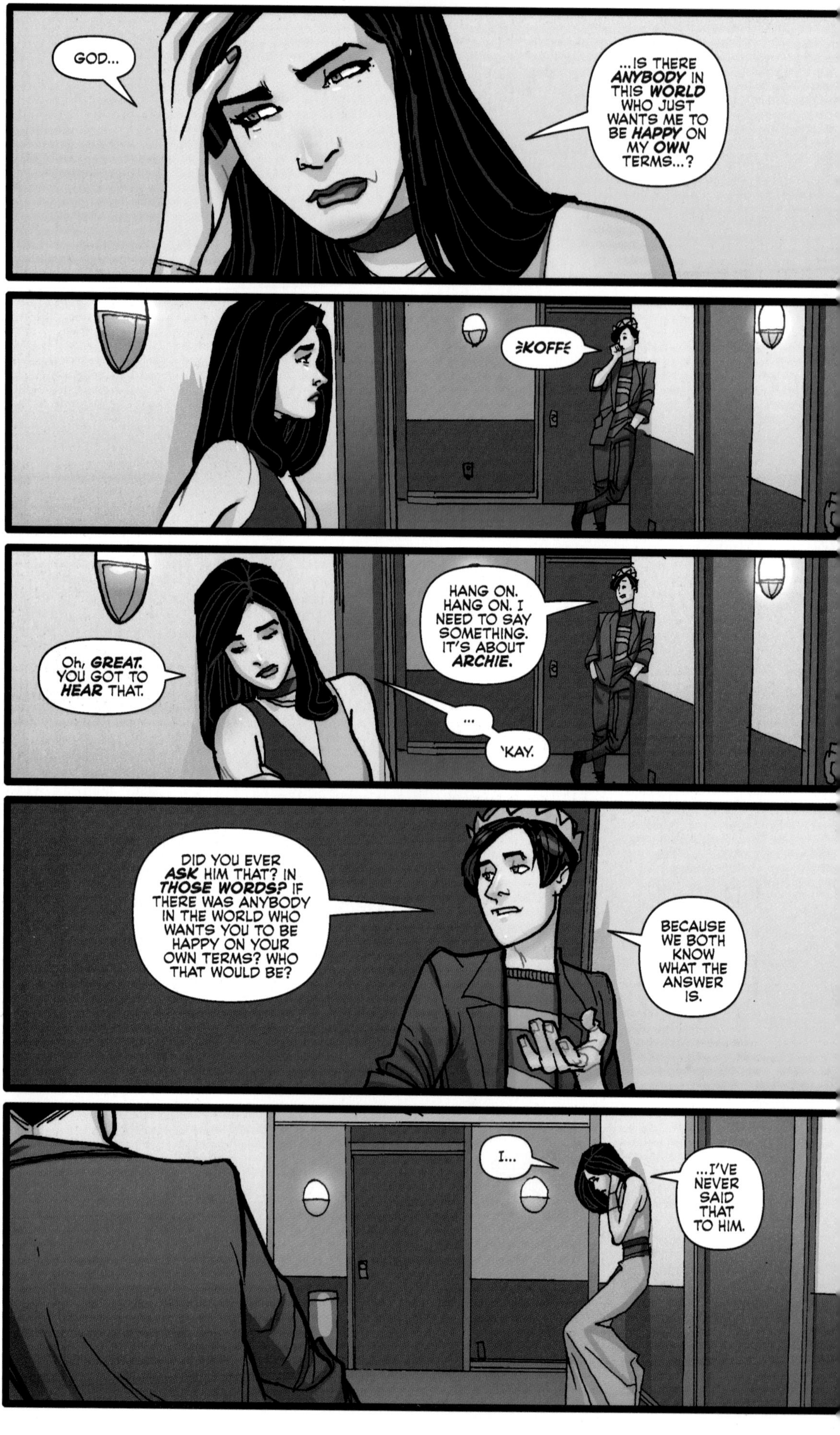
GOD...
...IS THERE ANYBODY IN THIS WORLD WHO JUST WANTS ME TO BE HAPPY ON MY OWN TERMS...?
KOFF
HANG ON. HANG ON. I NEED TO SAY SOMETHING. IT'S ABOUT ARCHIE.
Oh, GREAT. YOU GOT TO HEAR THAT.
...
'KAY.
DID YOU EVER ASK HIM THAT? IN THOSE WORDS? IF THERE WAS ANYBODY IN THE WORLD WHO WANTS YOU TO BE HAPPY ON YOUR OWN TERMS? WHO THAT WOULD BE?
BECAUSE WE BOTH KNOW WHAT THE ANSWER IS.
I...
...I'VE NEVER SAID THAT TO HIM.

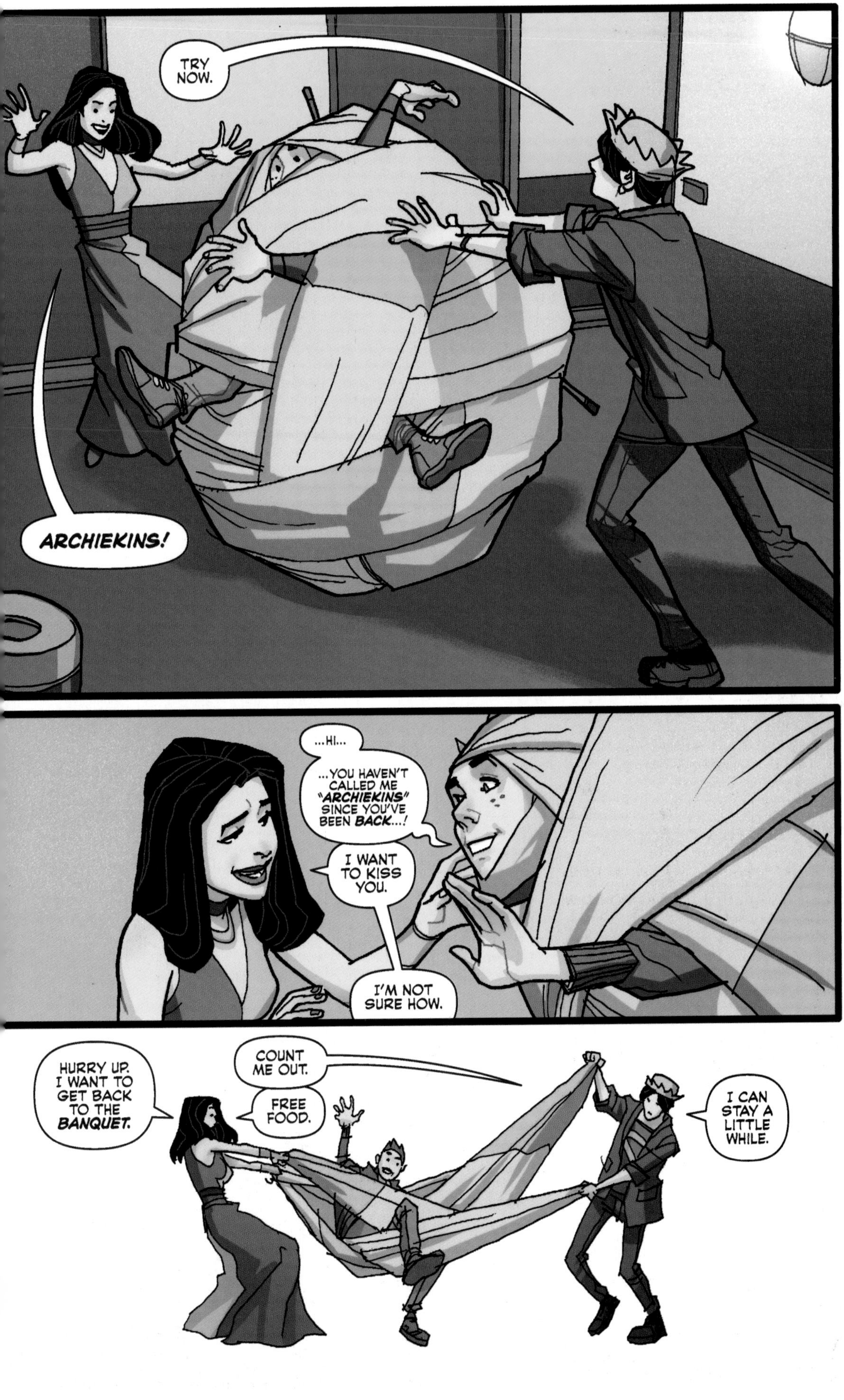
TRY NOW.
ARCHIEKINS!
...HI...
...YOU HAVEN'T CALLED ME "ARCHIEKINS" SINCE YOU'VE BEEN BACK...!
I WANT TO KISS YOU.
I'M NOT SURE HOW.
HURRY UP. I WANT TO GET BACK TO THE BANQUET.
COUNT ME OUT.
FREE FOOD.
I CAN STAY A LITTLE WHILE.

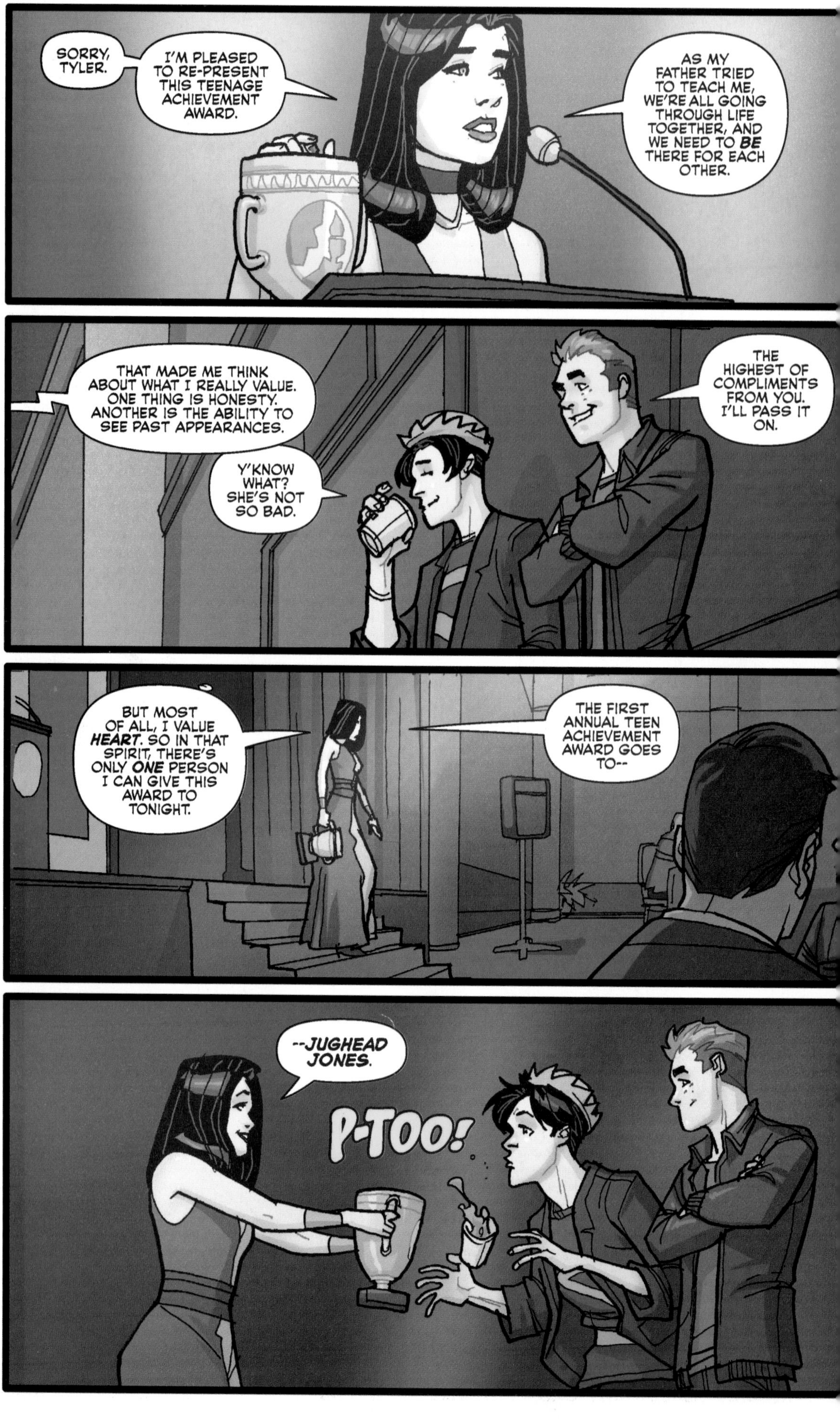
SORRY, TYLER.
I'M PLEASED TO RE-PRESENT THIS TEENAGE ACHIEVEMENT AWARD.
AS MY FATHER TRIED TO TEACH ME, WE'RE ALL GOING THROUGH LIFE TOGETHER, AND WE NEED TO **BE** THERE FOR EACH OTHER.
THAT MADE ME THINK ABOUT WHAT I REALLY VALUE. ONE THING IS HONESTY. ANOTHER IS THE ABILITY TO SEE PAST APPEARANCES.
THE HIGHEST OF COMPLIMENTS FROM YOU. I'LL PASS IT ON.
Y'KNOW WHAT? SHE'S NOT SO BAD.
BUT MOST OF ALL, I VALUE **HEART**. SO IN THAT SPIRIT, THERE'S ONLY **ONE** PERSON I CAN GIVE THIS AWARD TO TONIGHT.
THE FIRST ANNUAL TEEN ACHIEVEMENT AWARD GOES TO--
--JUGHEAD JONES.
P-TOO!

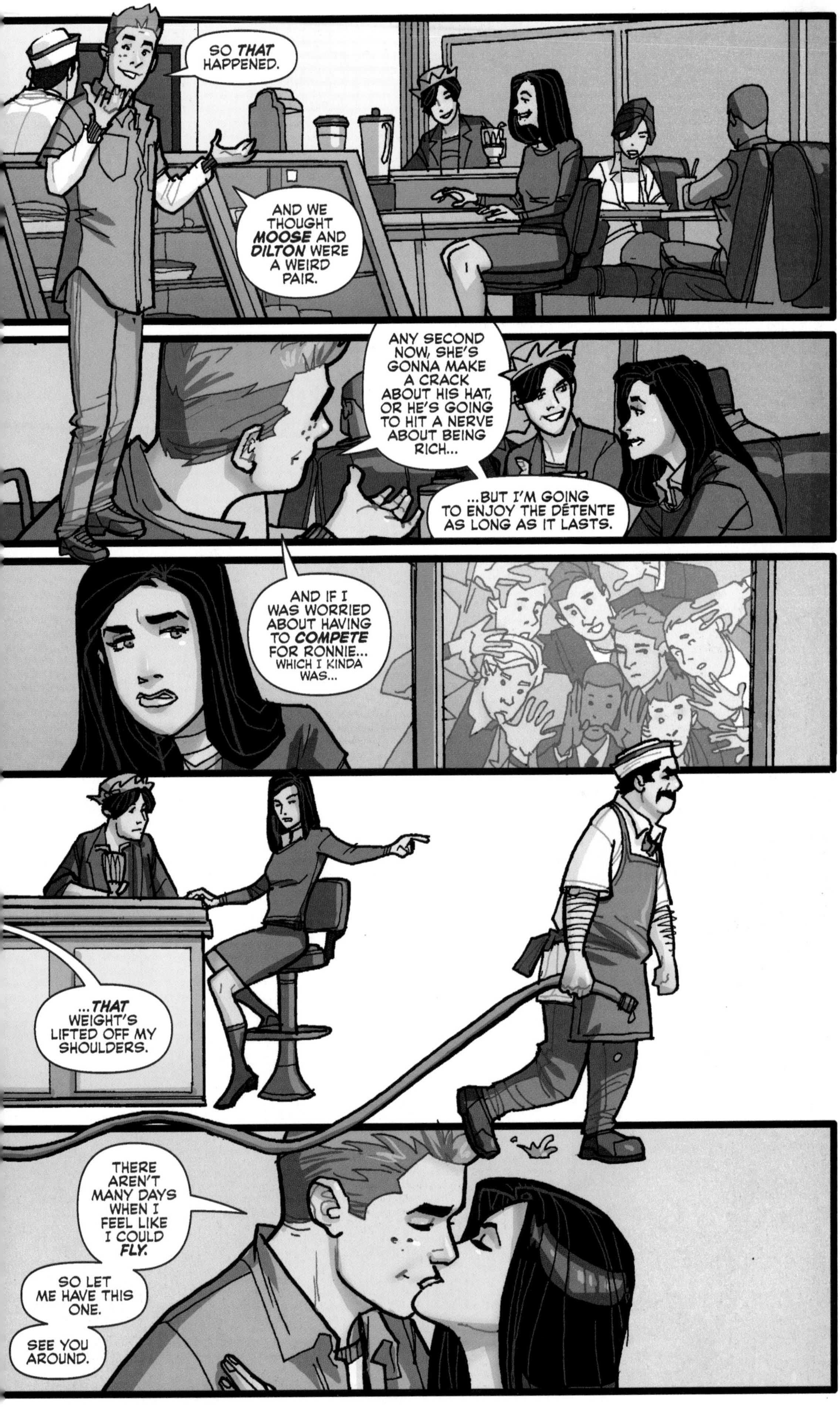
SO THAT HAPPENED.
AND WE THOUGHT MOOSE AND DILTON WERE A WEIRD PAIR.
ANY SECOND NOW, SHE'S GONNA MAKE A CRACK ABOUT HIS HAT, OR HE'S GOING TO HIT A NERVE ABOUT BEING RICH...
...BUT I'M GOING TO ENJOY THE DÉTENTE AS LONG AS IT LASTS.
AND IF I WAS WORRIED ABOUT HAVING TO COMPETE FOR RONNIE... WHICH I KINDA WAS...
...THAT WEIGHT'S LIFTED OFF MY SHOULDERS.
THERE AREN'T MANY DAYS WHEN I FEEL LIKE I COULD FLY.
SO LET ME HAVE THIS ONE.
SEE YOU AROUND.

CHAPTER FIVE: Dad?

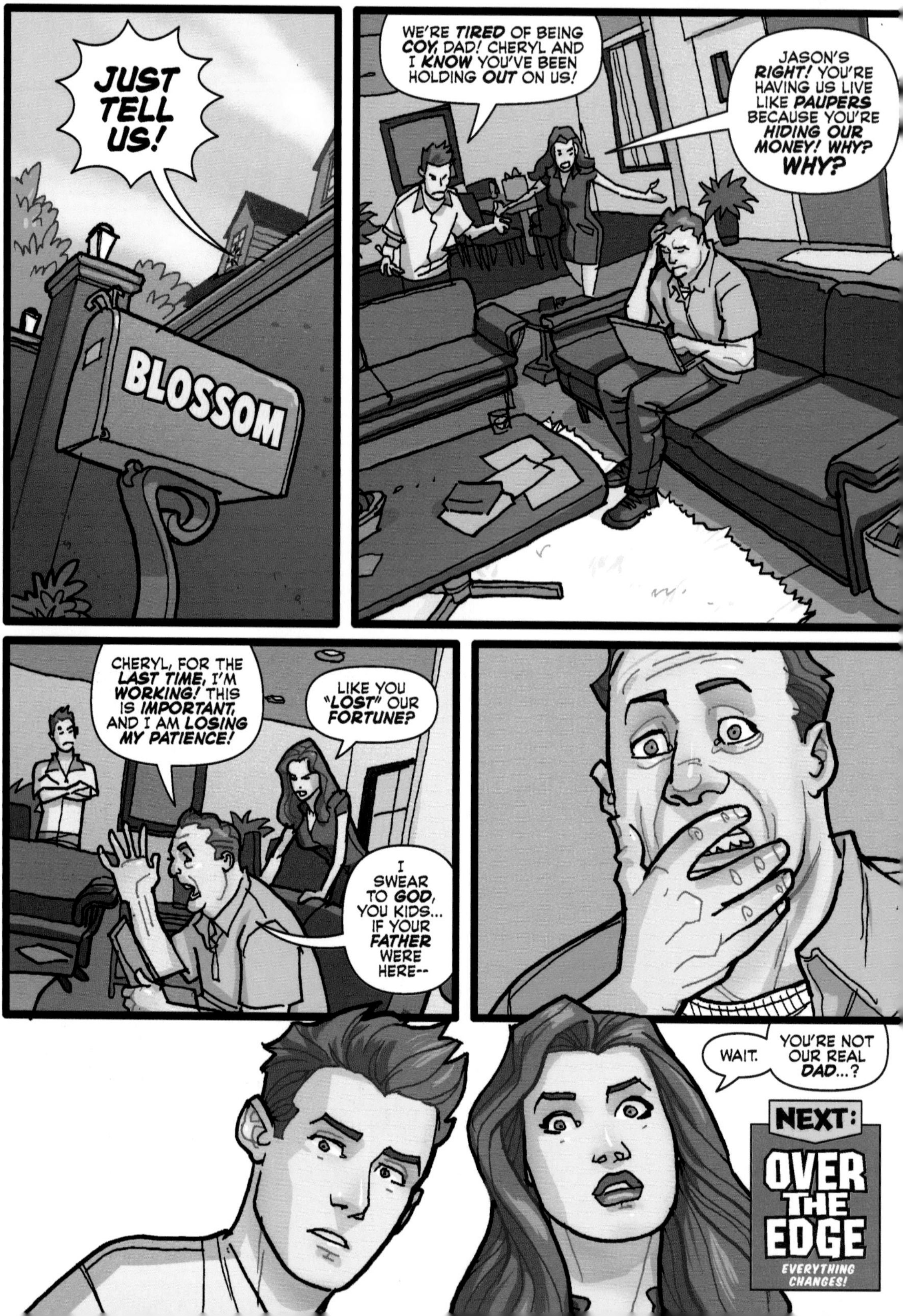
JUST TELL US!
BLOSSOM
WE'RE TIRED OF BEING COY, DAD! CHERYL AND I KNOW YOU'VE BEEN HOLDING OUT ON US!
JASON'S RIGHT! YOU'RE HAVING US LIVE LIKE PAUPERS BECAUSE YOU'RE HIDING OUR MONEY! WHY? WHY? WHY?
CHERYL, FOR THE LAST TIME, I'M WORKING! THIS IS IMPORTANT, AND I AM LOSING MY PATIENCE!
LIKE YOU "LOST" OUR FORTUNE?
I SWEAR TO GOD, YOU KIDS... IF YOUR FATHER WERE HERE--
WAIT.
YOU'RE NOT OUR REAL DAD...?
NEXT:
OVER THE EDGE
EVERYTHING CHANGES!

TO BE CONTINUED...

ISSUE TWENTY

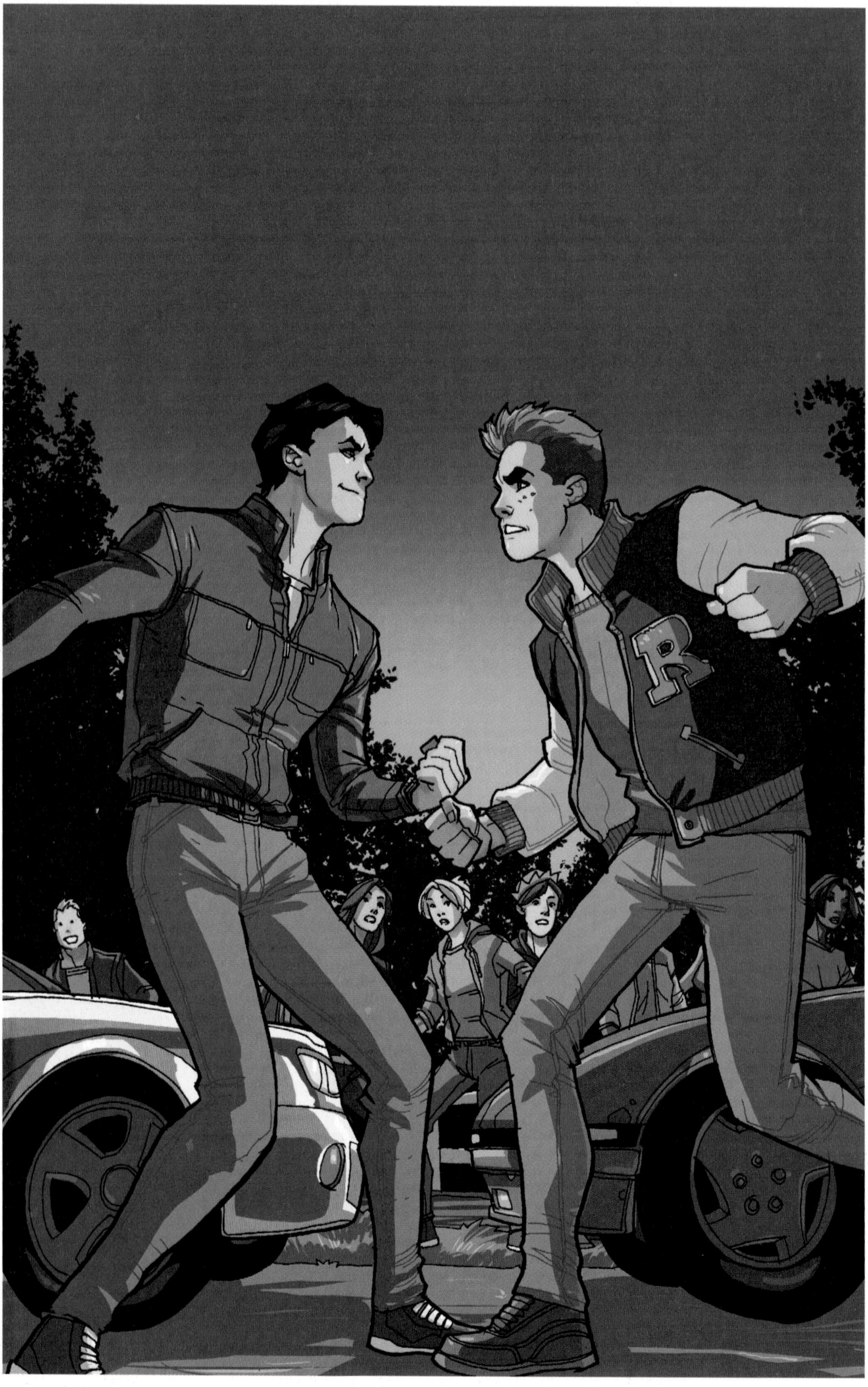

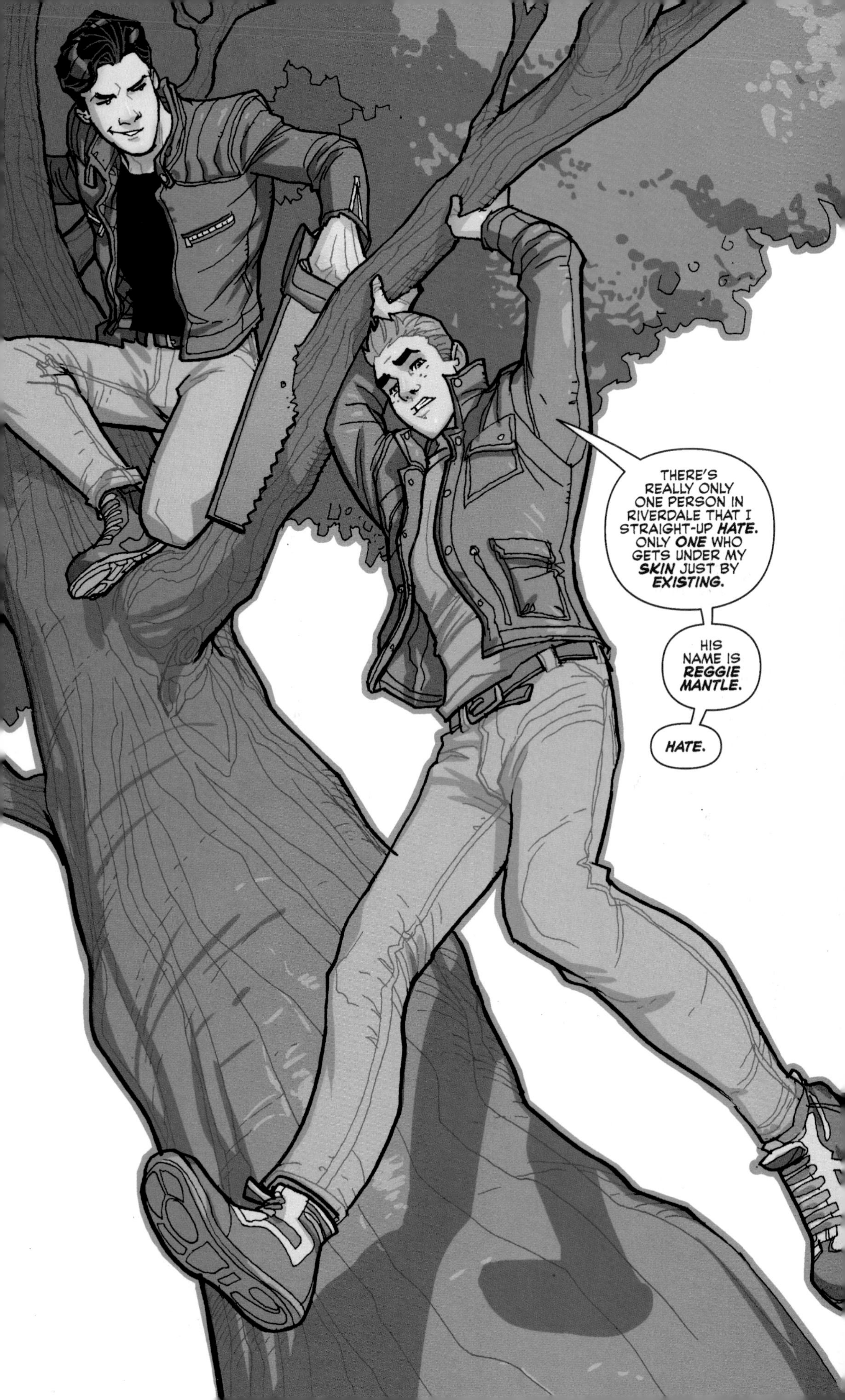
THERE'S REALLY ONLY ONE PERSON IN RIVERDALE THAT I STRAIGHT-UP **HATE.** ONLY **ONE** WHO GETS UNDER MY **SKIN** JUST BY **EXISTING.**
HIS NAME IS **REGGIE MANTLE.**
HATE.

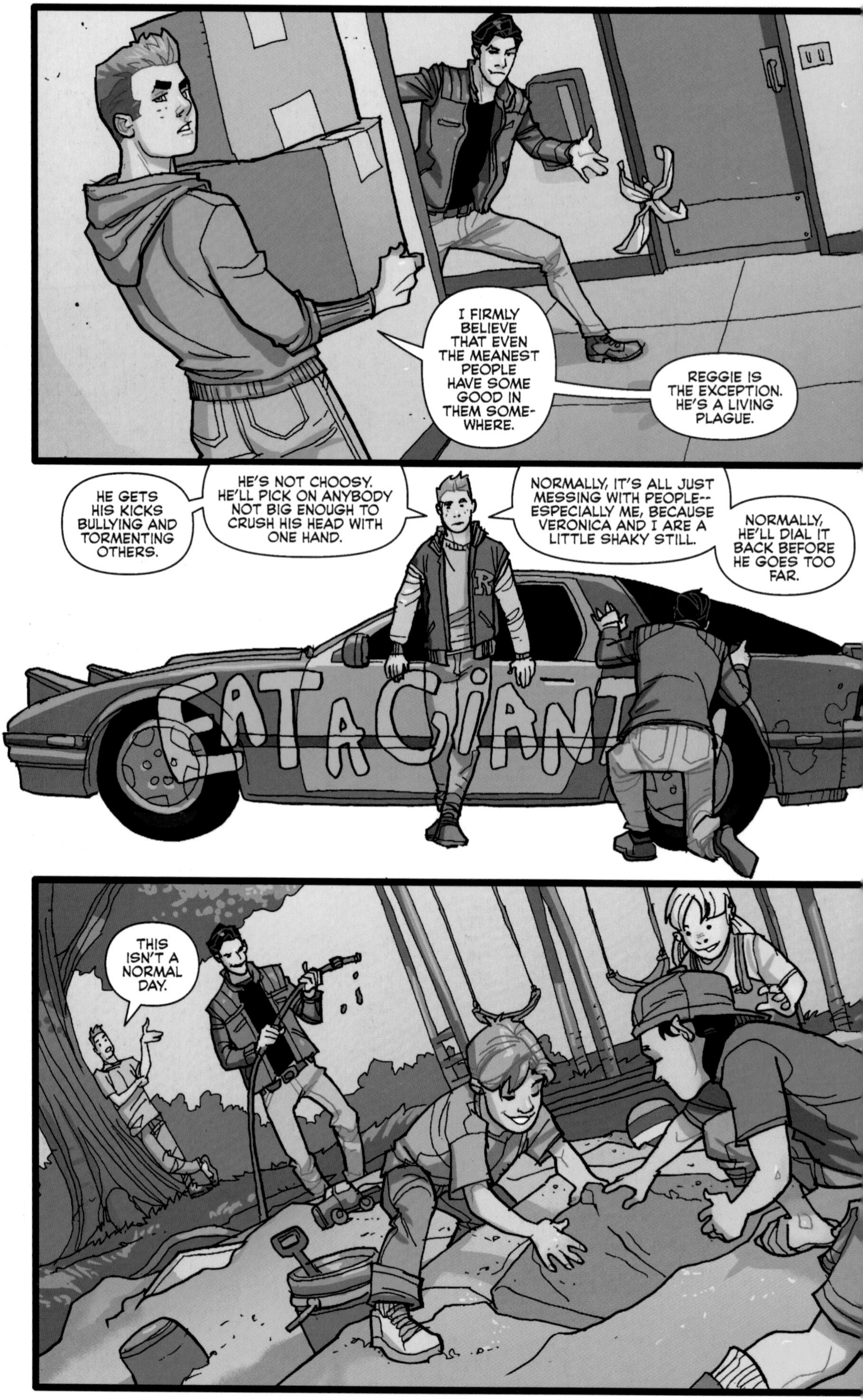
I FIRMLY BELIEVE THAT EVEN THE MEANEST PEOPLE HAVE SOME GOOD IN THEM SOMEWHERE.
REGGIE IS THE EXCEPTION. HE'S A LIVING PLAGUE.
HE GETS HIS KICKS BULLYING AND TORMENTING OTHERS.
HE'S NOT CHOOSY. HE'LL PICK ON ANYBODY NOT BIG ENOUGH TO CRUSH HIS HEAD WITH ONE HAND.
NORMALLY, IT'S ALL JUST MESSING WITH PEOPLE-- ESPECIALLY ME, BECAUSE VERONICA AND I ARE A LITTLE SHAKY STILL.
NORMALLY, HE'LL DIAL IT BACK BEFORE HE GOES TOO FAR.
FAT GIANT
THIS ISN'T A NORMAL DAY.

CHAPTER ONE: WHY NOT JUST BUY A NEW CAR?

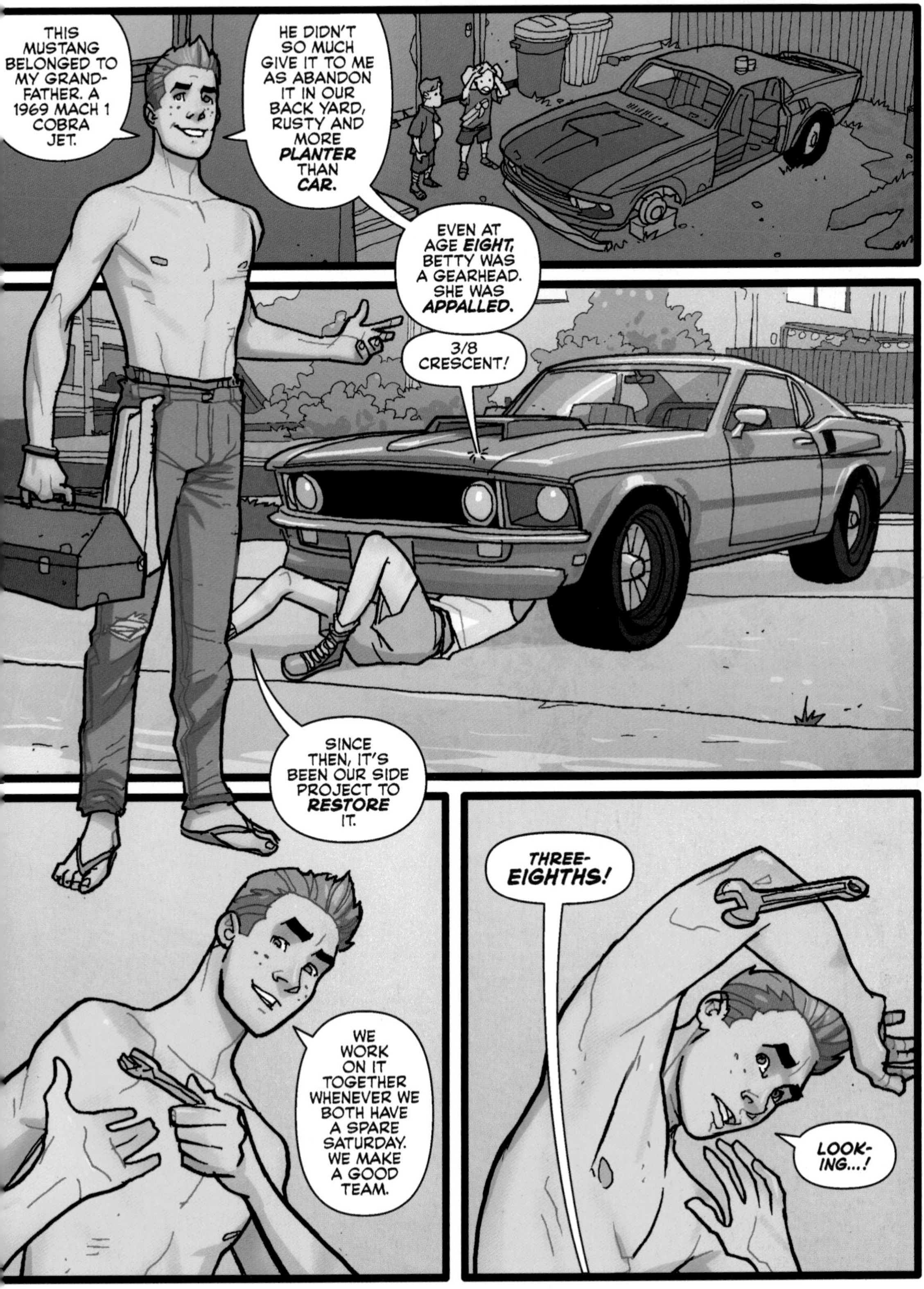
THIS MUSTANG BELONGED TO MY GRAND-FATHER. A 1969 MACH 1 COBRA JET.
HE DIDN'T SO MUCH GIVE IT TO ME AS ABANDON IT IN OUR BACK YARD, RUSTY AND MORE PLANTER THAN CAR.
EVEN AT AGE EIGHT, BETTY WAS A GEARHEAD. SHE WAS APPALLED.
3/8 CRESCENT!
SINCE THEN, IT'S BEEN OUR SIDE PROJECT TO RESTORE IT.
WE WORK ON IT TOGETHER WHENEVER WE BOTH HAVE A SPARE SATURDAY. WE MAKE A GOOD TEAM.
THREE-EIGHTHS!
LOOK-ING...!

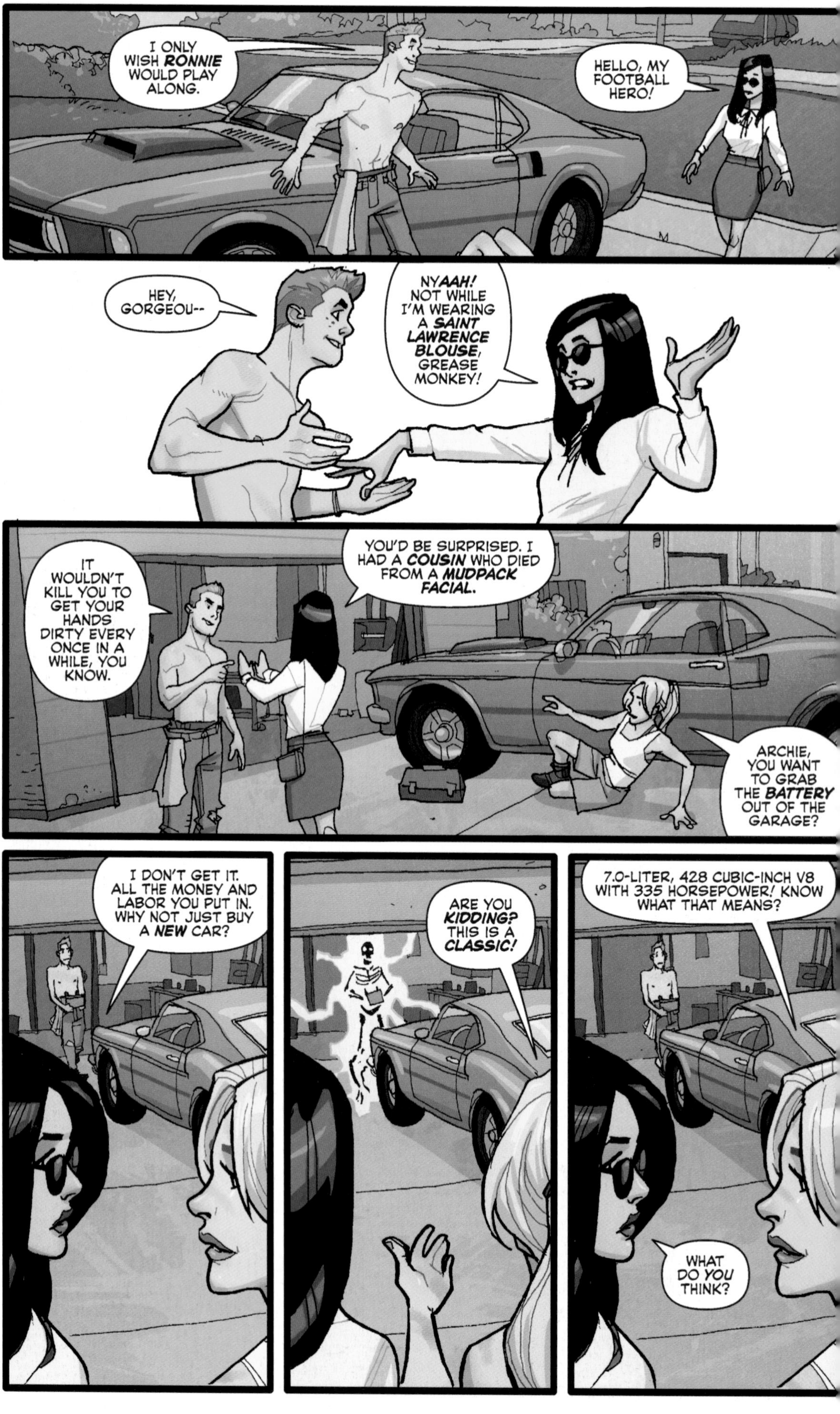
I ONLY WISH RONNIE WOULD PLAY ALONG.
HELLO, MY FOOTBALL HERO!
HEY, GORGEOU--
NYAAH! NOT WHILE I'M WEARING A SAINT LAWRENCE BLOUSE, GREASE MONKEY!
IT WOULDN'T KILL YOU TO GET YOUR HANDS DIRTY EVERY ONCE IN A WHILE, YOU KNOW.
YOU'D BE SURPRISED. I HAD A COUSIN WHO DIED FROM A MUDPACK FACIAL.
ARCHIE, YOU WANT TO GRAB THE BATTERY OUT OF THE GARAGE?
I DON'T GET IT. ALL THE MONEY AND LABOR YOU PUT IN. WHY NOT JUST BUY A NEW CAR?
ARE YOU KIDDING? THIS IS A CLASSIC!
7.0-LITER, 428 CUBIC-INCH V8 WITH 335 HORSEPOWER! KNOW WHAT THAT MEANS?
WHAT DO YOU THINK?

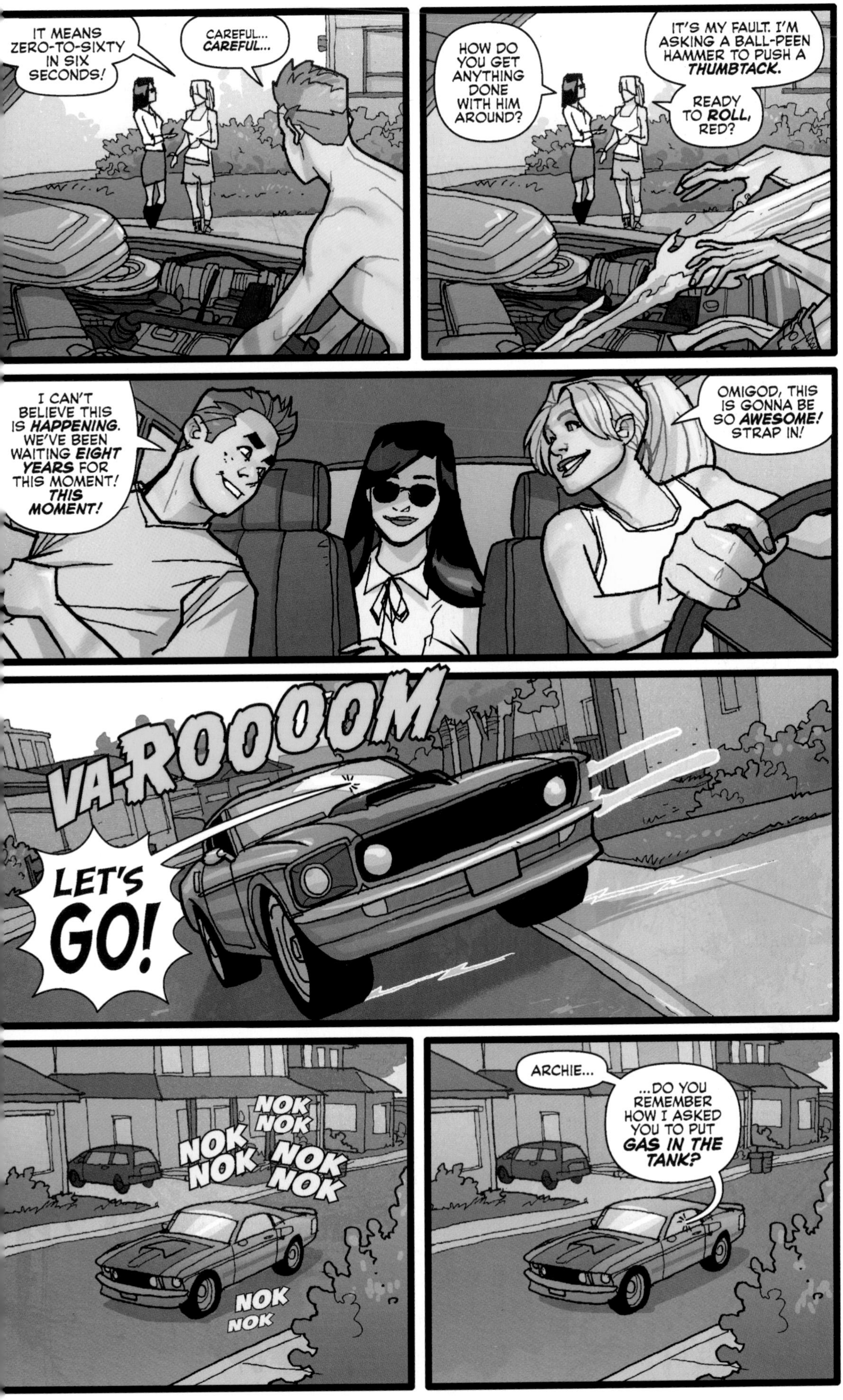
IT MEANS ZERO-TO-SIXTY IN SIX SECONDS!
CAREFUL... **CAREFUL...**
HOW DO YOU GET ANYTHING DONE WITH HIM AROUND?
IT'S MY FAULT. I'M ASKING A BALL-PEEN HAMMER TO PUSH A **THUMBTACK.**
READY TO **ROLL,** RED?
I CAN'T BELIEVE THIS IS **HAPPENING.** WE'VE BEEN WAITING **EIGHT YEARS** FOR THIS MOMENT! **THIS MOMENT!**
OMIGOD, THIS IS GONNA BE SO **AWESOME!** STRAP IN!
VA-ROOOOM
LET'S GO!
NOK NOK
NOK NOK
NOK NOK
NOK NOK
ARCHIE...
...DO YOU REMEMBER HOW I ASKED YOU TO PUT **GAS IN THE TANK?**

CHAPTER TWO: DON'T BEAT YOURSELF UP

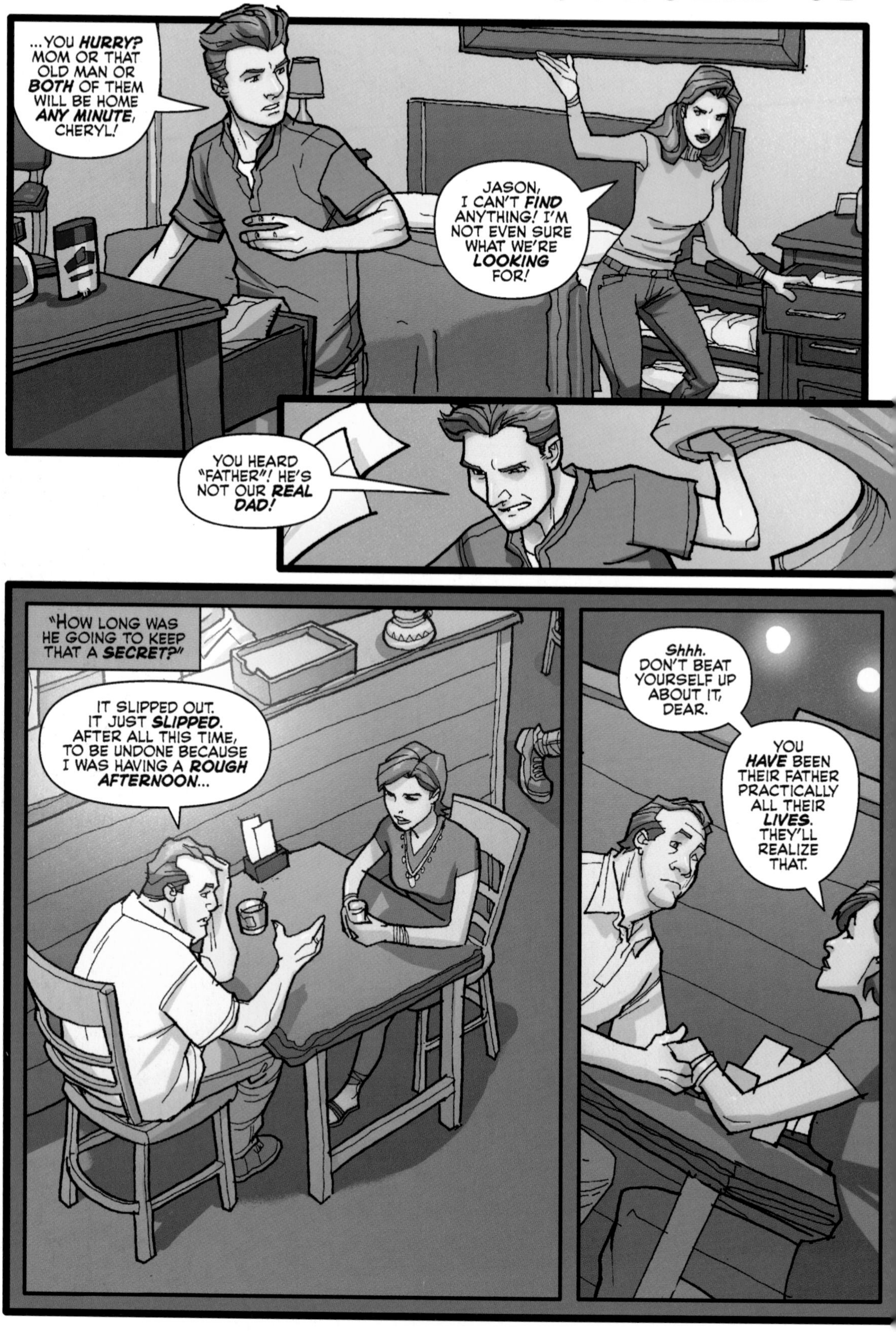
...YOU HURRY? MOM OR THAT OLD MAN OR BOTH OF THEM WILL BE HOME ANY MINUTE, CHERYL!
JASON, I CAN'T FIND ANYTHING! I'M NOT EVEN SURE WHAT WE'RE LOOKING FOR!
YOU HEARD "FATHER"! HE'S NOT OUR REAL DAD!
"HOW LONG WAS HE GOING TO KEEP THAT A SECRET?"
IT SLIPPED OUT. IT JUST SLIPPED. AFTER ALL THIS TIME, TO BE UNDONE BECAUSE I WAS HAVING A ROUGH AFTERNOON...
Shhh. DON'T BEAT YOURSELF UP ABOUT IT, DEAR.
YOU HAVE BEEN THEIR FATHER PRACTICALLY ALL THEIR LIVES. THEY'LL REALIZE THAT.

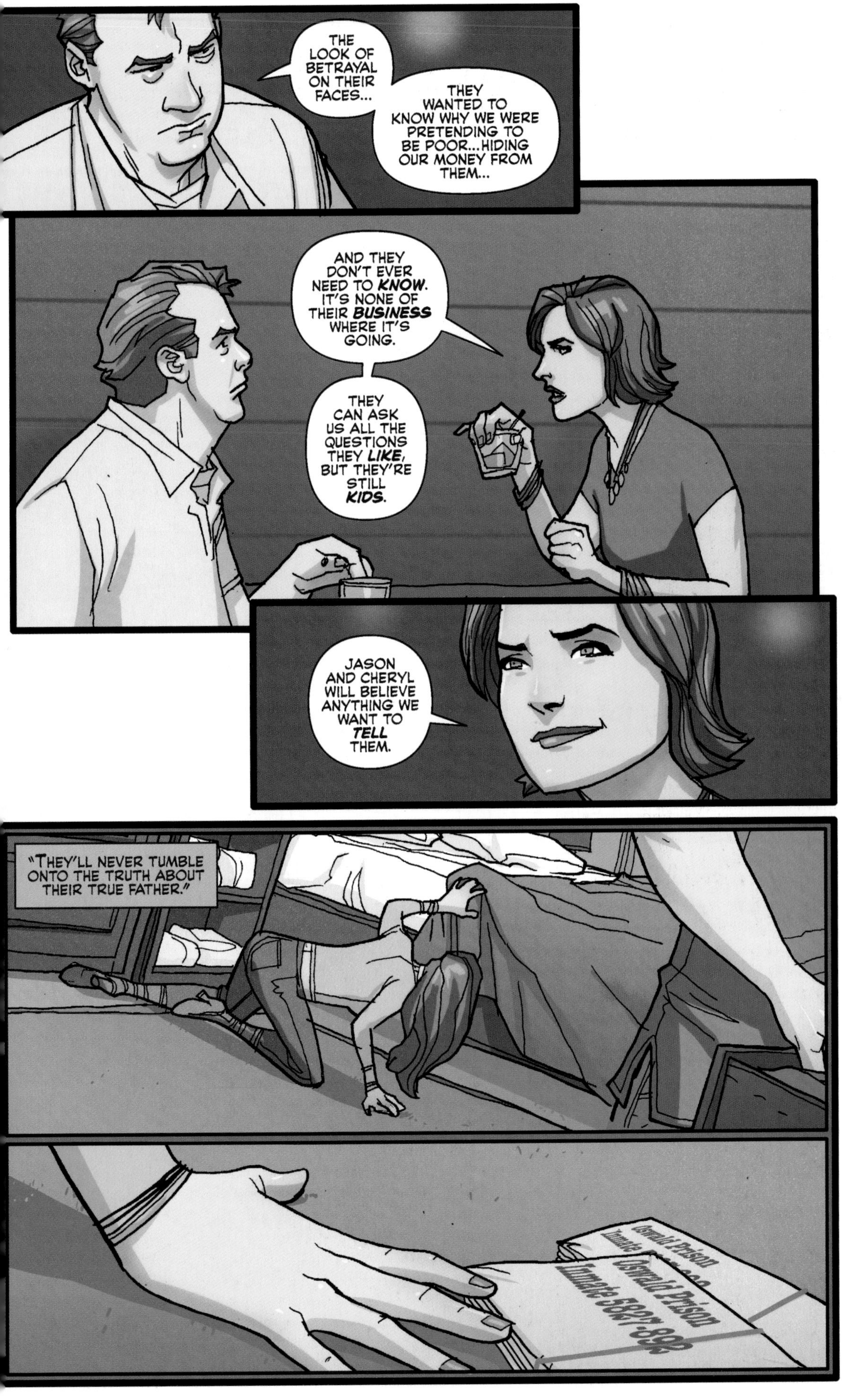
THE LOOK OF BETRAYAL ON THEIR FACES...
THEY WANTED TO KNOW WHY WE WERE PRETENDING TO BE POOR...HIDING OUR MONEY FROM THEM...
AND THEY DON'T EVER NEED TO ***KNOW***. IT'S NONE OF THEIR ***BUSINESS*** WHERE IT'S GOING.
THEY CAN ASK US ALL THE QUESTIONS THEY ***LIKE***, BUT THEY'RE STILL ***KIDS***.
JASON AND CHERYL WILL BELIEVE ANYTHING WE WANT TO ***TELL*** THEM.
"THEY'LL NEVER TUMBLE ONTO THE TRUTH ABOUT THEIR TRUE FATHER."
Oswald Prison
Oswald Prison
Inmate 5827-892

CHAPTER THREE: Widdle Archie

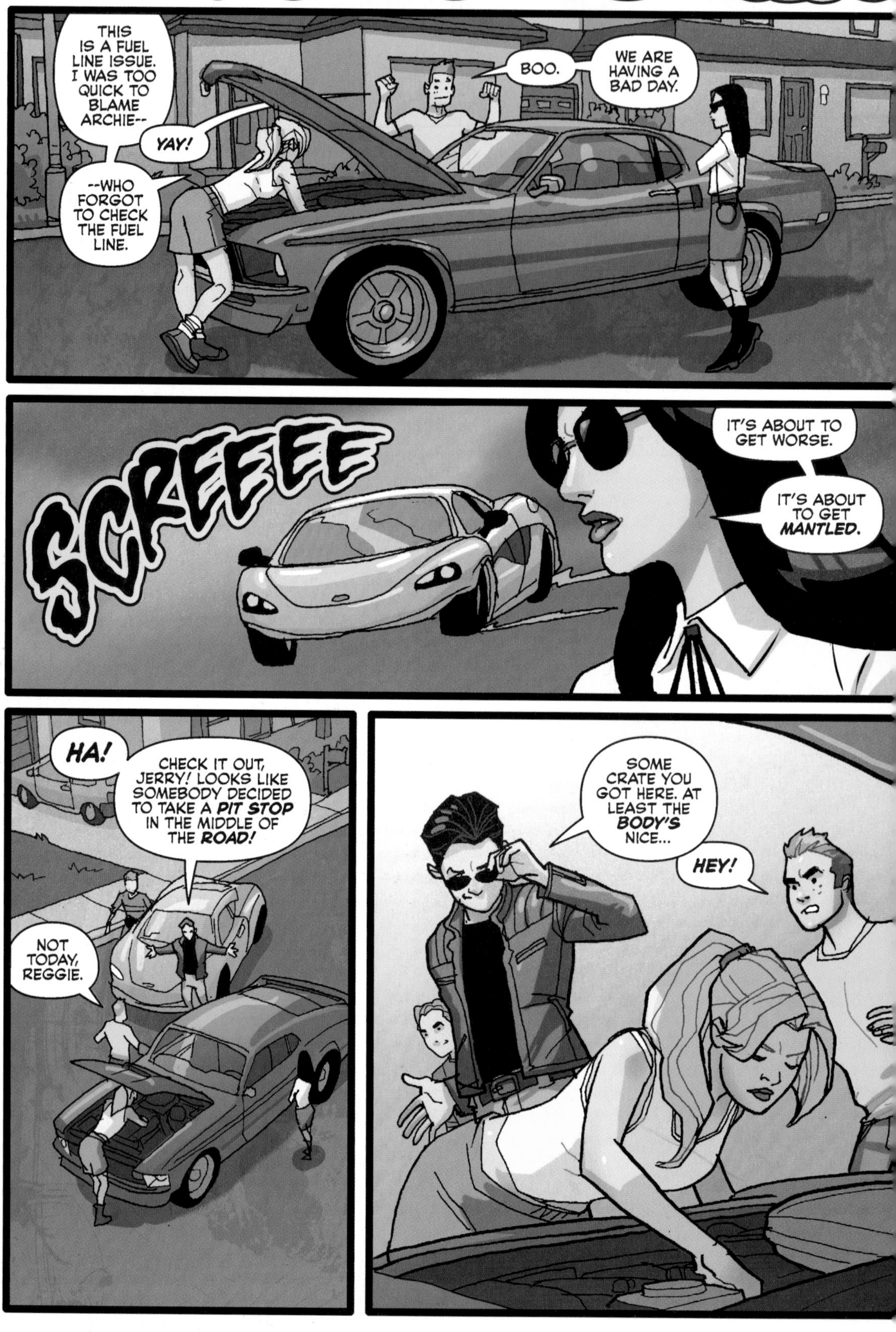

THIS IS A FUEL LINE ISSUE. I WAS TOO QUICK TO BLAME ARCHIE--
YAY!
--WHO FORGOT TO CHECK THE FUEL LINE.
BOO.
WE ARE HAVING A BAD DAY.
SCREEEE
IT'S ABOUT TO GET WORSE.
IT'S ABOUT TO GET MANTLED.
HA!
CHECK IT OUT, JERRY! LOOKS LIKE SOMEBODY DECIDED TO TAKE A PIT STOP IN THE MIDDLE OF THE ROAD!
NOT TODAY, REGGIE.
SOME CRATE YOU GOT HERE. AT LEAST THE BODY'S NICE...
HEY!

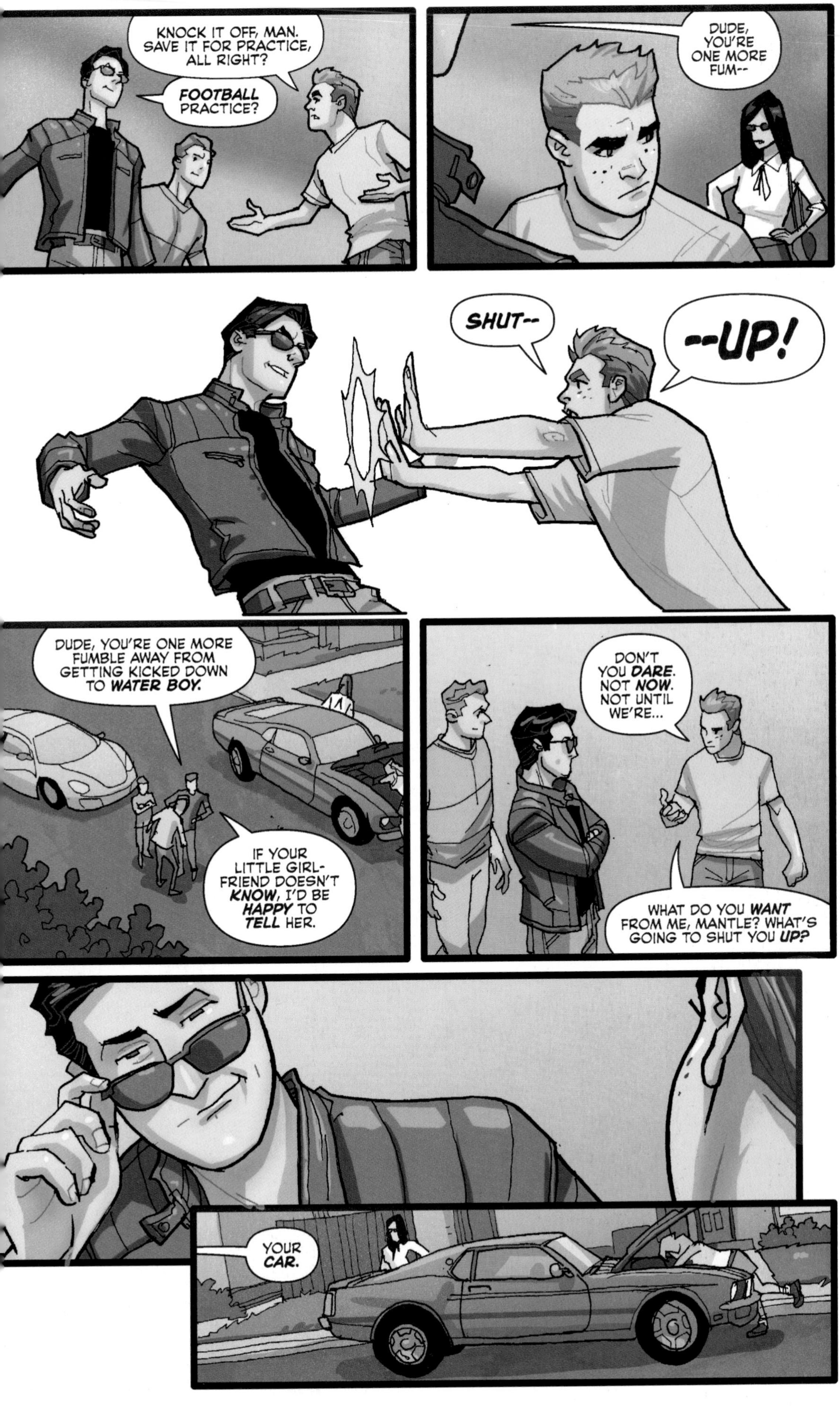
KNOCK IT OFF, MAN. SAVE IT FOR PRACTICE, ALL RIGHT?
FOOTBALL PRACTICE?
DUDE, YOU'RE ONE MORE FUM--
SHUT--
--UP!
DUDE, YOU'RE ONE MORE FUMBLE AWAY FROM GETTING KICKED DOWN TO WATER BOY.
IF YOUR LITTLE GIRL-FRIEND DOESN'T KNOW, I'D BE HAPPY TO TELL HER.
DON'T YOU DARE. NOT NOW. NOT UNTIL WE'RE...
WHAT DO YOU WANT FROM ME, MANTLE? WHAT'S GOING TO SHUT YOU UP?
YOUR CAR.

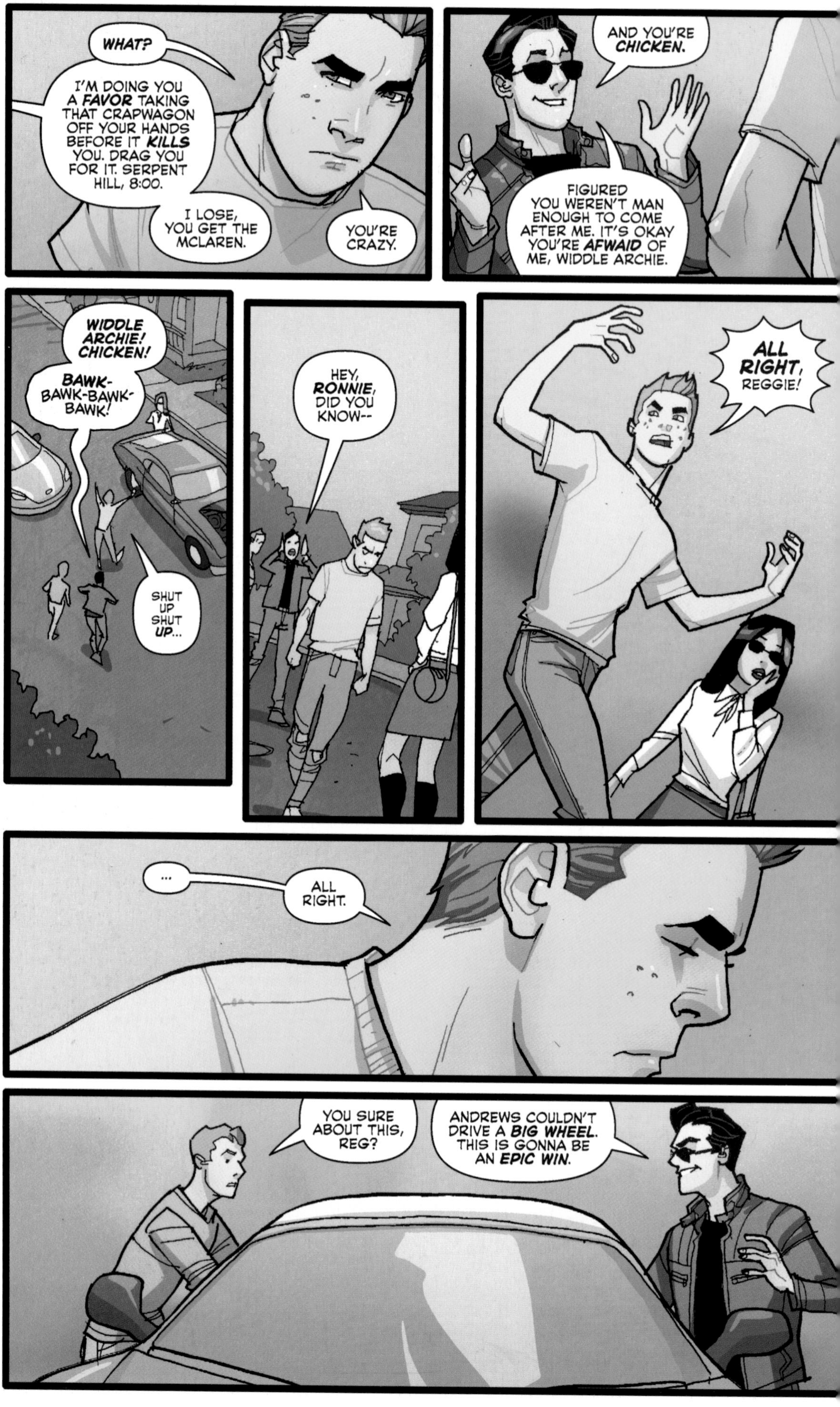
WHAT?
I'M DOING YOU A FAVOR TAKING THAT CRAPWAGON OFF YOUR HANDS BEFORE IT KILLS YOU. DRAG YOU FOR IT. SERPENT HILL, 8:00.
I LOSE, YOU GET THE MCLAREN.
YOU'RE CRAZY.
AND YOU'RE CHICKEN.
FIGURED YOU WEREN'T MAN ENOUGH TO COME AFTER ME. IT'S OKAY YOU'RE AFWAID OF ME, WIDDLE ARCHIE.
WIDDLE ARCHIE! CHICKEN!
BAWK-BAWK-BAWK-BAWK!
SHUT UP SHUT UP...
HEY, RONNIE, DID YOU KNOW--
ALL RIGHT, REGGIE!
...
ALL RIGHT.
YOU SURE ABOUT THIS, REG?
ANDREWS COULDN'T DRIVE A BIG WHEEL. THIS IS GONNA BE AN EPIC WIN.

CHAPTER FOUR: LIKE A TIGER

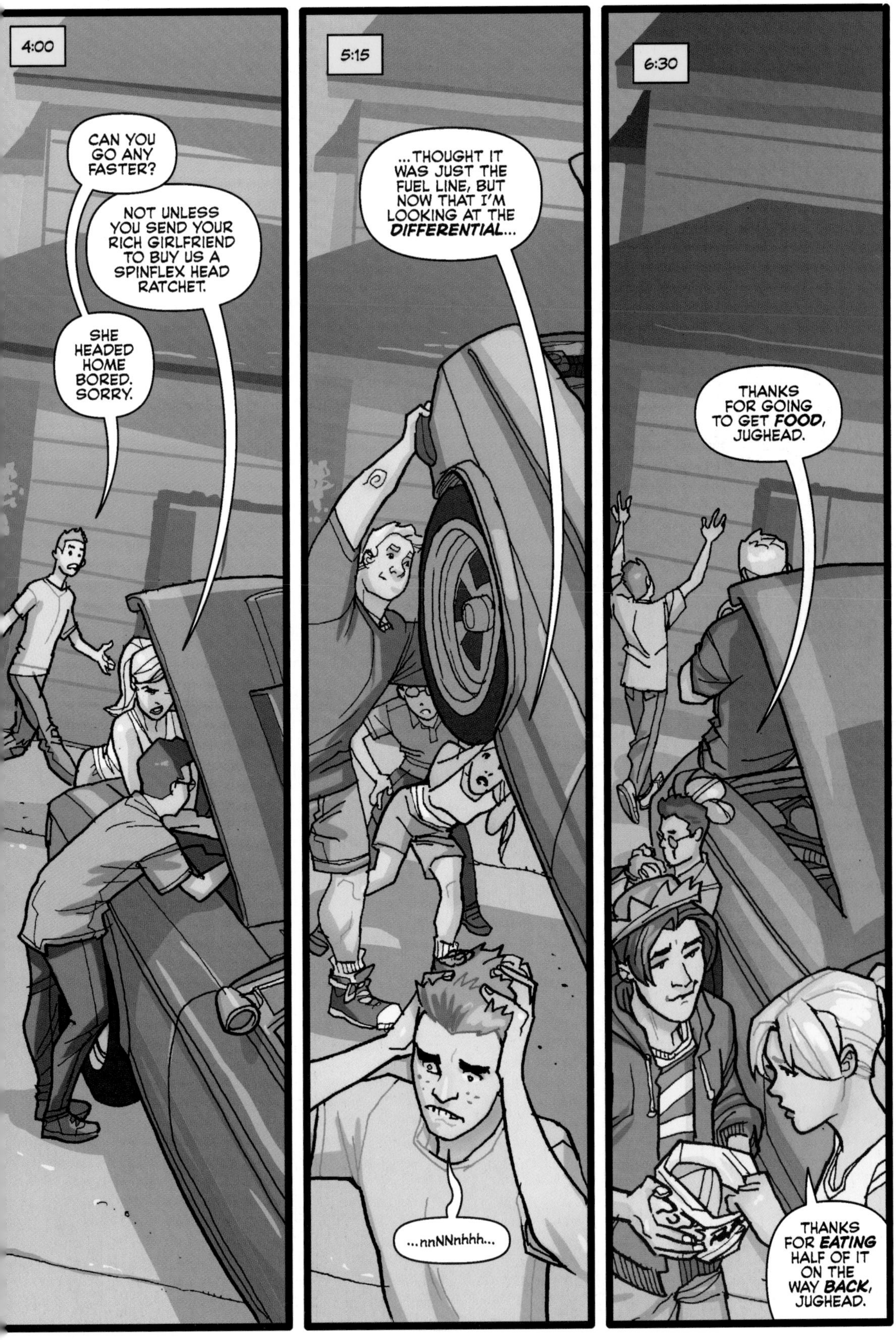

4:00
CAN YOU GO ANY FASTER?
NOT UNLESS YOU SEND YOUR RICH GIRLFRIEND TO BUY US A SPINFLEX HEAD RATCHET.
SHE HEADED HOME BORED. SORRY.
5:15
...THOUGHT IT WAS JUST THE FUEL LINE, BUT NOW THAT I'M LOOKING AT THE DIFFERENTIAL...
...nnNNnhhh...
6:30
THANKS FOR GOING TO GET FOOD, JUGHEAD.
THANKS FOR EATING HALF OF IT ON THE WAY BACK, JUGHEAD.

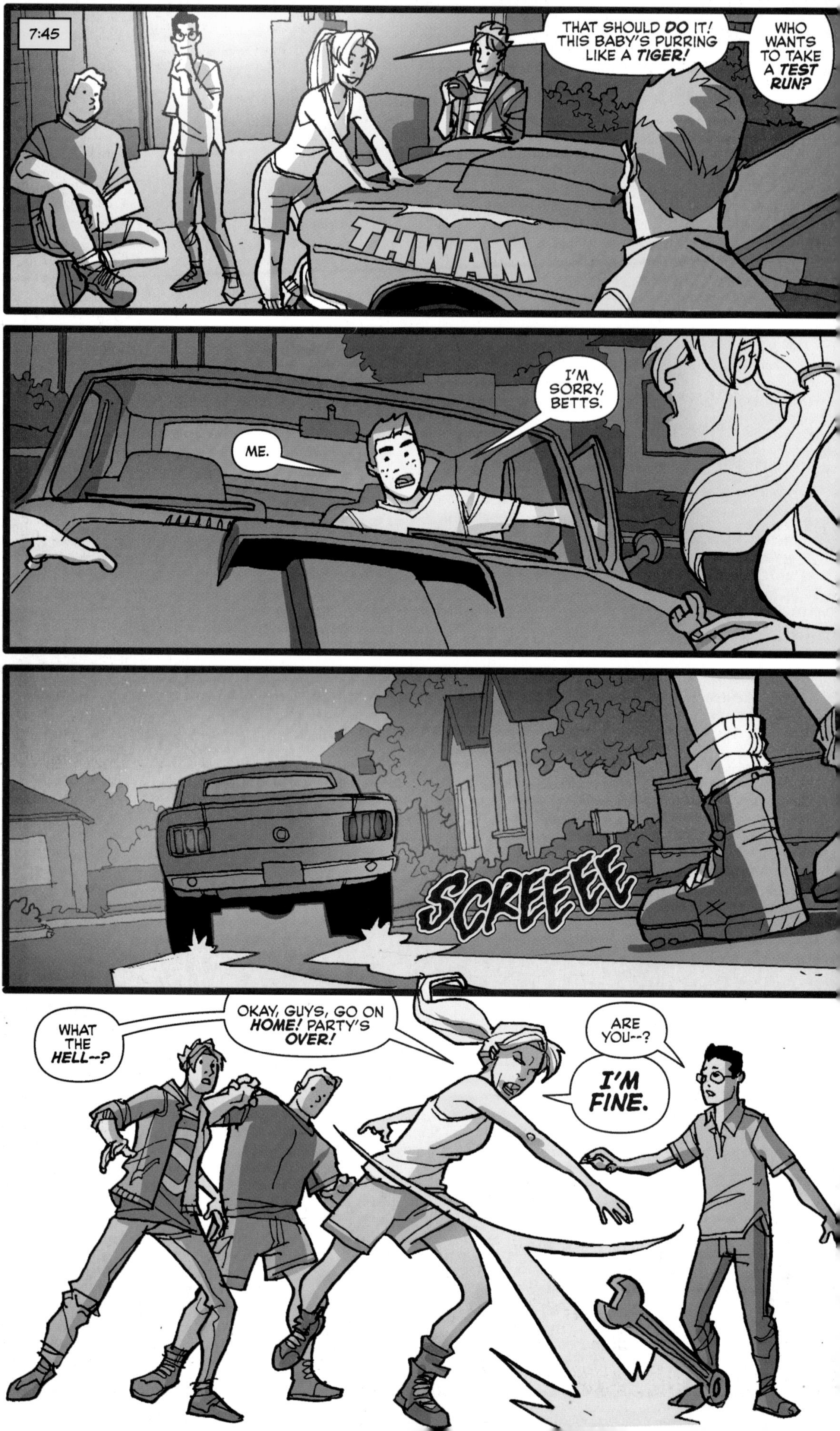
7:45
THAT SHOULD DO IT! THIS BABY'S PURRING LIKE A TIGER!
WHO WANTS TO TAKE A TEST RUN?
THWAM
ME.
I'M SORRY, BETTS.
SCREEEE
WHAT THE HELL--?
OKAY, GUYS, GO ON HOME! PARTY'S OVER!
ARE YOU--?
I'M FINE.

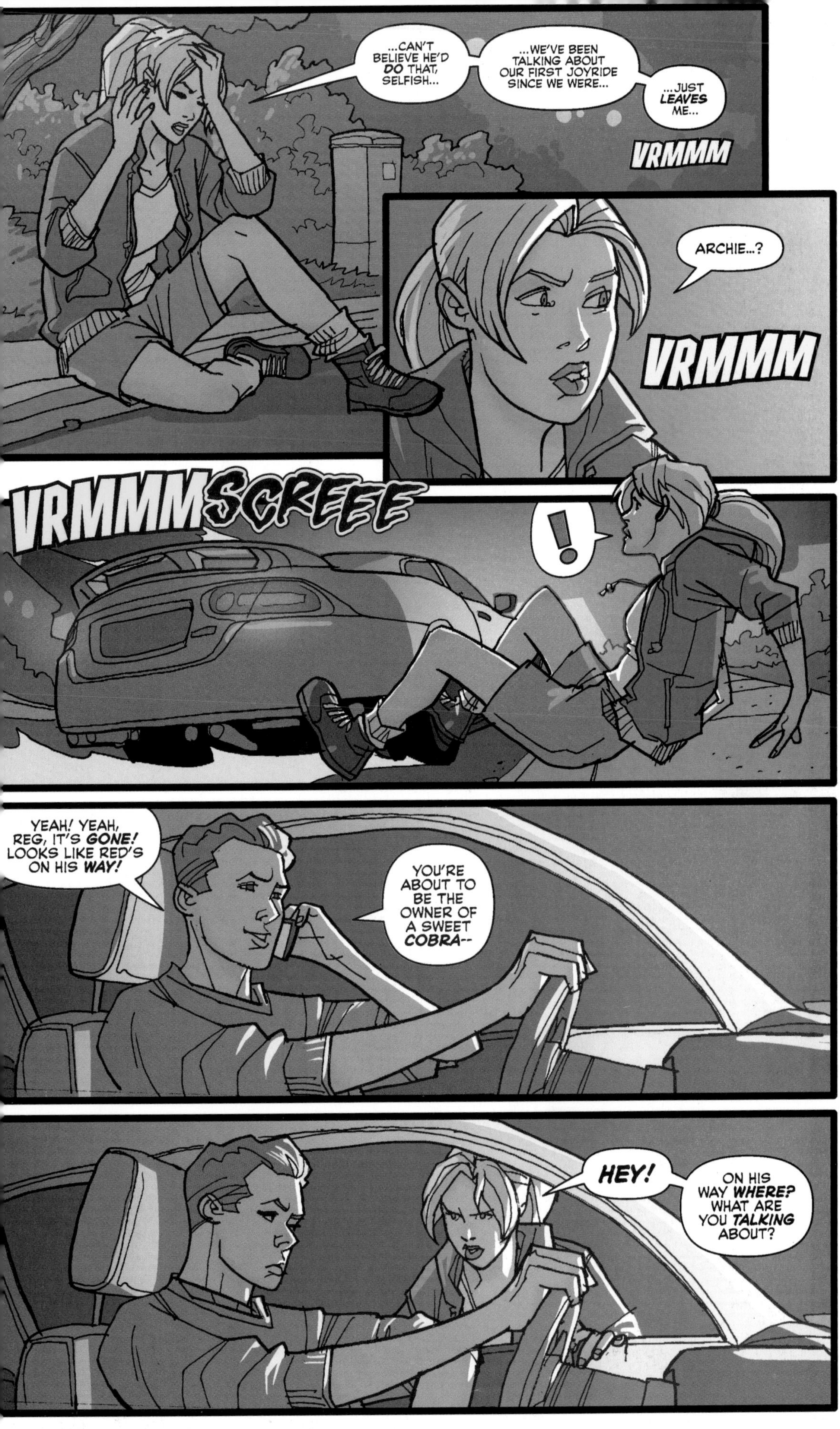
...CAN'T BELIEVE HE'D DO THAT, SELFISH...
...WE'VE BEEN TALKING ABOUT OUR FIRST JOYRIDE SINCE WE WERE...
...JUST LEAVES ME...
VRMMM
ARCHIE...?
VRMMM
VRMMMSCREEE
!
YEAH! YEAH, REG, IT'S GONE! LOOKS LIKE RED'S ON HIS WAY!
YOU'RE ABOUT TO BE THE OWNER OF A SWEET COBRA--
HEY!
ON HIS WAY WHERE? WHAT ARE YOU TALKING ABOUT?

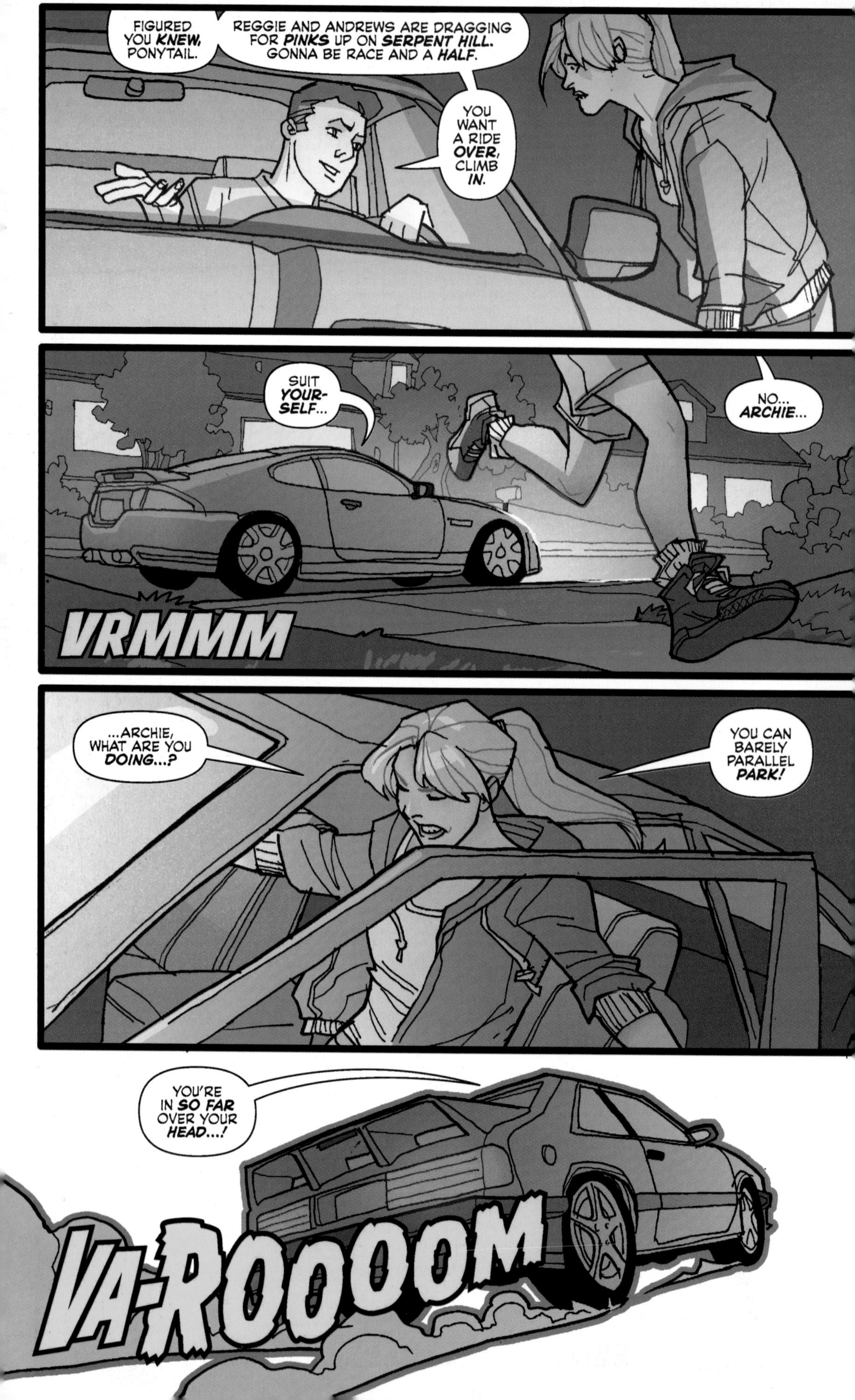
FIGURED YOU KNEW, PONYTAIL.
REGGIE AND ANDREWS ARE DRAGGING FOR PINKS UP ON SERPENT HILL. GONNA BE RACE AND A HALF.
YOU WANT A RIDE OVER, CLIMB IN.
SUIT YOURSELF...
NO... ARCHIE...
VRMMM
...ARCHIE, WHAT ARE YOU DOING...?
YOU CAN BARELY PARALLEL PARK!
YOU'RE IN SO FAR OVER YOUR HEAD...!
VA-ROOOOOM

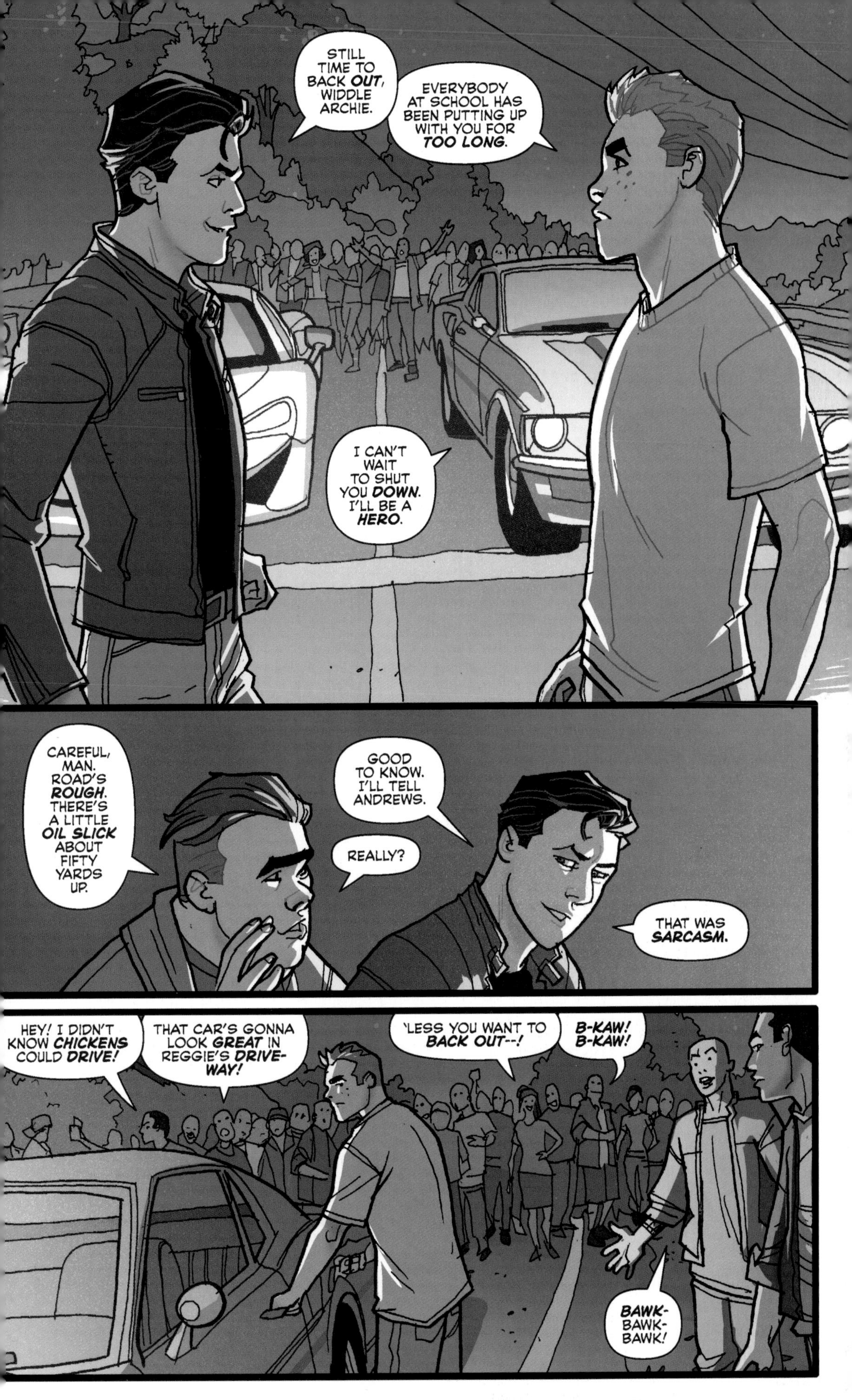
STILL TIME TO BACK OUT, WIDDLE ARCHIE.
EVERYBODY AT SCHOOL HAS BEEN PUTTING UP WITH YOU FOR TOO LONG.
I CAN'T WAIT TO SHUT YOU DOWN. I'LL BE A HERO.
CAREFUL, MAN. ROAD'S ROUGH. THERE'S A LITTLE OIL SLICK ABOUT FIFTY YARDS UP.
GOOD TO KNOW. I'LL TELL ANDREWS.
REALLY?
THAT WAS SARCASM.
HEY! I DIDN'T KNOW CHICKENS COULD DRIVE!
THAT CAR'S GONNA LOOK GREAT IN REGGIE'S DRIVE-WAY!
'LESS YOU WANT TO BACK OUT--!
B-KAW! B-KAW!
BAWK-BAWK-BAWK!

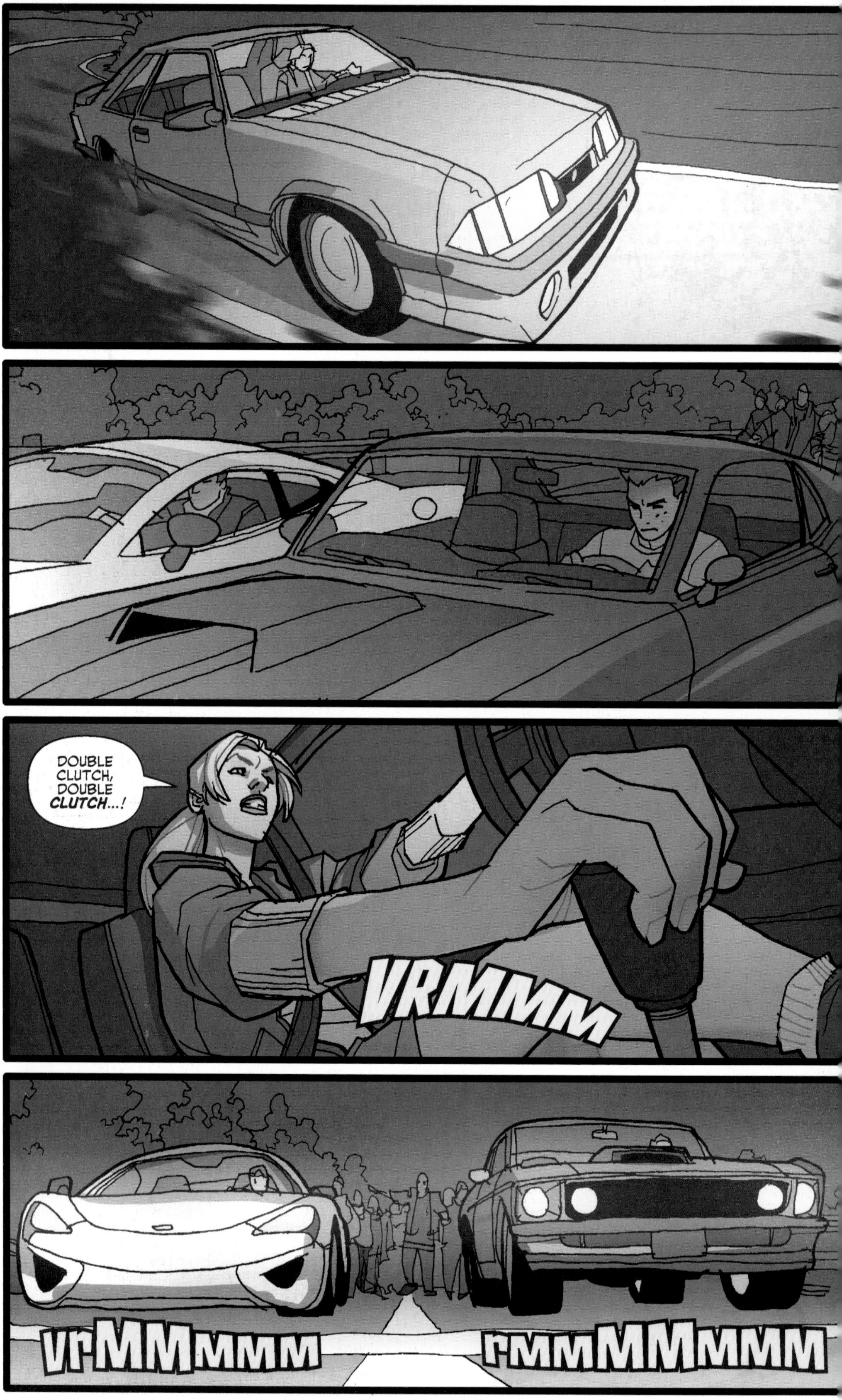
DOUBLE CLUTCH, DOUBLE CLUTCH...!
VRMMMM
vrMMmmm
rmmMMMmmm

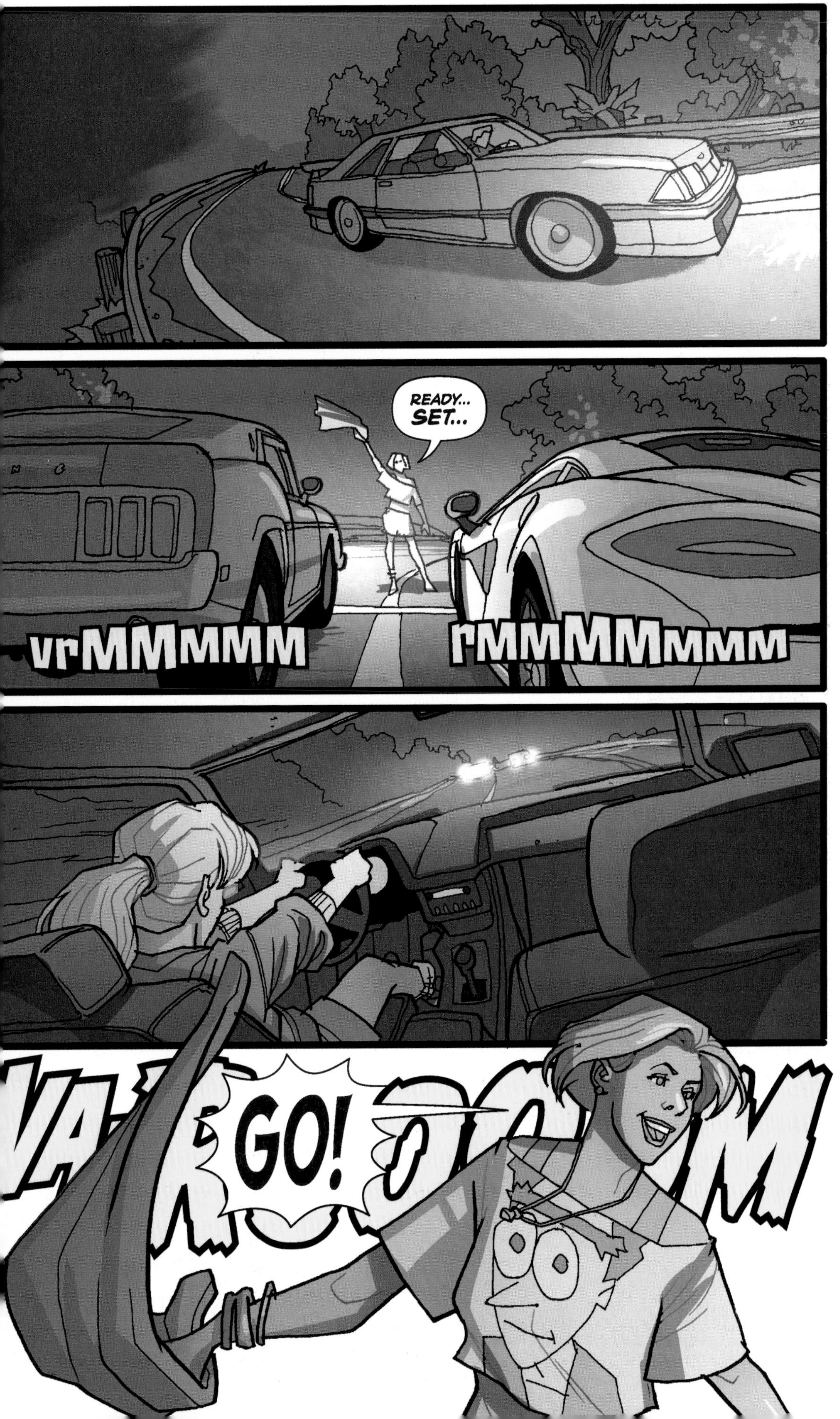
READY... SET...
VrMMMMMM
rMMMMMMMMM
GO!

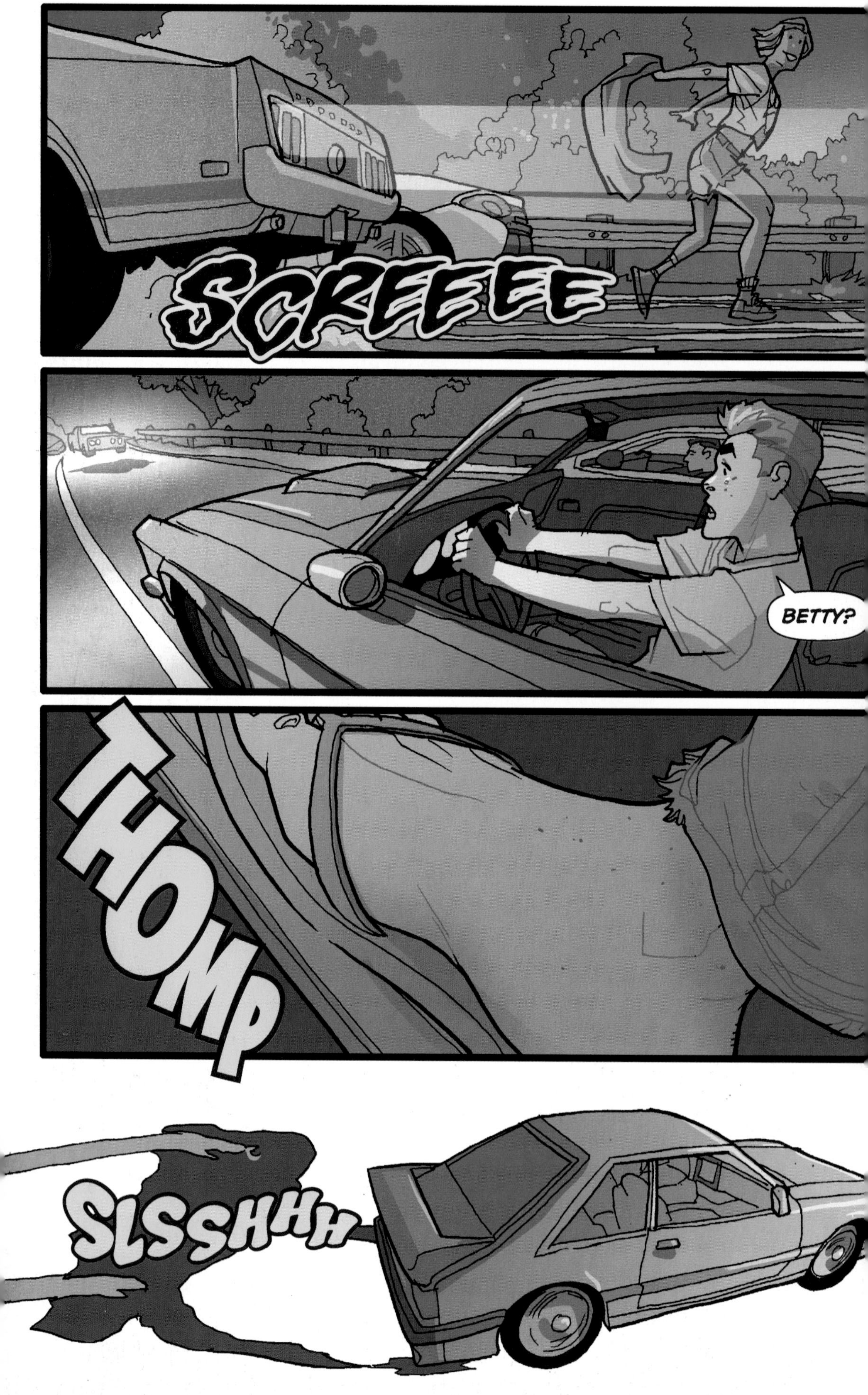
SCREEEE
BETTY?
THOMP
SLSSHHH

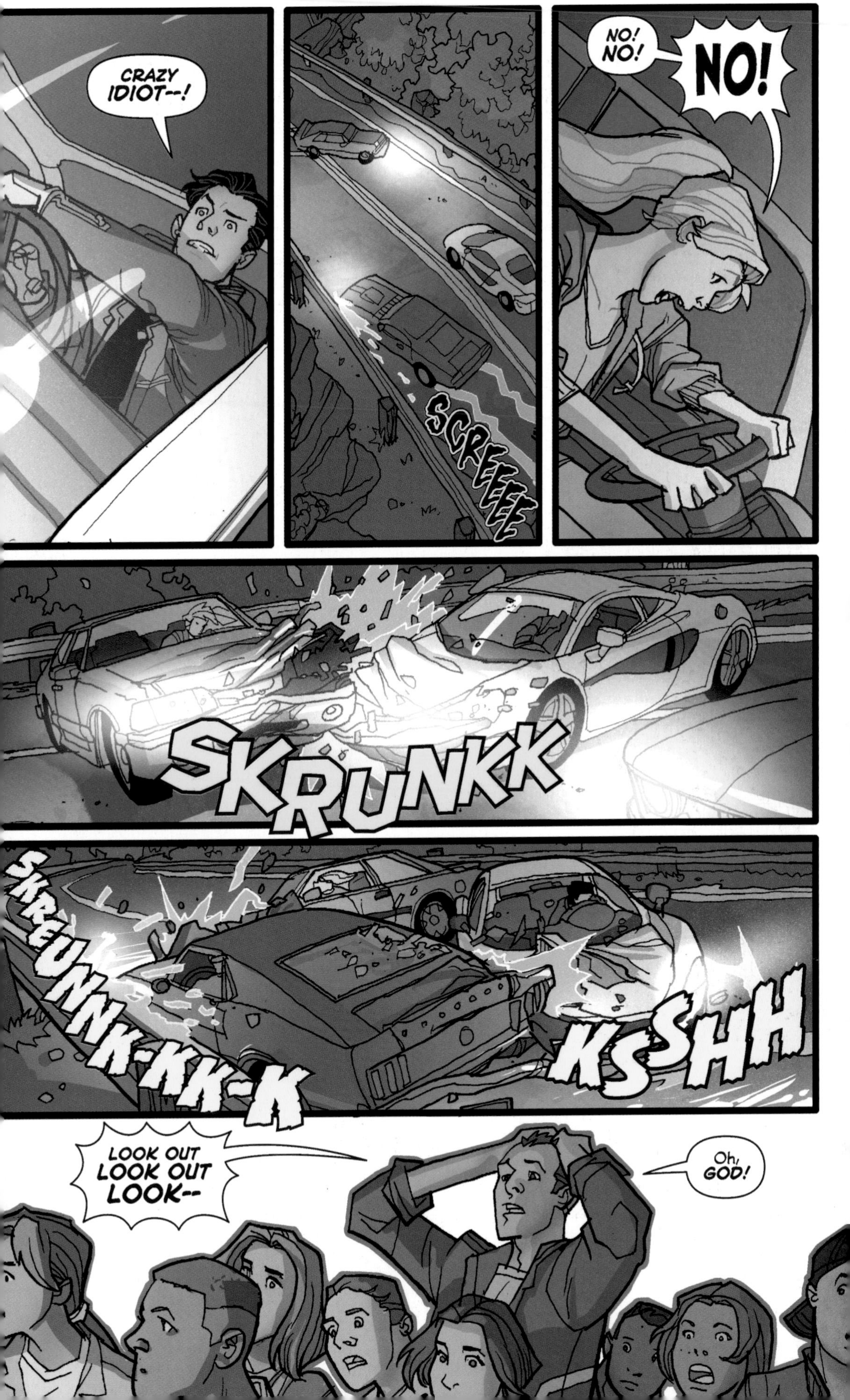
CRAZY IDIOT--!
SCREEEEE
NO! NO!
NO!
SKRUNKK
SKREUNNK-KK-K
KSSHH
LOOK OUT LOOK OUT LOOK--
Oh, GOD!

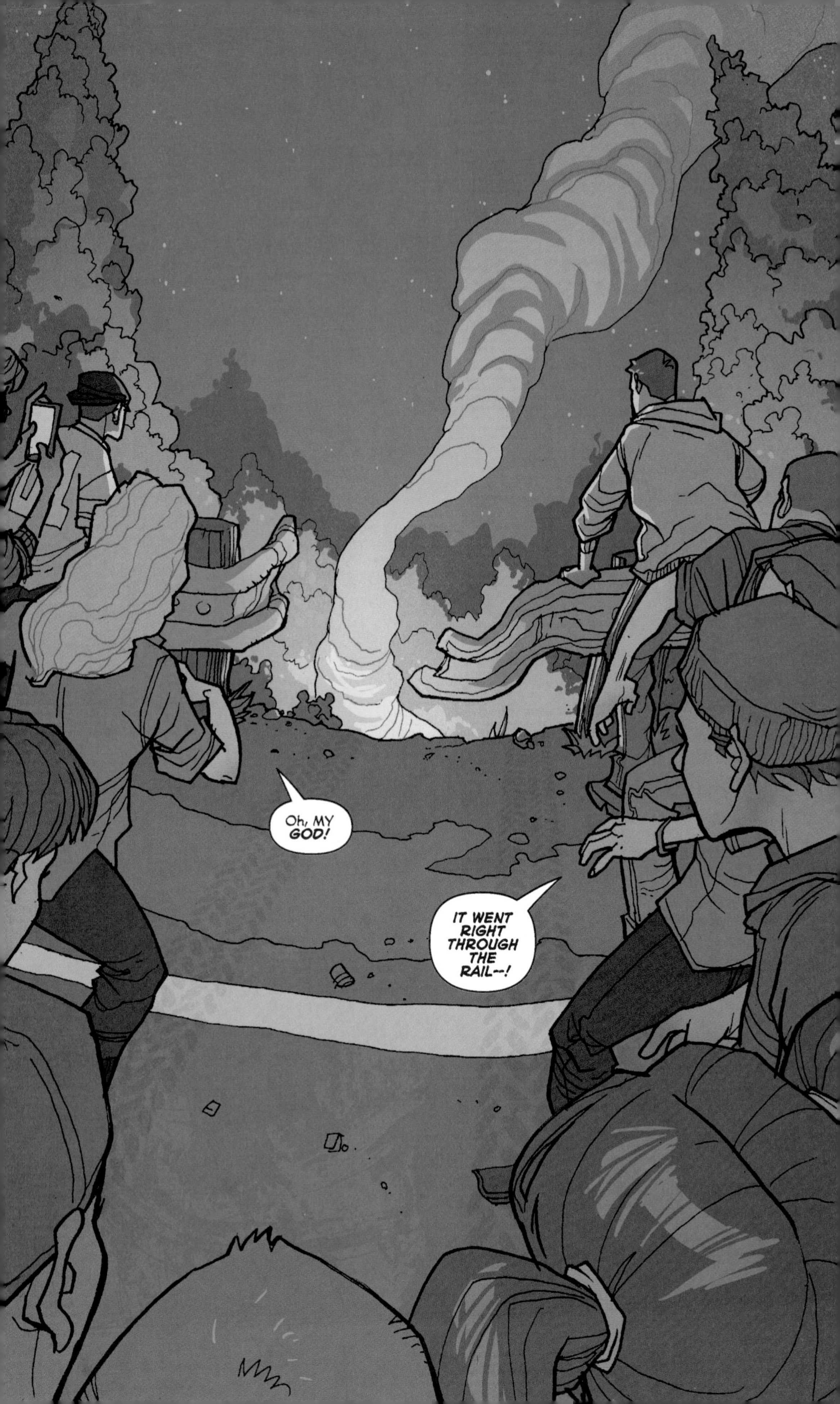
Oh, MY GOD!
IT WENT RIGHT THROUGH THE RAIL--!

TO BE CONTINUED...

ISSUE TWENTY ONE

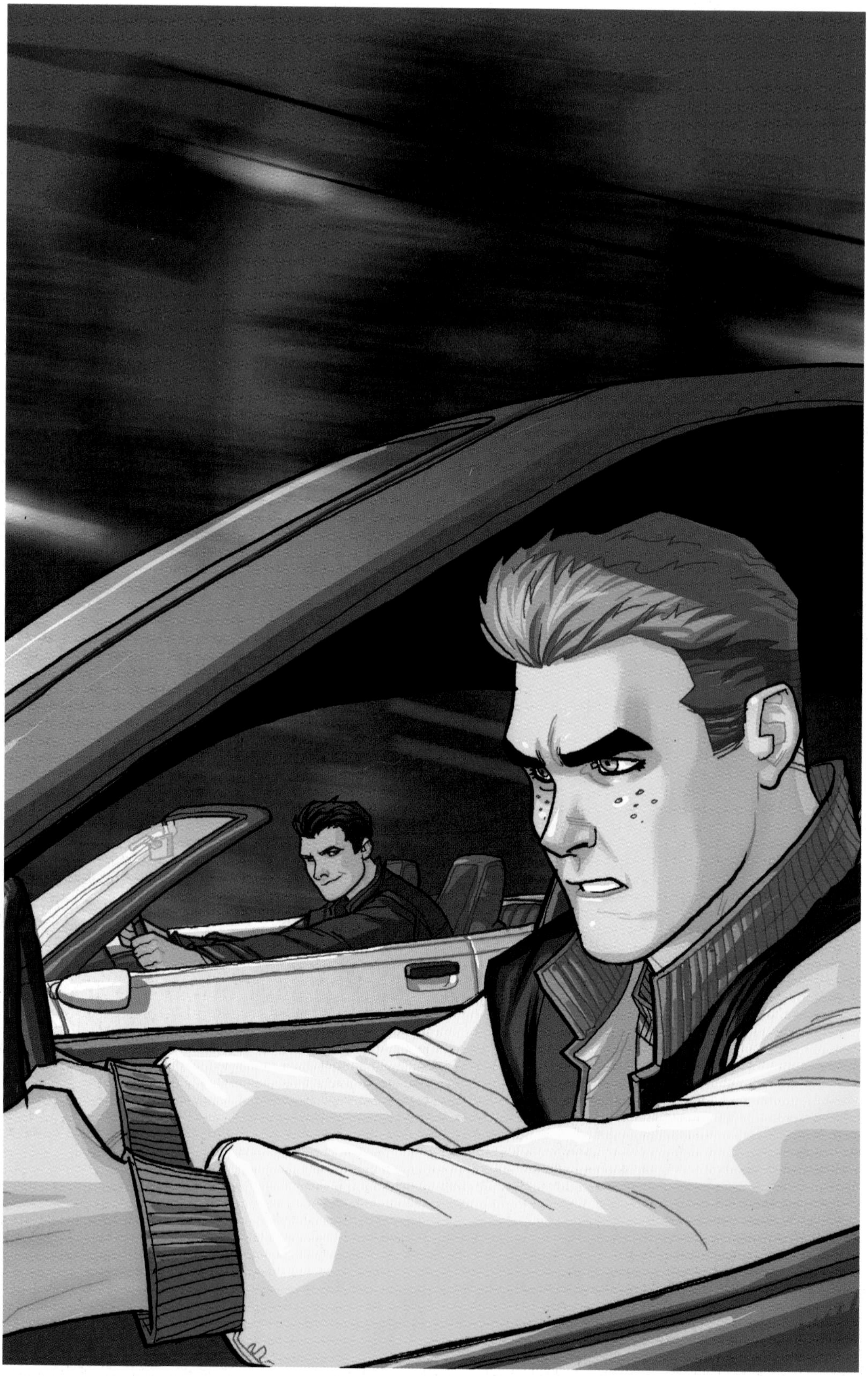

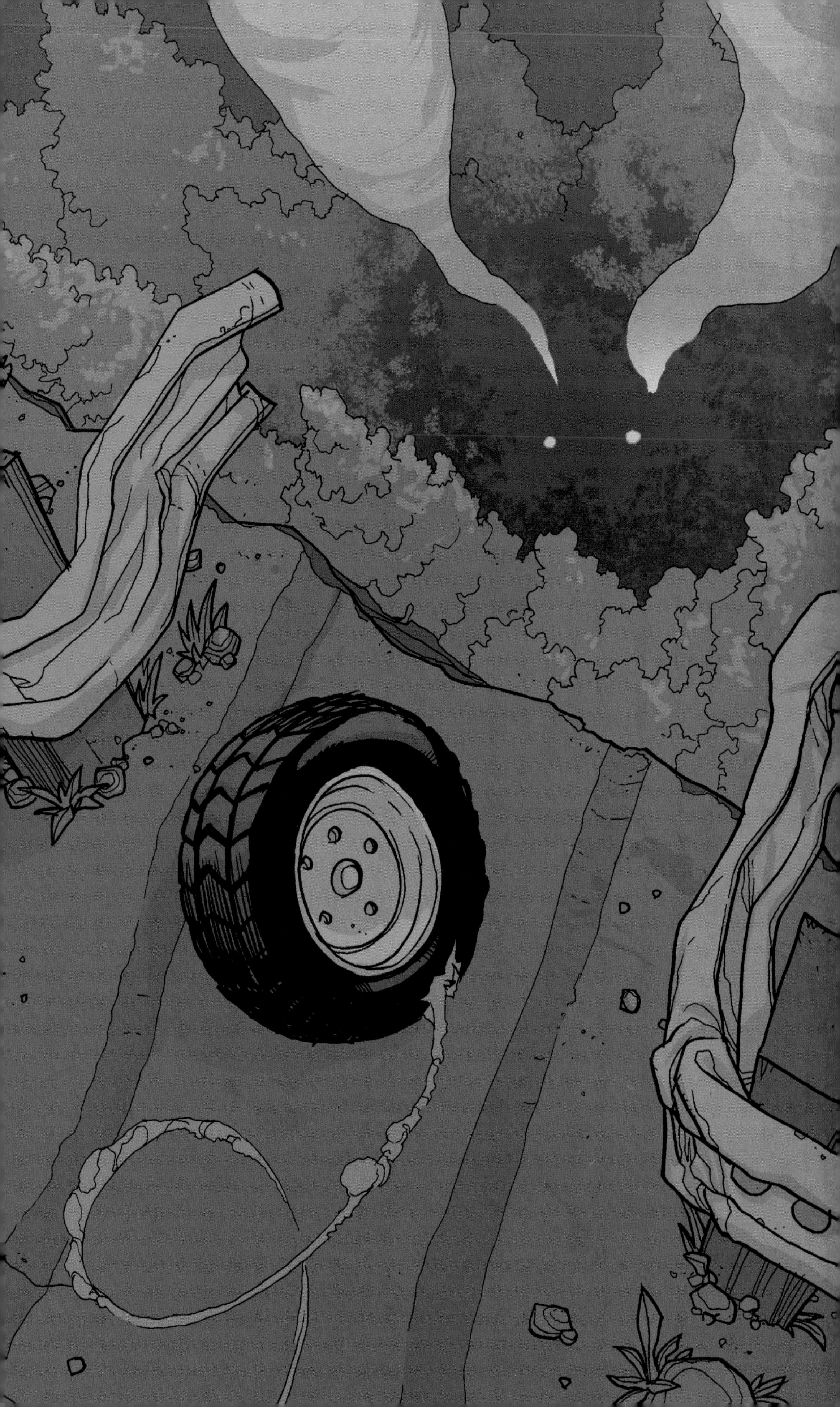

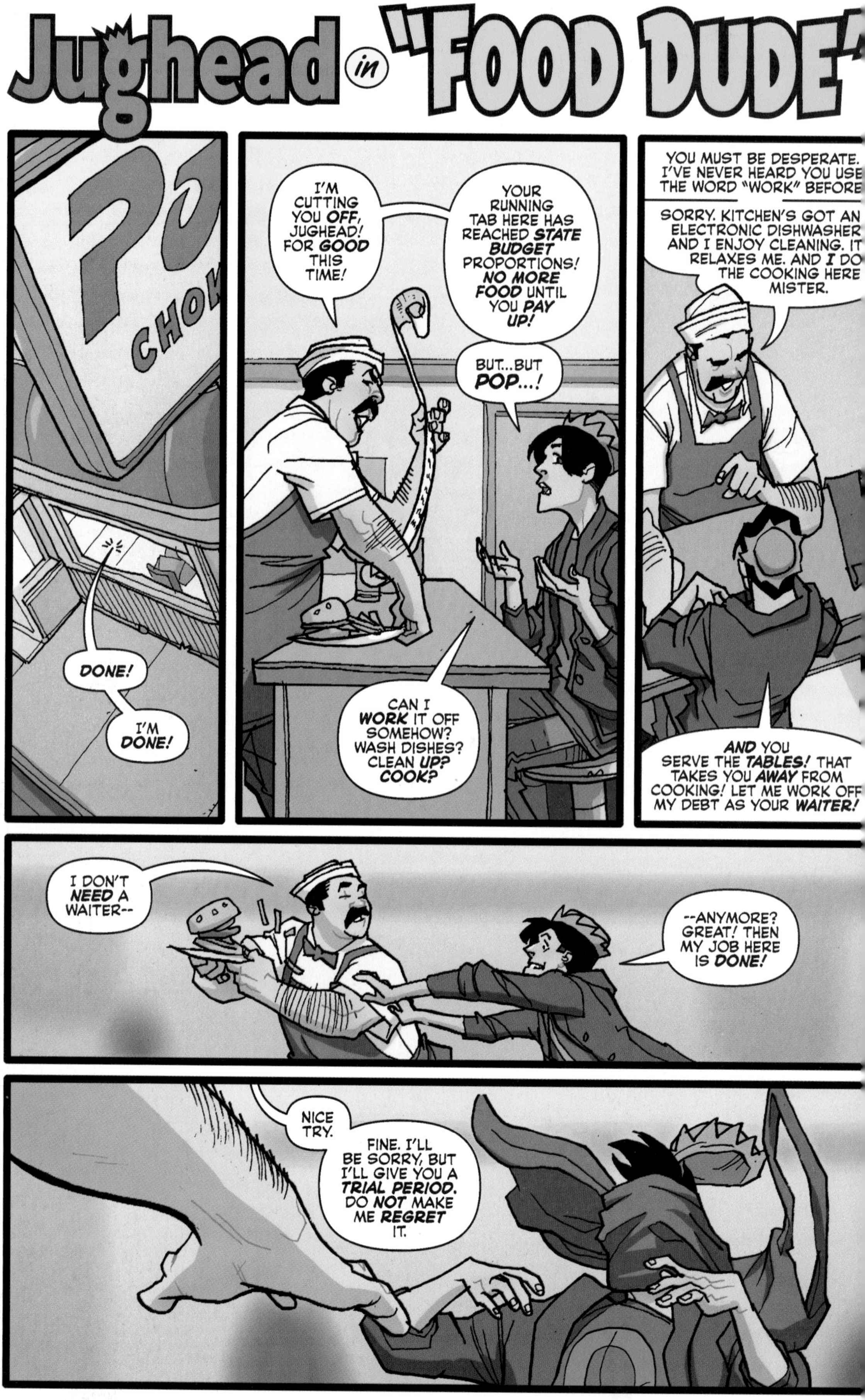

Jughead in "FOOD DUDE"
POP'S CHOK
DONE!
I'M DONE!
I'M CUTTING YOU OFF, JUGHEAD! FOR GOOD THIS TIME!
YOUR RUNNING TAB HERE HAS REACHED STATE BUDGET PROPORTIONS! NO MORE FOOD UNTIL YOU PAY UP!
BUT...BUT POP...!
CAN I WORK IT OFF SOMEHOW? WASH DISHES? CLEAN UP? COOK?
YOU MUST BE DESPERATE. I'VE NEVER HEARD YOU USE THE WORD "WORK" BEFORE
SORRY. KITCHEN'S GOT AN ELECTRONIC DISHWASHER AND I ENJOY CLEANING. IT RELAXES ME. AND I DO THE COOKING HERE, MISTER.
AND YOU SERVE THE TABLES! THAT TAKES YOU AWAY FROM COOKING! LET ME WORK OFF MY DEBT AS YOUR WAITER!
I DON'T NEED A WAITER--
--ANYMORE? GREAT! THEN MY JOB HERE IS DONE!
NICE TRY.
FINE. I'LL BE SORRY, BUT I'LL GIVE YOU A TRIAL PERIOD. DO NOT MAKE ME REGRET IT.

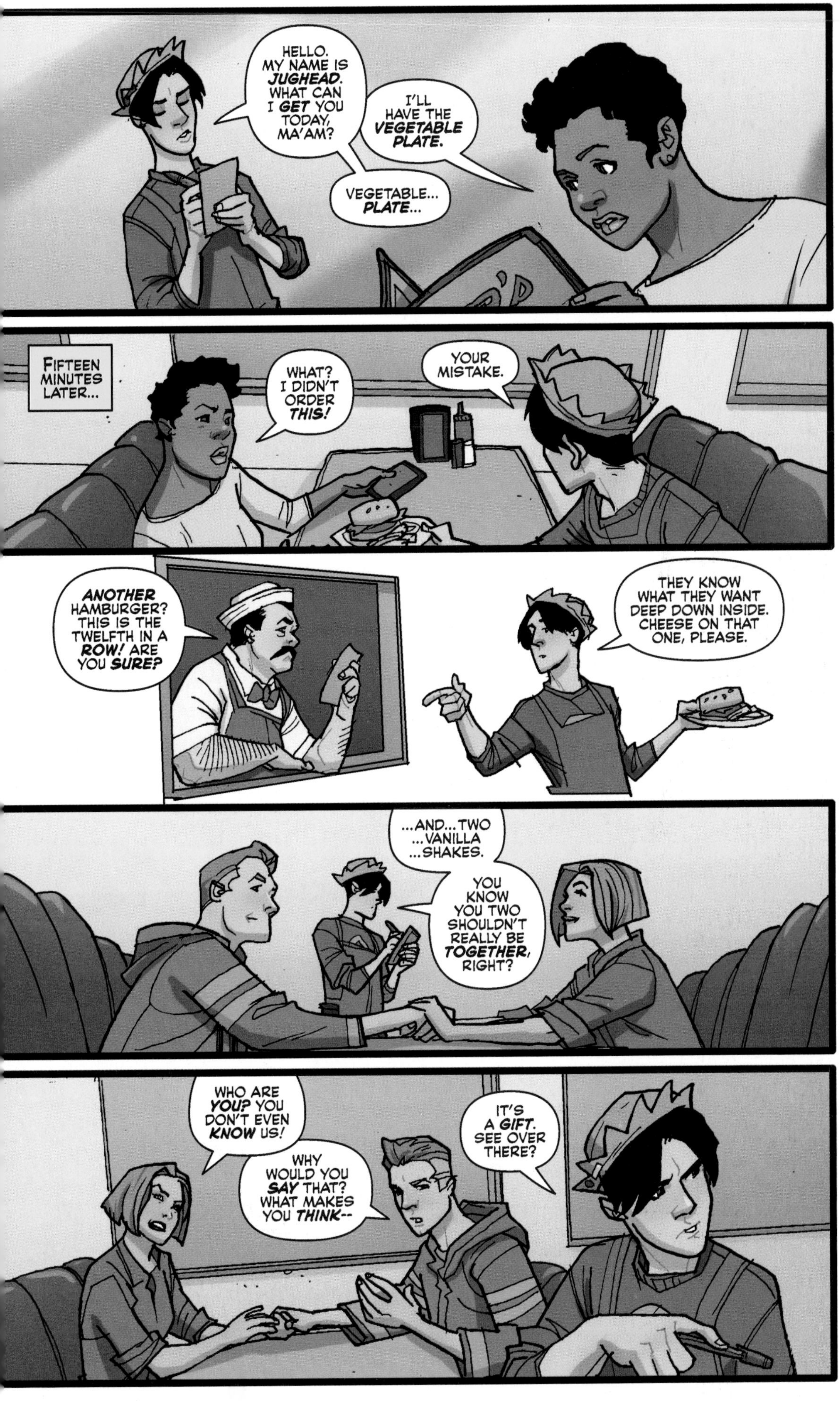
HELLO. MY NAME IS JUGHEAD. WHAT CAN I GET YOU TODAY, MA'AM?
I'LL HAVE THE VEGETABLE PLATE.
VEGETABLE... PLATE...
FIFTEEN MINUTES LATER...
WHAT? I DIDN'T ORDER THIS!
YOUR MISTAKE.
ANOTHER HAMBURGER? THIS IS THE TWELFTH IN A ROW! ARE YOU SURE?
THEY KNOW WHAT THEY WANT DEEP DOWN INSIDE. CHEESE ON THAT ONE, PLEASE.
...AND...TWO ...VANILLA ...SHAKES.
YOU KNOW YOU TWO SHOULDN'T REALLY BE TOGETHER, RIGHT?
WHO ARE YOU? YOU DON'T EVEN KNOW US!
WHY WOULD YOU SAY THAT? WHAT MAKES YOU THINK--
IT'S A GIFT. SEE OVER THERE?

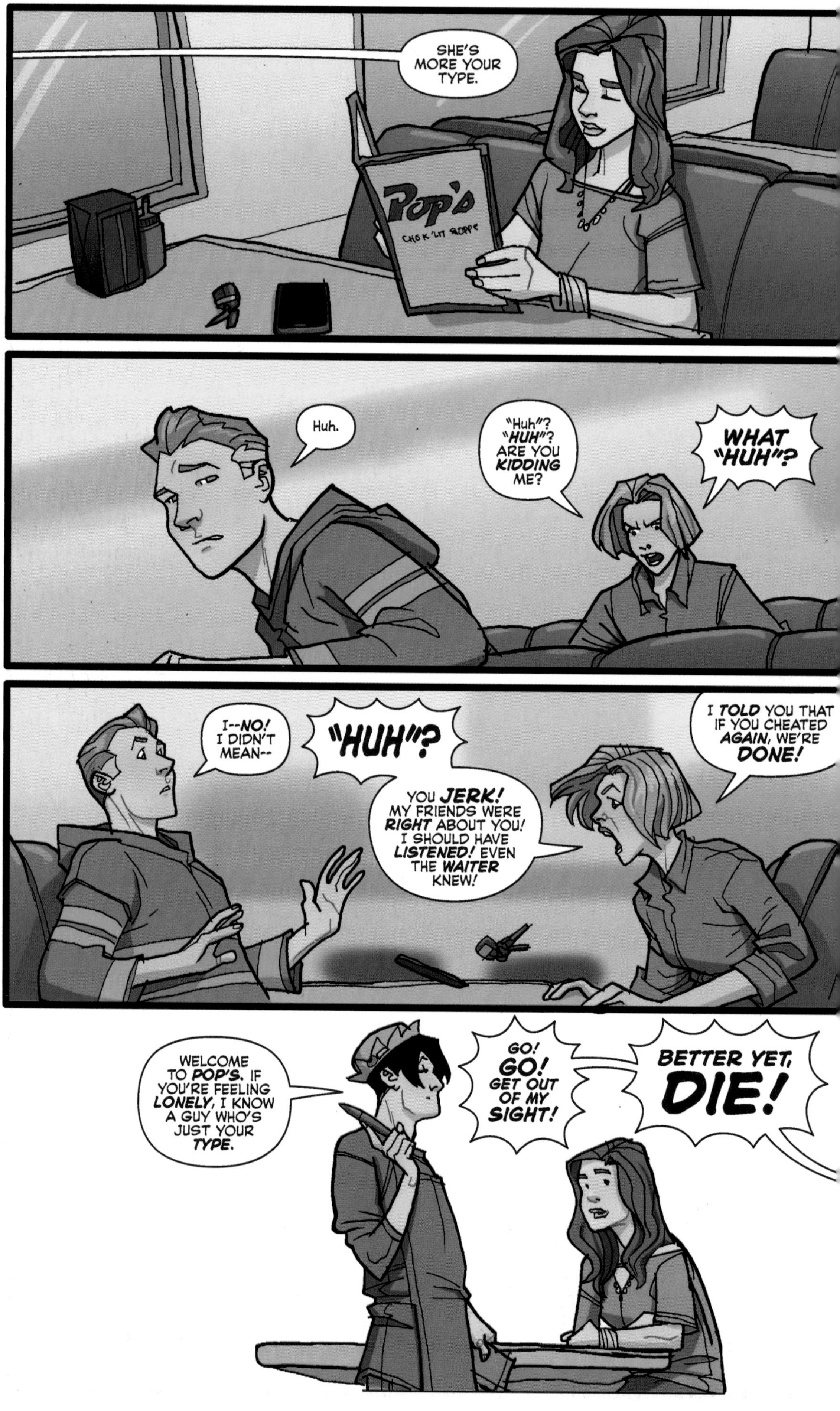
SHE'S MORE YOUR TYPE.
Pop's
CHOK'LIT SHOPPE
Huh.
"Huh"? "HUH"? ARE YOU KIDDING ME?
WHAT "HUH"?
I--NO! I DIDN'T MEAN--
"HUH"?
YOU JERK! MY FRIENDS WERE RIGHT ABOUT YOU! I SHOULD HAVE LISTENED! EVEN THE WAITER KNEW!
I TOLD YOU THAT IF YOU CHEATED AGAIN, WE'RE DONE!
WELCOME TO POP'S. IF YOU'RE FEELING LONELY, I KNOW A GUY WHO'S JUST YOUR TYPE.
GO! GO! GET OUT OF MY SIGHT!
BETTER YET, DIE!

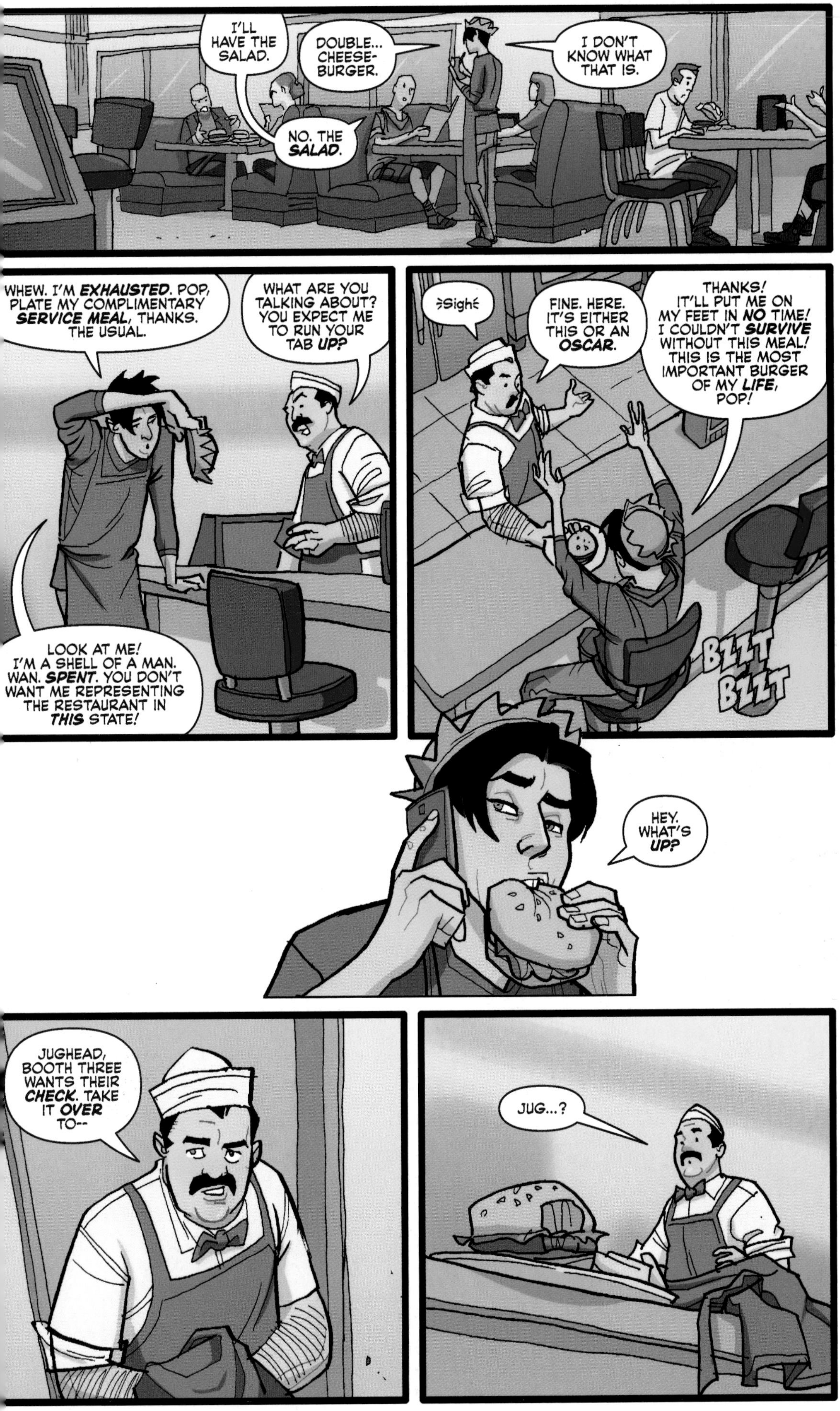
I'LL HAVE THE SALAD.
DOUBLE... CHEESE-BURGER.
I DON'T KNOW WHAT THAT IS.
NO. THE SALAD.
WHEW. I'M EXHAUSTED. POP, PLATE MY COMPLIMENTARY SERVICE MEAL, THANKS. THE USUAL.
WHAT ARE YOU TALKING ABOUT? YOU EXPECT ME TO RUN YOUR TAB UP?
LOOK AT ME! I'M A SHELL OF A MAN. WAN. SPENT. YOU DON'T WANT ME REPRESENTING THE RESTAURANT IN THIS STATE!
Sigh
FINE. HERE. IT'S EITHER THIS OR AN OSCAR.
THANKS! IT'LL PUT ME ON MY FEET IN NO TIME! I COULDN'T SURVIVE WITHOUT THIS MEAL! THIS IS THE MOST IMPORTANT BURGER OF MY LIFE, POP!
BZZT BZZT
HEY. WHAT'S UP?
JUGHEAD, BOOTH THREE WANTS THEIR CHECK. TAKE IT OVER TO--
JUG...?

Raj in "CREATURE TEACHER"

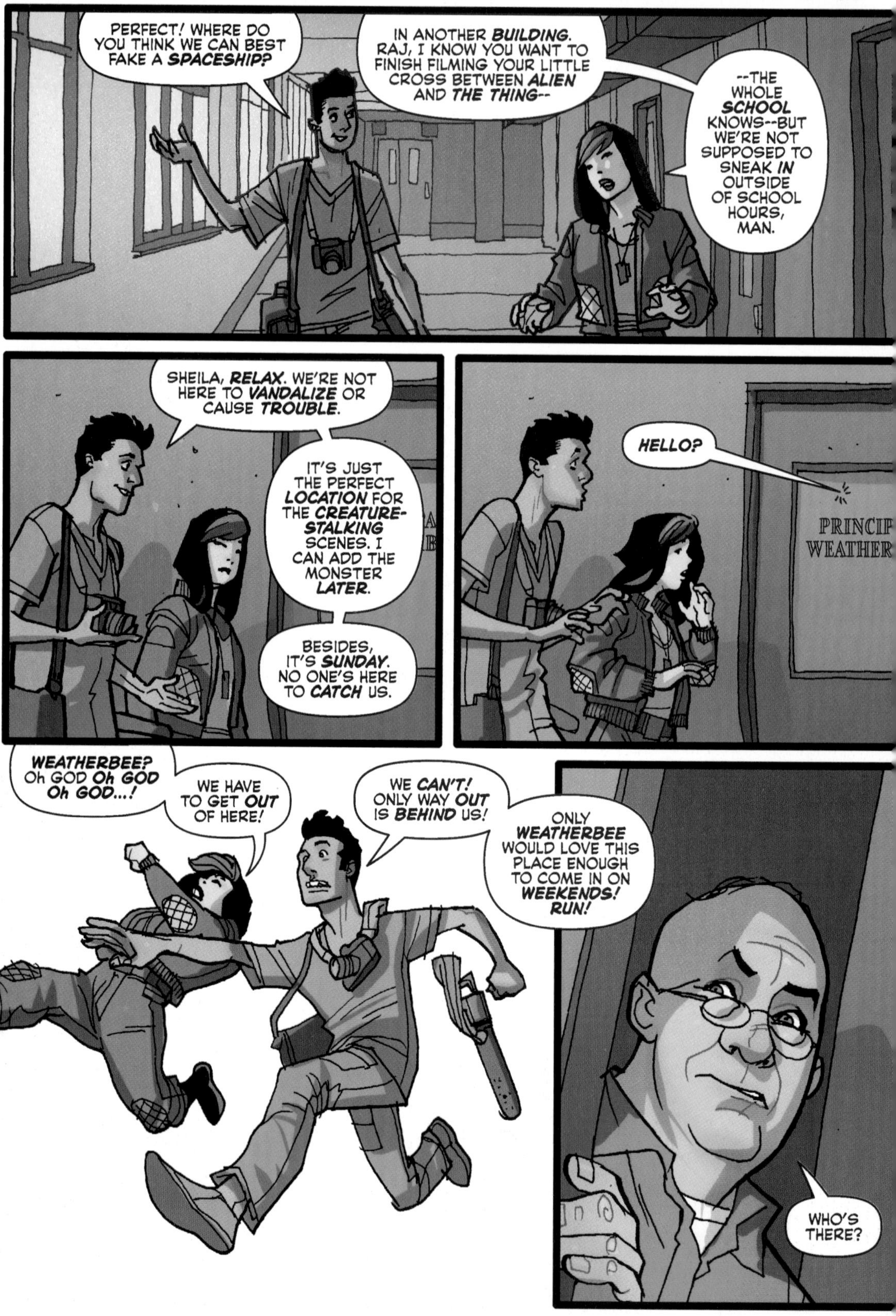
PERFECT! WHERE DO YOU THINK WE CAN BEST FAKE A SPACESHIP?
IN ANOTHER BUILDING. RAJ, I KNOW YOU WANT TO FINISH FILMING YOUR LITTLE CROSS BETWEEN ALIEN AND THE THING--
--THE WHOLE SCHOOL KNOWS--BUT WE'RE NOT SUPPOSED TO SNEAK IN OUTSIDE OF SCHOOL HOURS, MAN.
SHEILA, RELAX. WE'RE NOT HERE TO VANDALIZE OR CAUSE TROUBLE.
IT'S JUST THE PERFECT LOCATION FOR THE CREATURE-STALKING SCENES. I CAN ADD THE MONSTER LATER.
BESIDES, IT'S SUNDAY. NO ONE'S HERE TO CATCH US.
HELLO?
PRINCIP
WEATHER
WEATHERBEE? Oh GOD Oh GOD Oh GOD...!
WE HAVE TO GET OUT OF HERE!
WE CAN'T! ONLY WAY OUT IS BEHIND US!
ONLY WEATHERBEE WOULD LOVE THIS PLACE ENOUGH TO COME IN ON WEEKENDS! RUN!
WHO'S THERE?

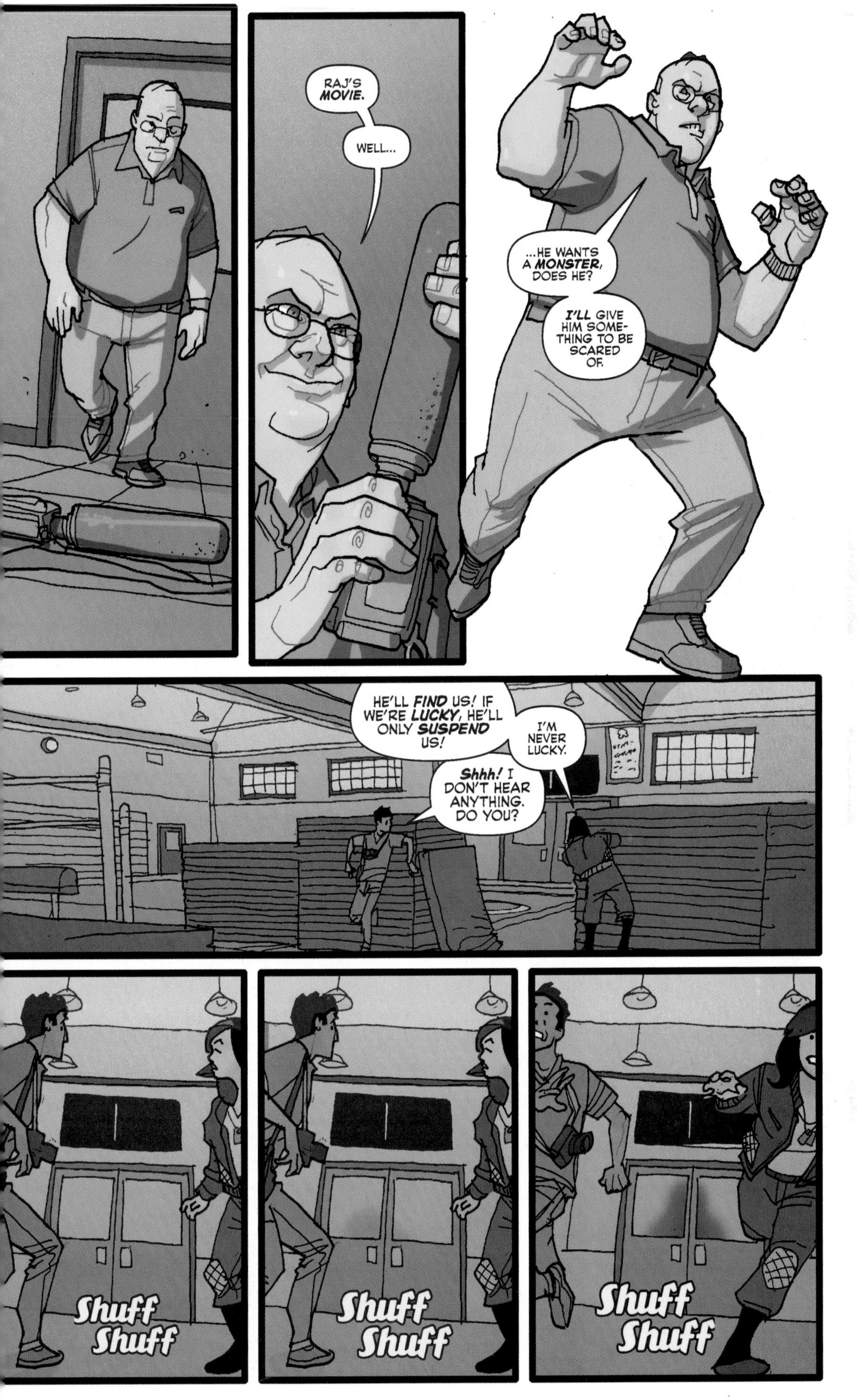

RAJ'S MOVIE.
WELL...
...HE WANTS A MONSTER, DOES HE?
I'LL GIVE HIM SOME-THING TO BE SCARED OF.
HE'LL FIND US! IF WE'RE LUCKY, HE'LL ONLY SUSPEND US!
I'M NEVER LUCKY.
Shhh! I DON'T HEAR ANYTHING. DO YOU?
Shuff Shuff
Shuff Shuff
Shuff Shuff

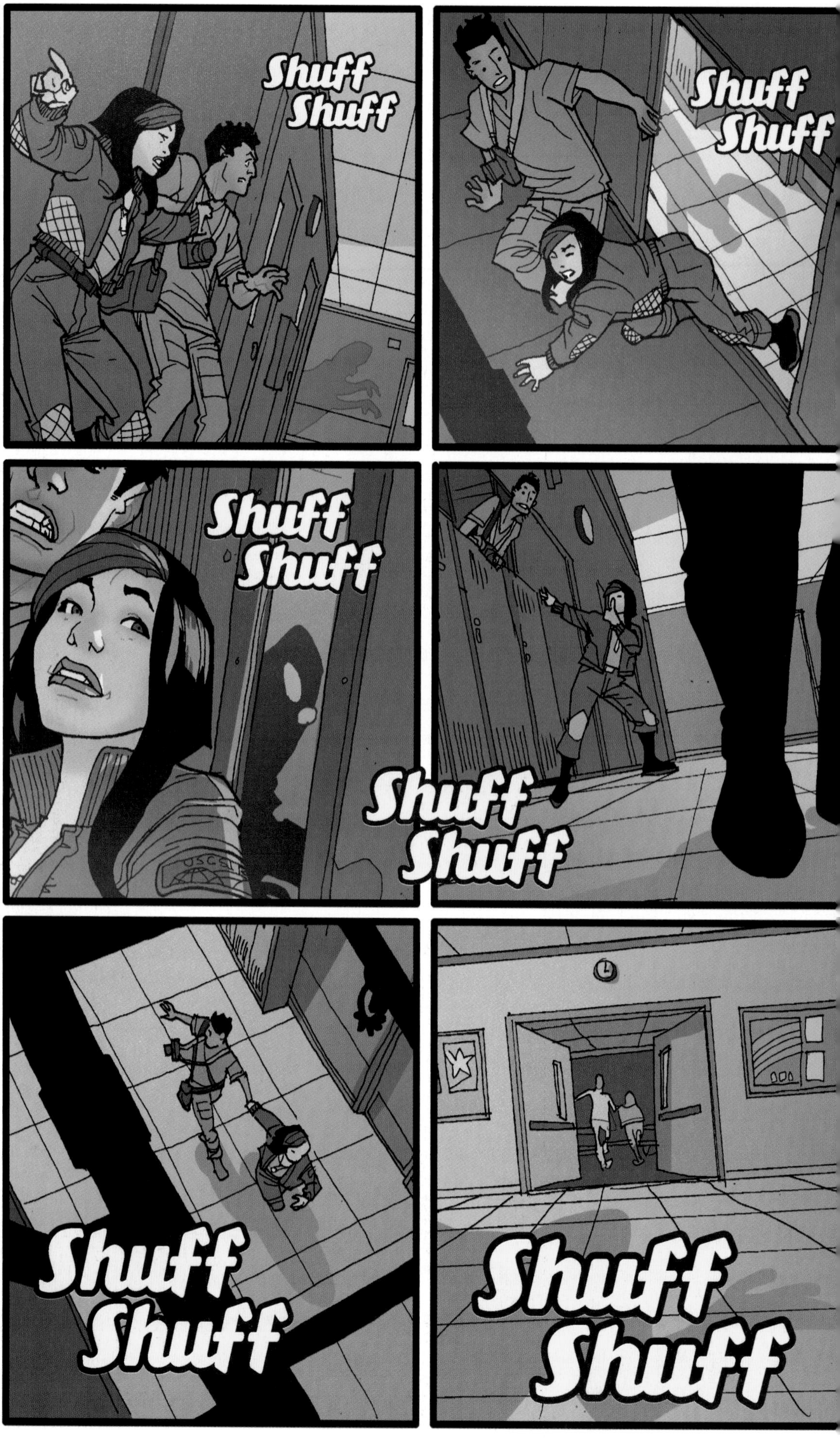
Shuff
Shuff
Shuff
Shuff
Shuff
Shuff
Shuff
Shuff
Shuff
Shuff
Shuff
Shuff

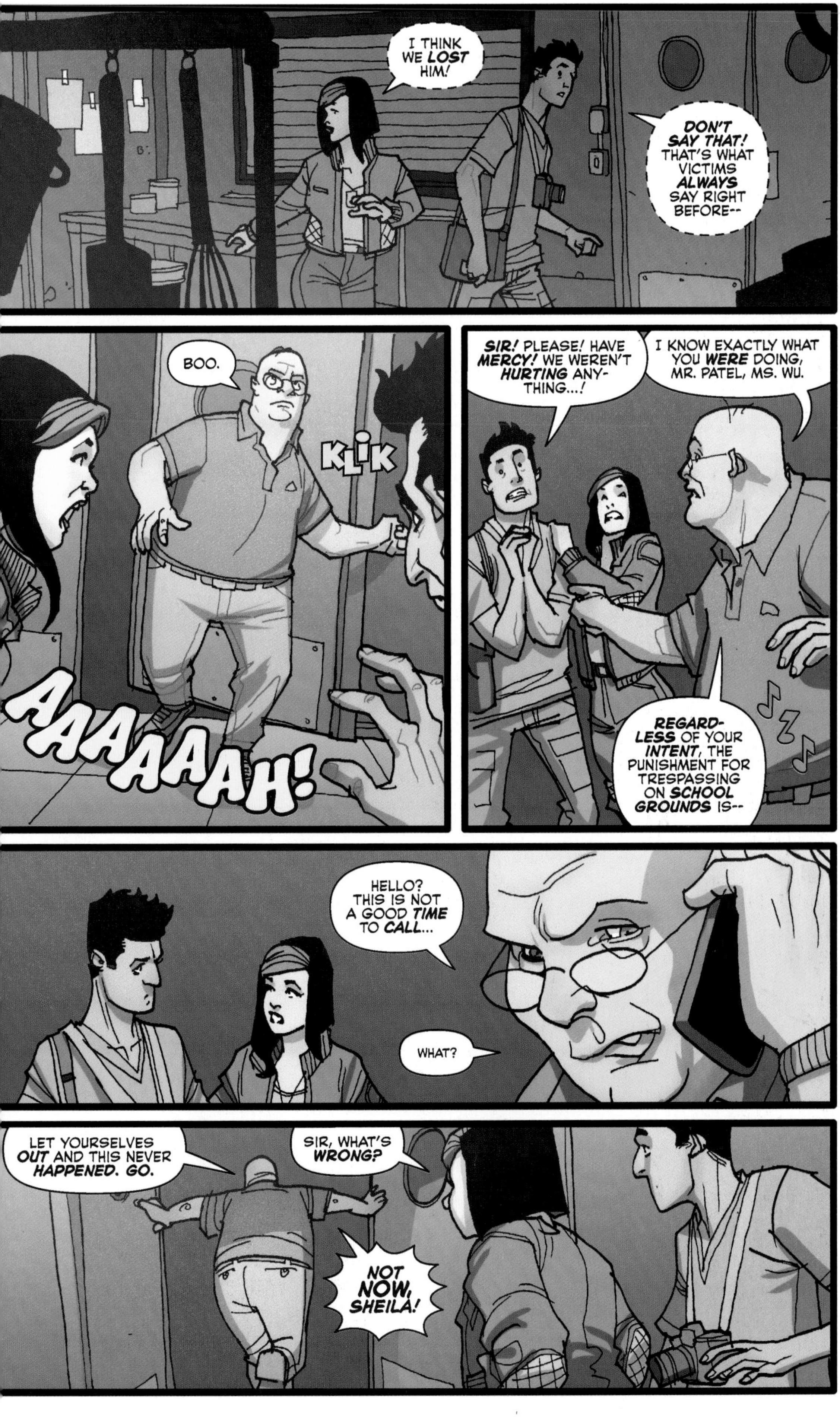
I THINK WE LOST HIM!
DON'T SAY THAT! THAT'S WHAT VICTIMS ALWAYS SAY RIGHT BEFORE--
BOO.
KLIK
AAAAAAAH!
SIR! PLEASE! HAVE MERCY! WE WEREN'T HURTING ANY-THING...!
I KNOW EXACTLY WHAT YOU WERE DOING, MR. PATEL, MS. WU.
REGARD-LESS OF YOUR INTENT, THE PUNISHMENT FOR TRESPASSING ON SCHOOL GROUNDS IS--
HELLO? THIS IS NOT A GOOD TIME TO CALL...
WHAT?
LET YOURSELVES OUT AND THIS NEVER HAPPENED. GO.
SIR, WHAT'S WRONG?
NOT NOW, SHEILA!

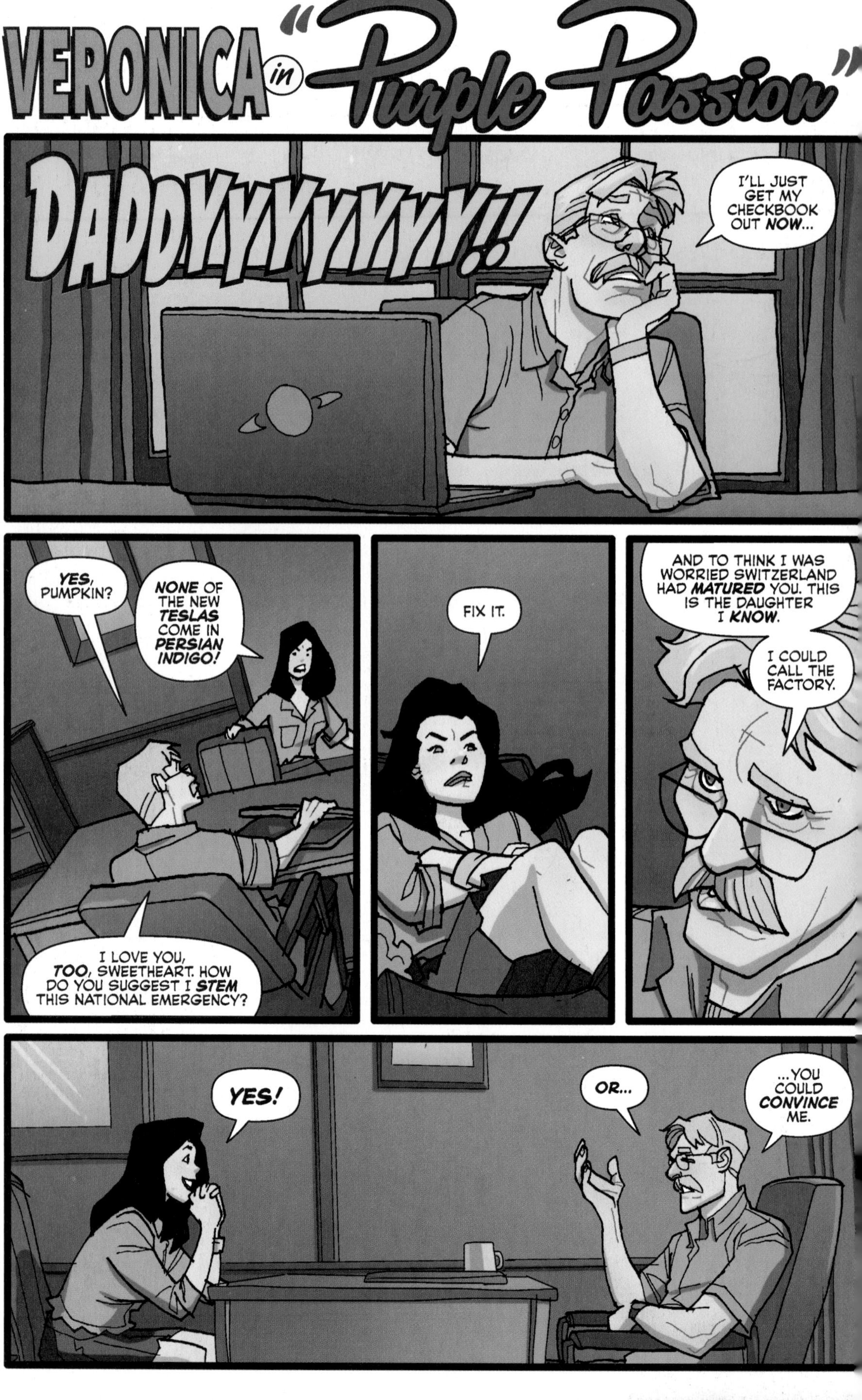
VERONICA in "Purple Passion"
DADDYYYYYYYY!!
I'LL JUST GET MY CHECKBOOK OUT NOW...
YES, PUMPKIN?
NONE OF THE NEW TESLAS COME IN PERSIAN INDIGO!
I LOVE YOU, TOO, SWEETHEART. HOW DO YOU SUGGEST I STEM THIS NATIONAL EMERGENCY?
FIX IT.
AND TO THINK I WAS WORRIED SWITZERLAND HAD MATURED YOU. THIS IS THE DAUGHTER I KNOW.
I COULD CALL THE FACTORY.
YES!
OR...
...YOU COULD CONVINCE ME.

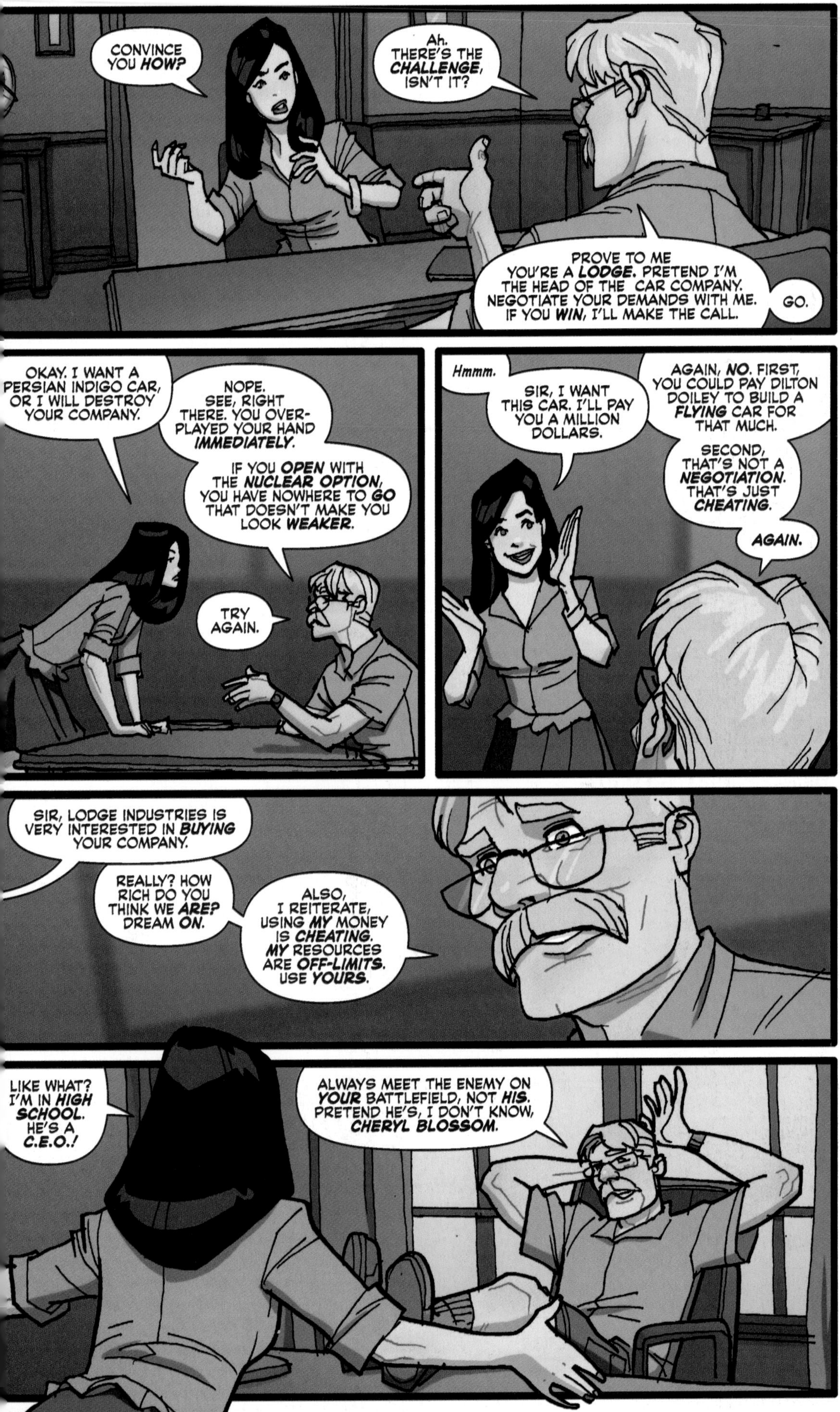

CONVINCE YOU HOW?
Ah. THERE'S THE CHALLENGE, ISN'T IT?
PROVE TO ME YOU'RE A LODGE. PRETEND I'M THE HEAD OF THE CAR COMPANY. NEGOTIATE YOUR DEMANDS WITH ME. IF YOU WIN, I'LL MAKE THE CALL.
GO.
OKAY. I WANT A PERSIAN INDIGO CAR, OR I WILL DESTROY YOUR COMPANY.
NOPE. SEE, RIGHT THERE. YOU OVER-PLAYED YOUR HAND IMMEDIATELY.
IF YOU OPEN WITH THE NUCLEAR OPTION, YOU HAVE NOWHERE TO GO THAT DOESN'T MAKE YOU LOOK WEAKER.
TRY AGAIN.
Hmmm.
SIR, I WANT THIS CAR. I'LL PAY YOU A MILLION DOLLARS.
AGAIN, NO. FIRST, YOU COULD PAY DILTON DOILEY TO BUILD A FLYING CAR FOR THAT MUCH.
SECOND, THAT'S NOT A NEGOTIATION. THAT'S JUST CHEATING.
AGAIN.
SIR, LODGE INDUSTRIES IS VERY INTERESTED IN BUYING YOUR COMPANY.
REALLY? HOW RICH DO YOU THINK WE ARE? DREAM ON.
ALSO, I REITERATE, USING MY MONEY IS CHEATING. MY RESOURCES ARE OFF-LIMITS. USE YOURS.
LIKE WHAT? I'M IN HIGH SCHOOL. HE'S A C.E.O.!
ALWAYS MEET THE ENEMY ON YOUR BATTLEFIELD, NOT HIS. PRETEND HE'S, I DON'T KNOW, CHERYL BLOSSOM.

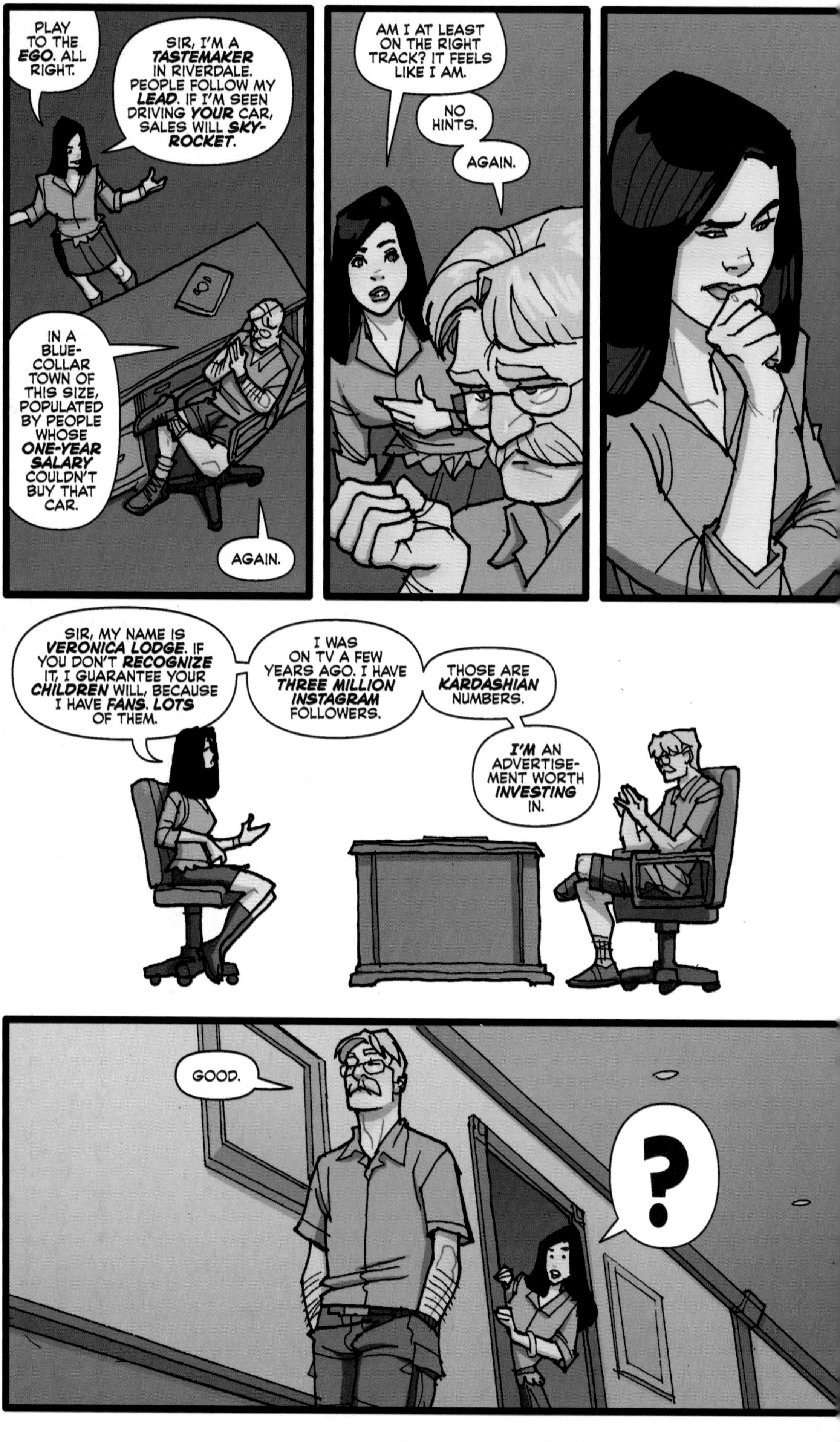
PLAY TO THE EGO. ALL RIGHT.
SIR, I'M A TASTEMAKER IN RIVERDALE. PEOPLE FOLLOW MY LEAD. IF I'M SEEN DRIVING YOUR CAR, SALES WILL SKY-ROCKET.
IN A BLUE-COLLAR TOWN OF THIS SIZE, POPULATED BY PEOPLE WHOSE ONE-YEAR SALARY COULDN'T BUY THAT CAR.
AGAIN.
AM I AT LEAST ON THE RIGHT TRACK? IT FEELS LIKE I AM.
NO HINTS.
AGAIN.
SIR, MY NAME IS VERONICA LODGE. IF YOU DON'T RECOGNIZE IT, I GUARANTEE YOUR CHILDREN WILL, BECAUSE I HAVE FANS. LOTS OF THEM.
I WAS ON TV A FEW YEARS AGO. I HAVE THREE MILLION INSTAGRAM FOLLOWERS.
THOSE ARE KARDASHIAN NUMBERS.
I'M AN ADVERTISE-MENT WORTH INVESTING IN.
GOOD.
?

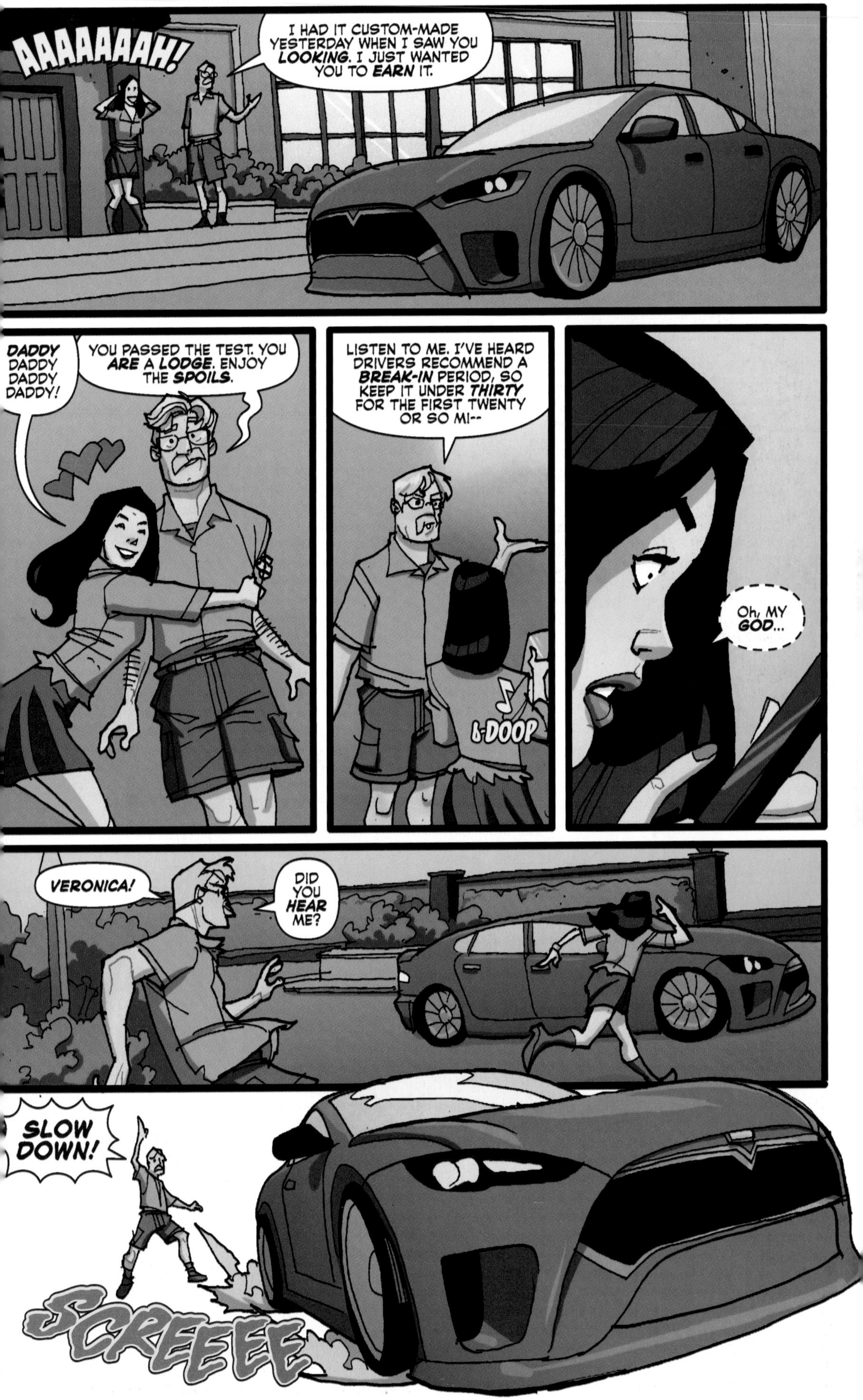
AAAAAAAH!
I HAD IT CUSTOM-MADE YESTERDAY WHEN I SAW YOU LOOKING. I JUST WANTED YOU TO EARN IT.
DADDY DADDY DADDY DADDY!
YOU PASSED THE TEST. YOU ARE A LODGE. ENJOY THE SPOILS.
LISTEN TO ME. I'VE HEARD DRIVERS RECOMMEND A BREAK-IN PERIOD, SO KEEP IT UNDER THIRTY FOR THE FIRST TWENTY OR SO MI--
b-DOOP
Oh, MY GOD...
VERONICA!
DID YOU HEAR ME?
SLOW DOWN!
SCREEEE

Dilton in "BRAIN DRAIN"

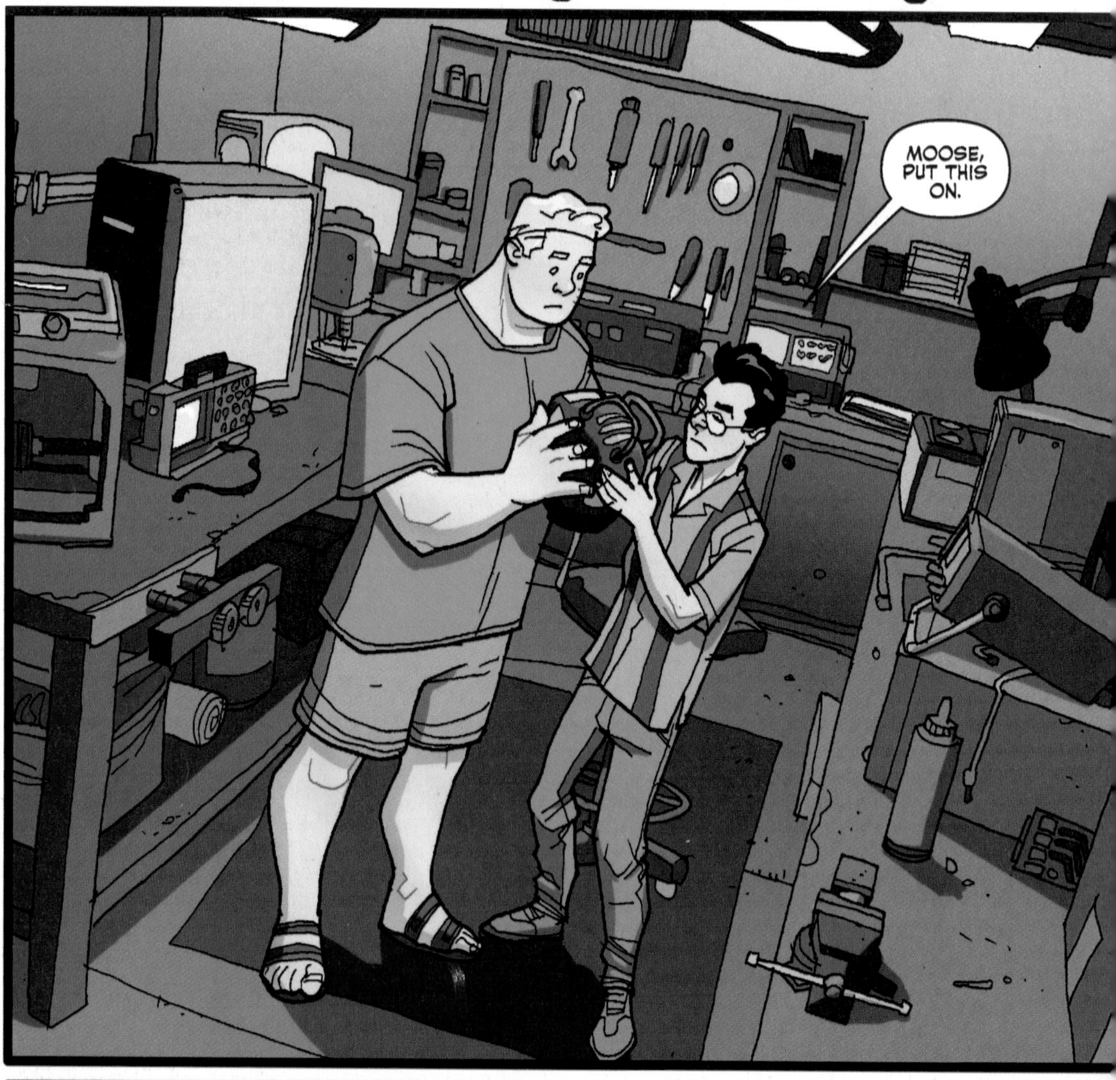
MOOSE, PUT THIS ON.

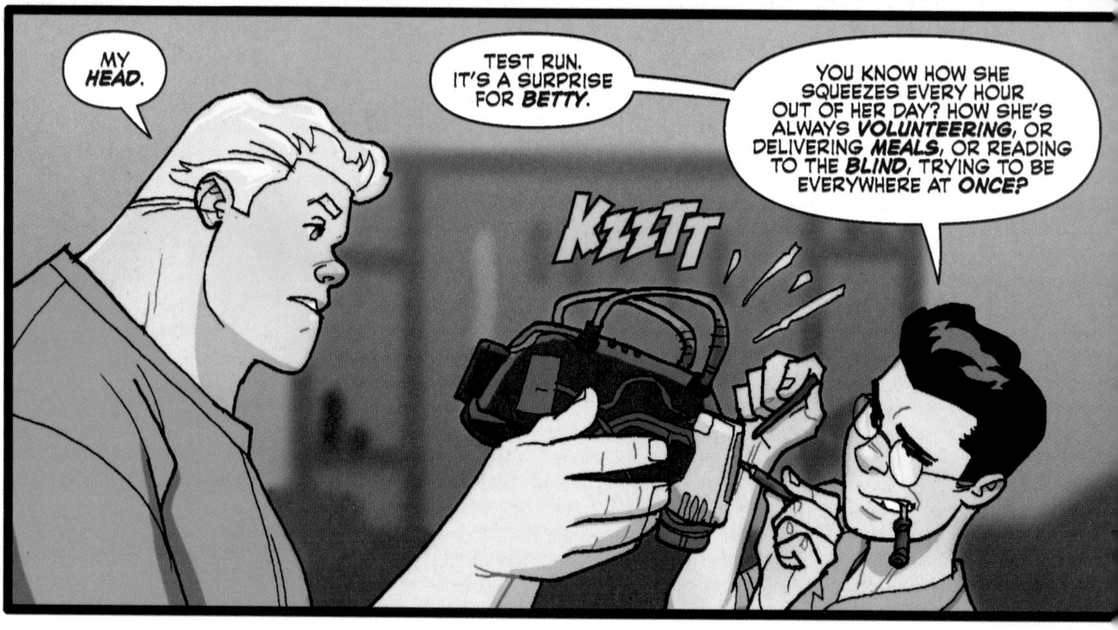
MY HEAD.
TEST RUN. IT'S A SURPRISE FOR BETTY.
YOU KNOW HOW SHE SQUEEZES EVERY HOUR OUT OF HER DAY? HOW SHE'S ALWAYS VOLUNTEERING, OR DELIVERING MEALS, OR READING TO THE BLIND, TRYING TO BE EVERYWHERE AT ONCE?
KZZTT

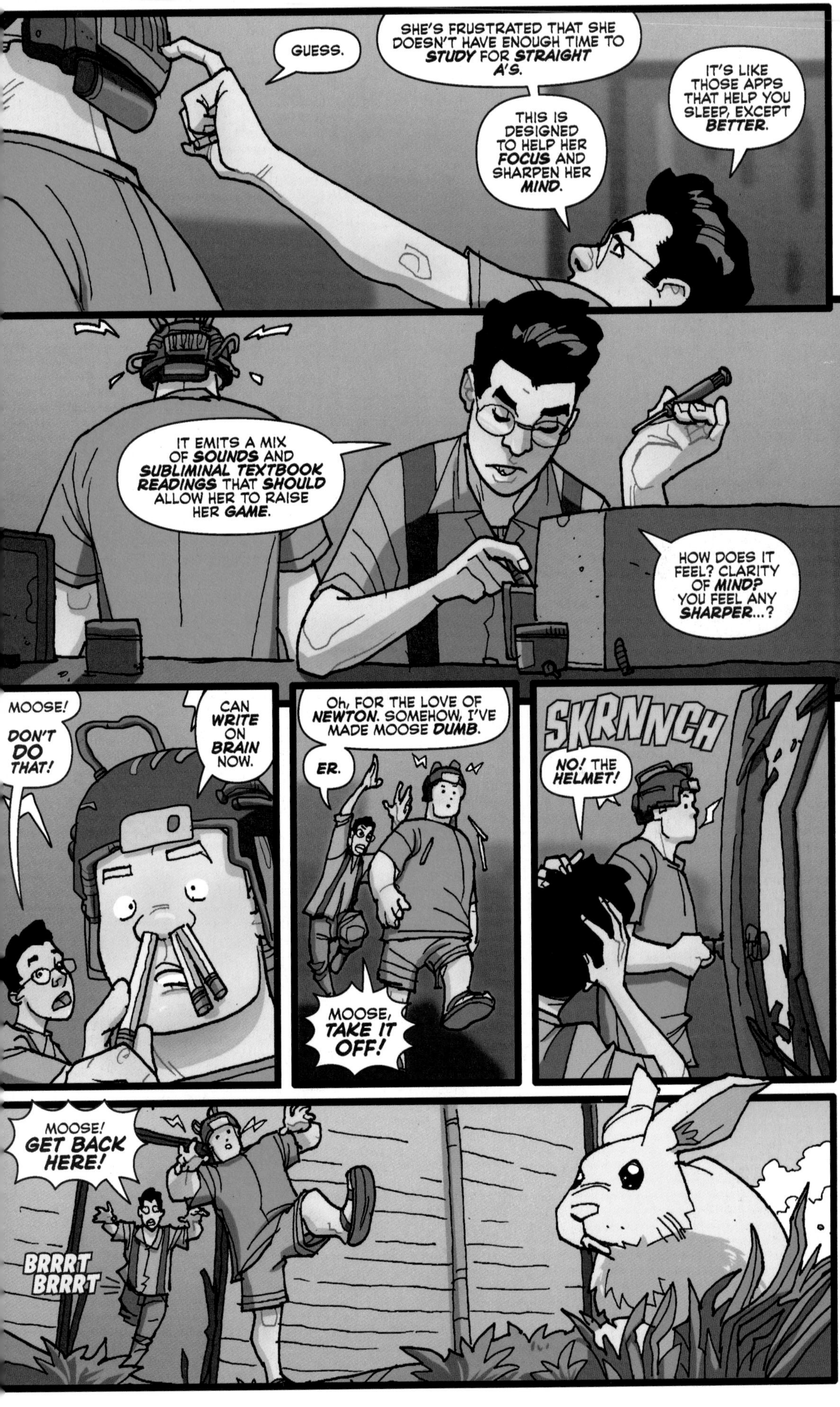

GUESS.
SHE'S FRUSTRATED THAT SHE DOESN'T HAVE ENOUGH TIME TO STUDY FOR STRAIGHT A'S.
THIS IS DESIGNED TO HELP HER FOCUS AND SHARPEN HER MIND.
IT'S LIKE THOSE APPS THAT HELP YOU SLEEP, EXCEPT BETTER.
IT EMITS A MIX OF SOUNDS AND SUBLIMINAL TEXTBOOK READINGS THAT SHOULD ALLOW HER TO RAISE HER GAME.
HOW DOES IT FEEL? CLARITY OF MIND? YOU FEEL ANY SHARPER...?
MOOSE! DON'T DO THAT!
CAN WRITE ON BRAIN NOW.
Oh, FOR THE LOVE OF NEWTON. SOMEHOW, I'VE MADE MOOSE DUMB.
ER.
MOOSE, TAKE IT OFF!
SKRNNCH
NO! THE HELMET!
MOOSE! GET BACK HERE!
BRRRT BRRRT

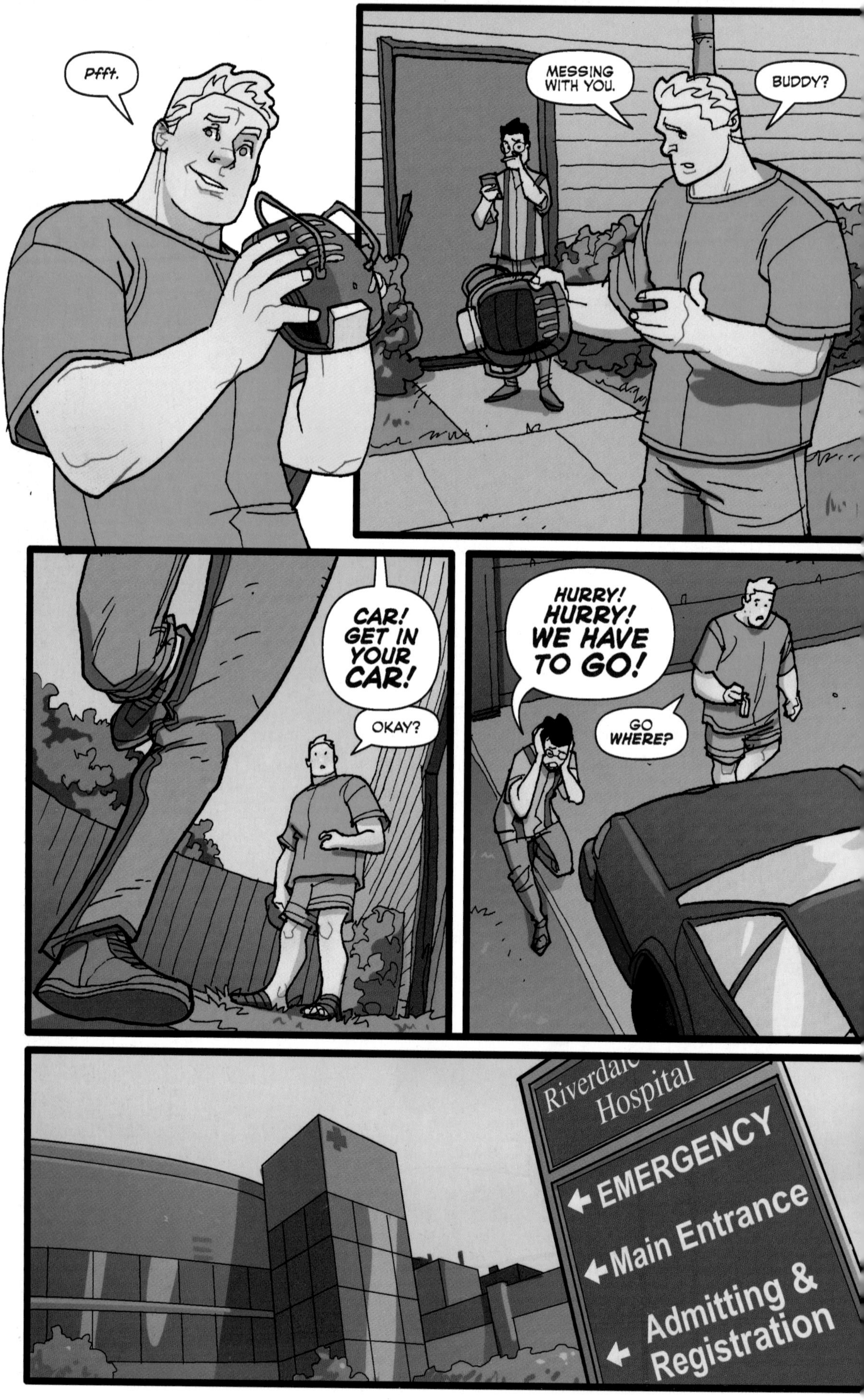
Pfft.
MESSING WITH YOU.
BUDDY?
CAR! GET IN YOUR CAR!
OKAY?
HURRY! HURRY! WE HAVE TO GO!
GO WHERE?
Riverdale Hospital
EMERGENCY
Main Entrance
Admitting & Registration

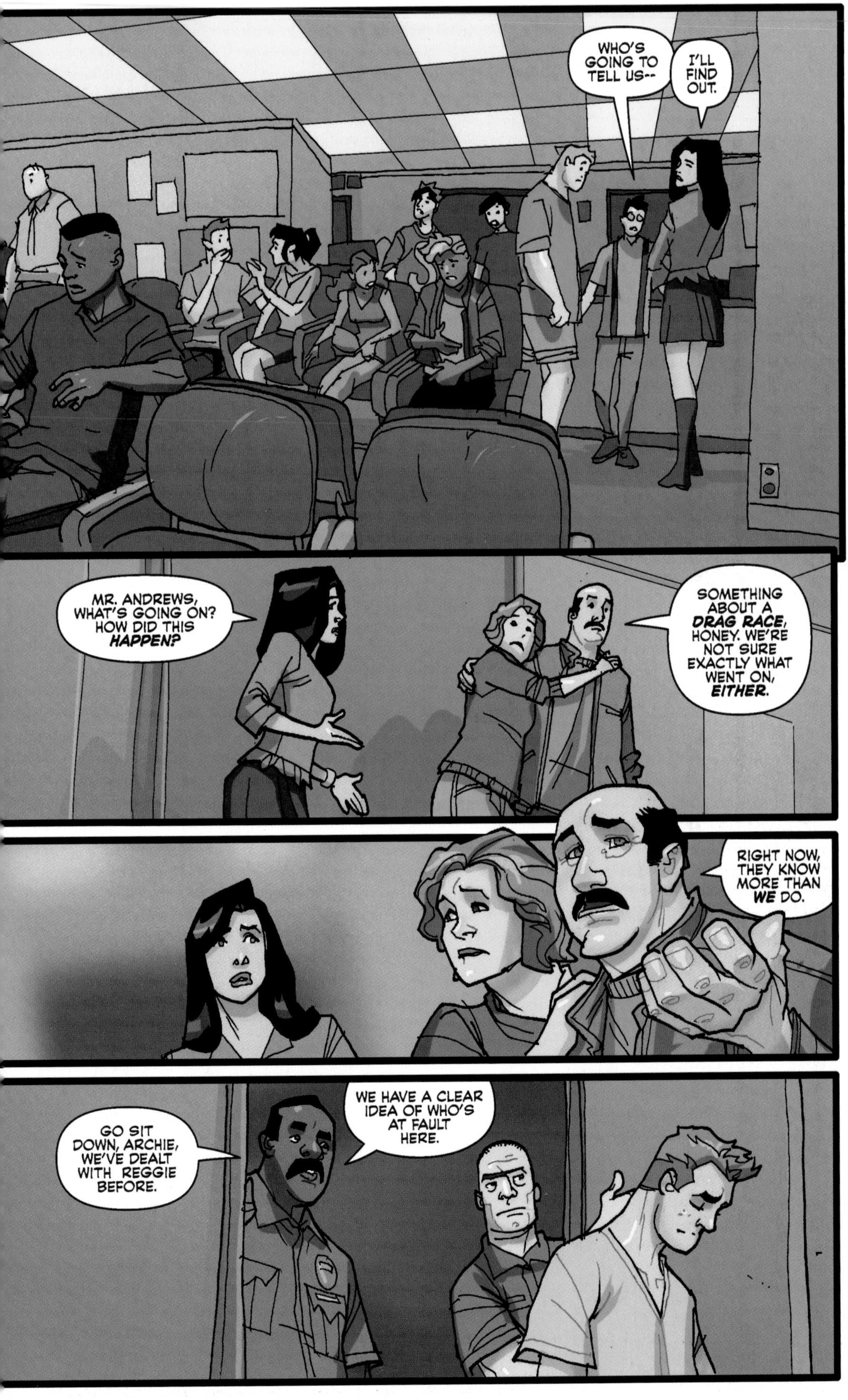
WHO'S GOING TO TELL US--
I'LL FIND OUT.
MR. ANDREWS, WHAT'S GOING ON? HOW DID THIS HAPPEN?
SOMETHING ABOUT A DRAG RACE, HONEY. WE'RE NOT SURE EXACTLY WHAT WENT ON, EITHER.
RIGHT NOW, THEY KNOW MORE THAN WE DO.
GO SIT DOWN, ARCHIE, WE'VE DEALT WITH REGGIE BEFORE.
WE HAVE A CLEAR IDEA OF WHO'S AT FAULT HERE.

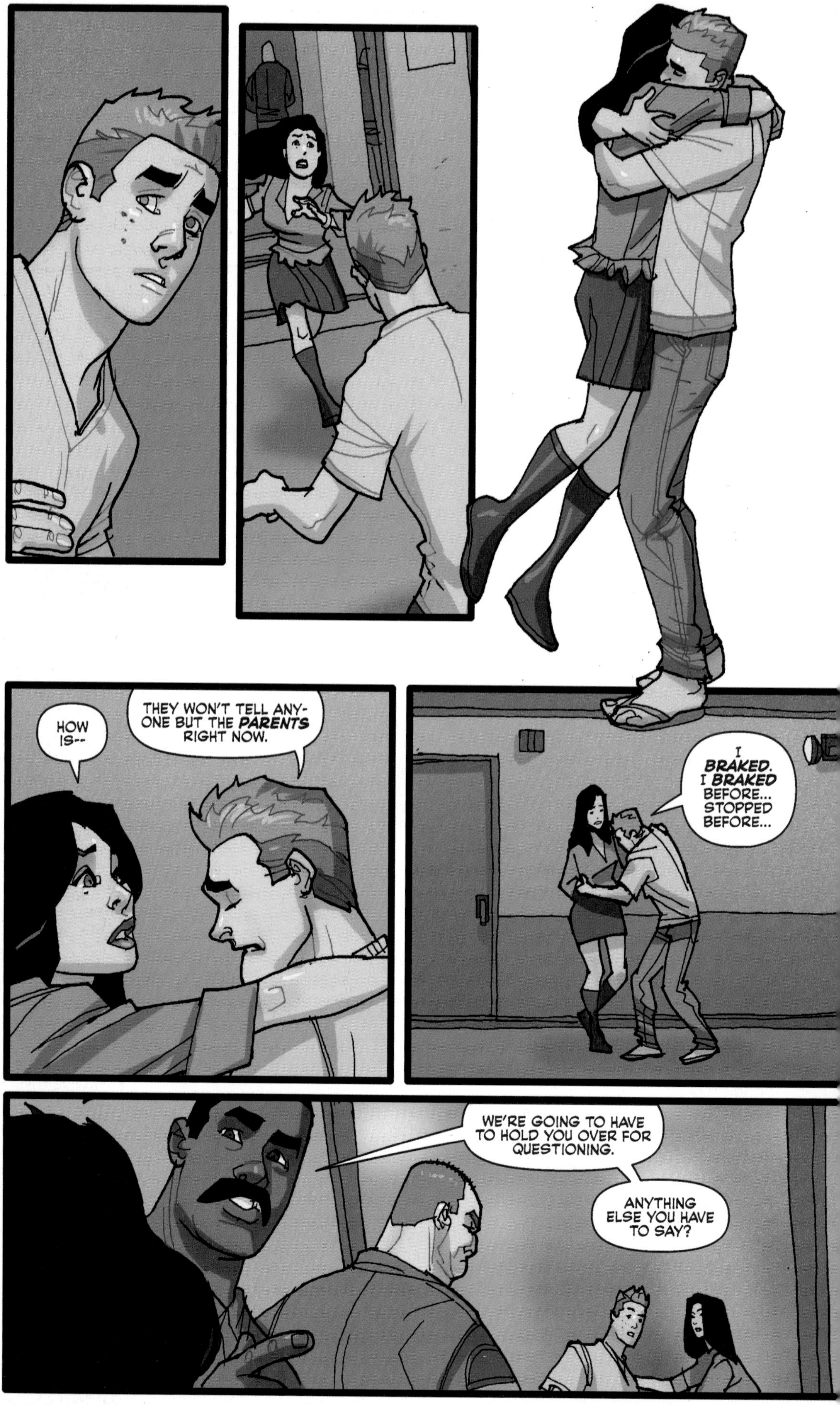
HOW IS--
THEY WON'T TELL ANYONE BUT THE PARENTS RIGHT NOW.
I BRAKED. I BRAKED BEFORE... STOPPED BEFORE...
WE'RE GOING TO HAVE TO HOLD YOU OVER FOR QUESTIONING.
ANYTHING ELSE YOU HAVE TO SAY?

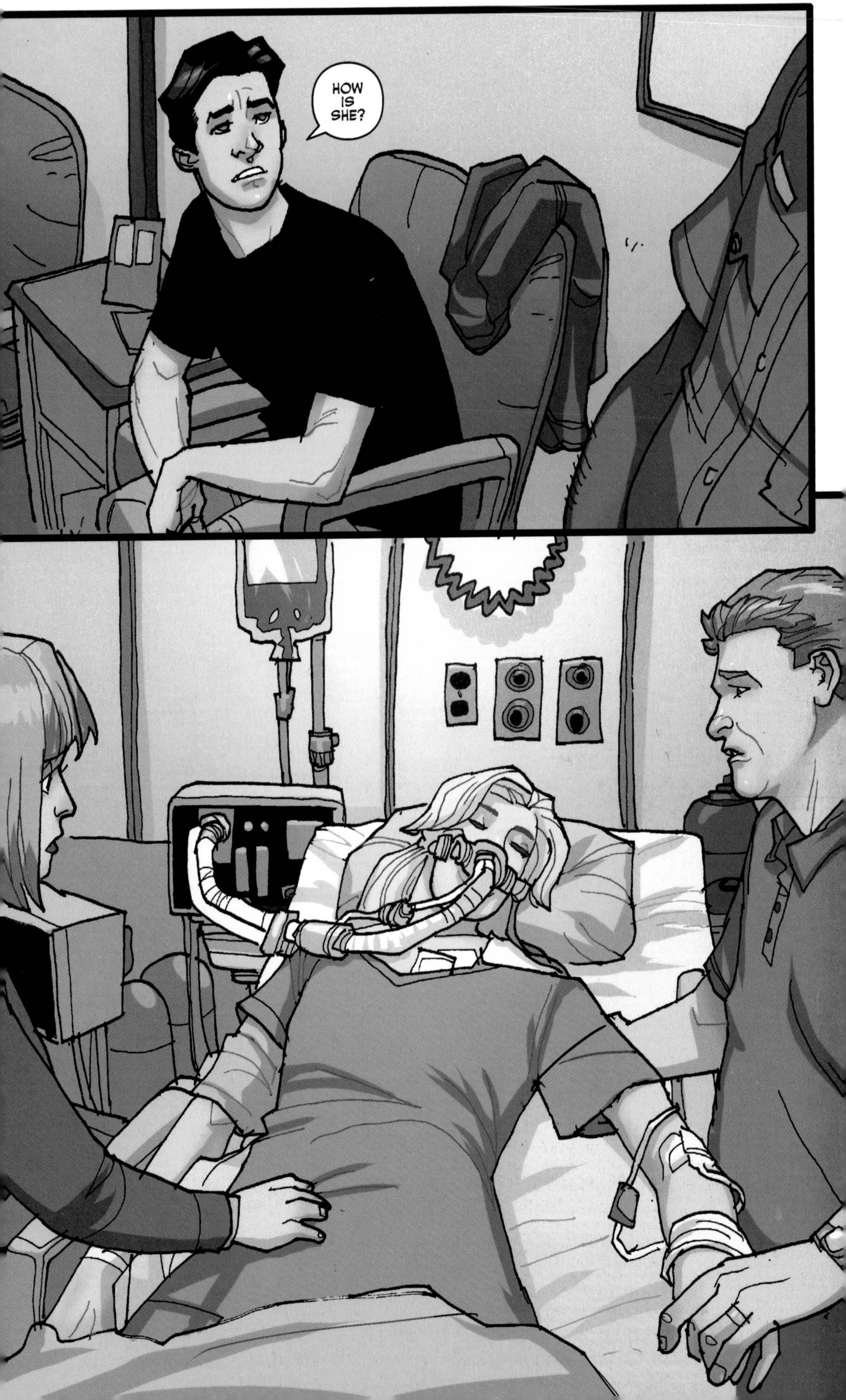
HOW IS SHE?

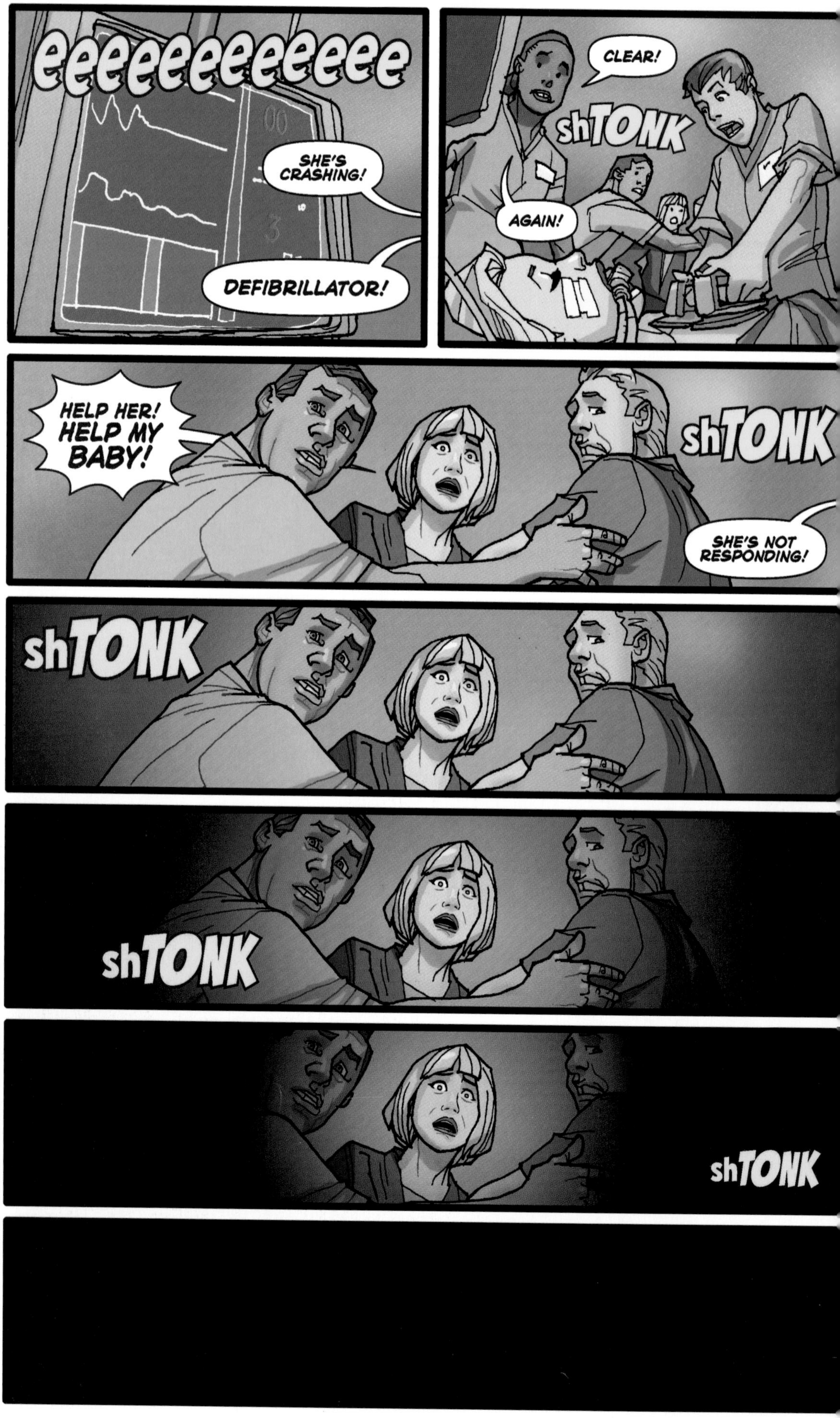
eeeeeeeeeeeee
SHE'S CRASHING!
DEFIBRILLATOR!
CLEAR!
shTONK
AGAIN!
HELP HER! HELP MY BABY!
shTONK
SHE'S NOT RESPONDING!
shTONK
shTONK
shTONK

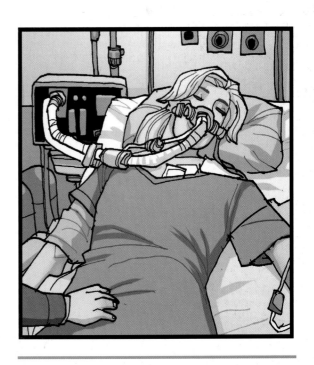

TO BE CONTINUED...

ISSUE TWENTY TWO

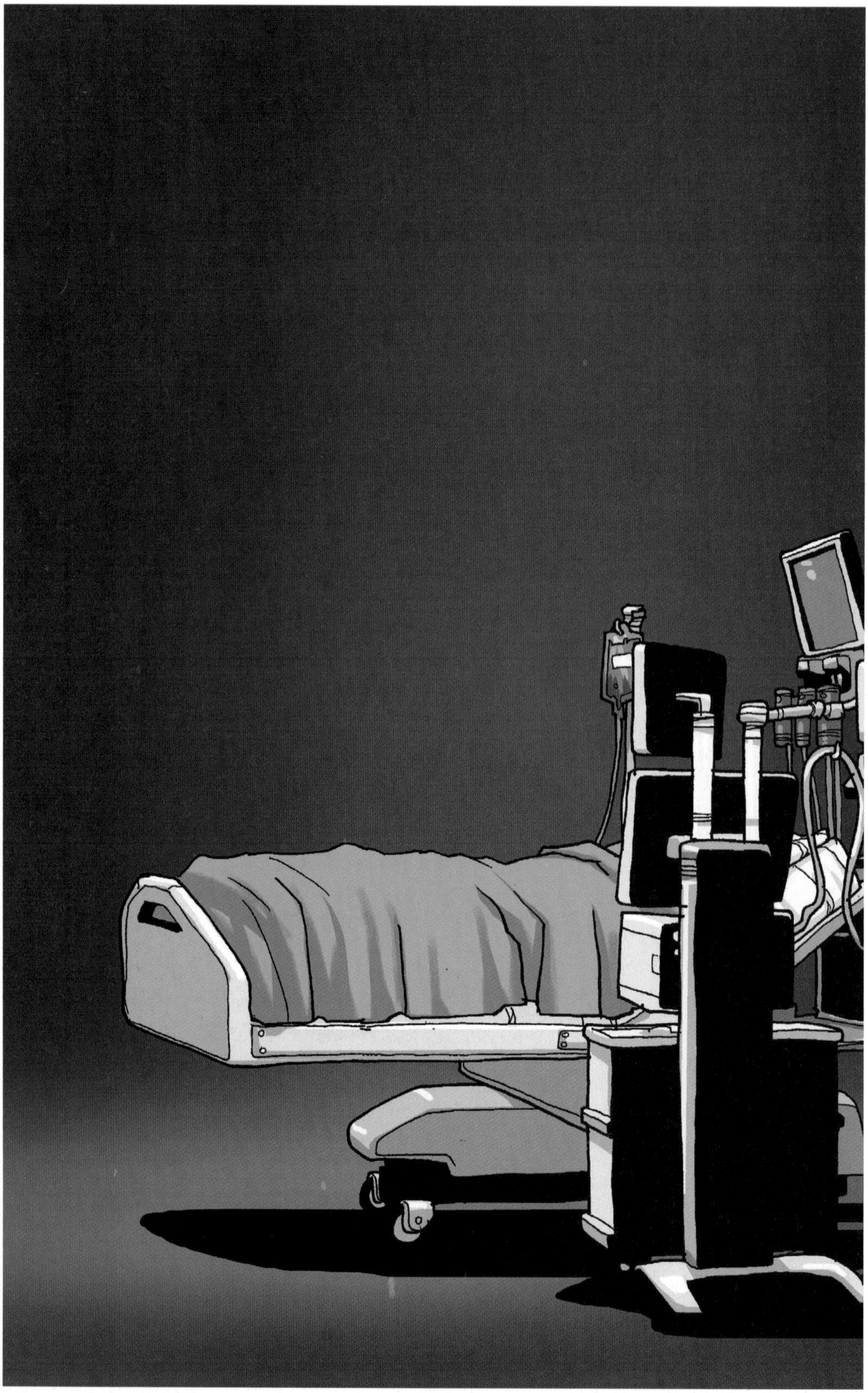

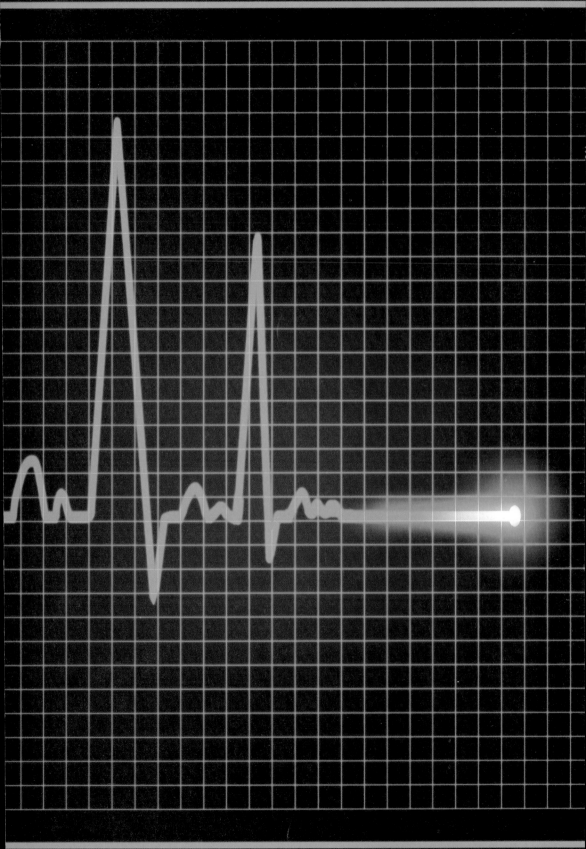

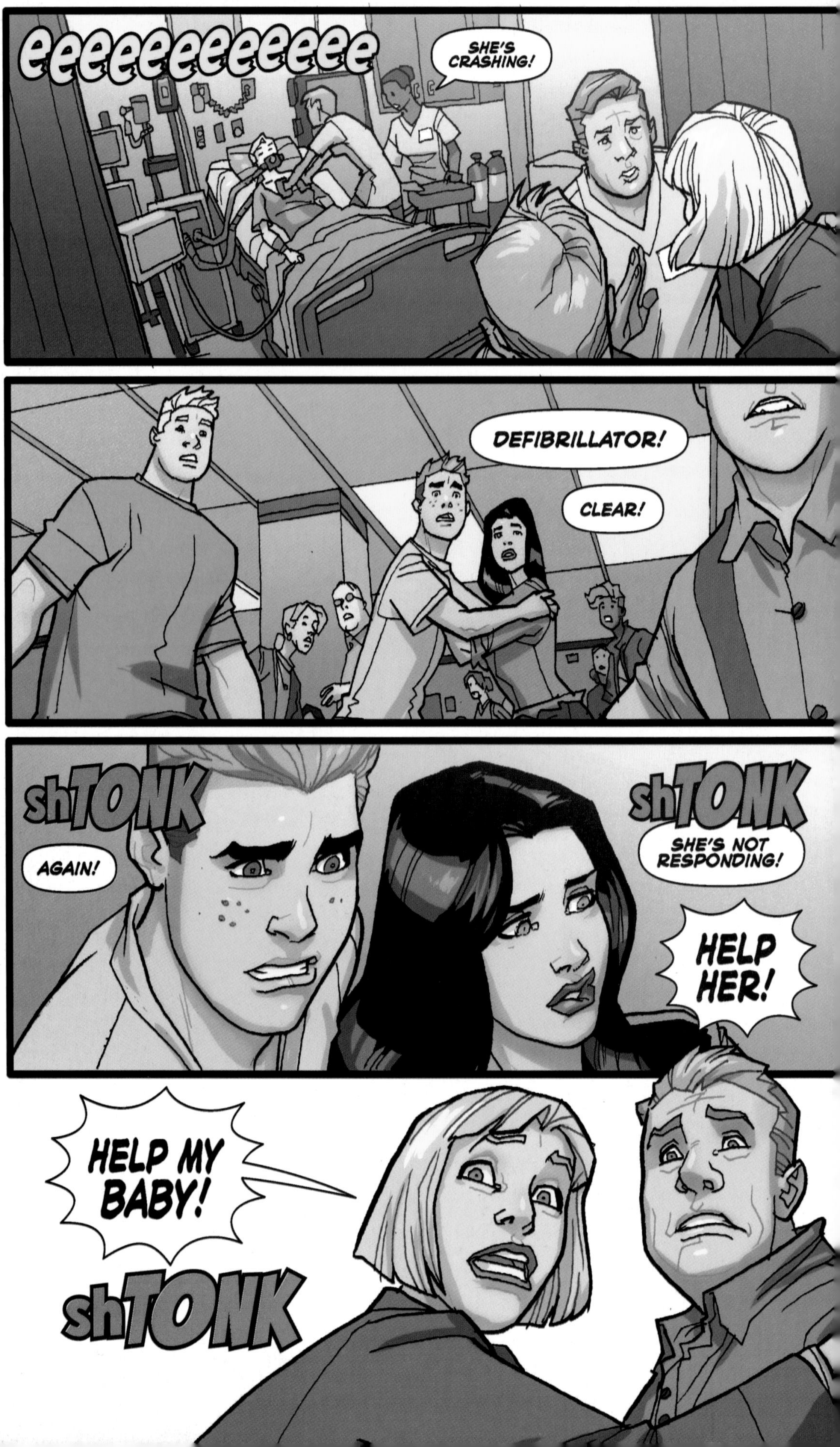
eeeeeeeeeeee
SHE'S CRASHING!
DEFIBRILLATOR!
CLEAR!
shTONK
AGAIN!
shTONK
SHE'S NOT RESPONDING!
HELP HER!
HELP MY BABY!
shTONK

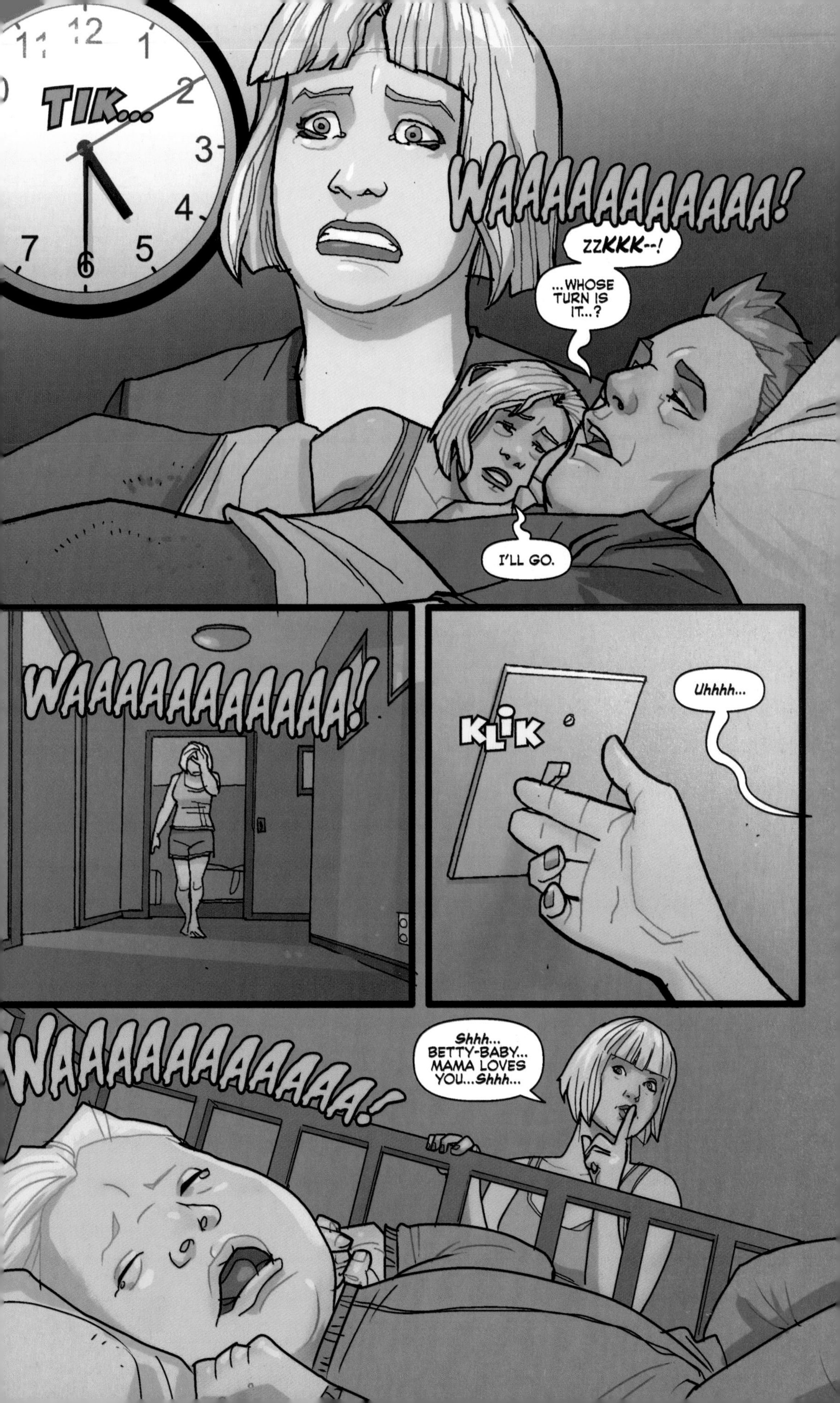
TIK...
WAAAAAAAAAAAA!
ZZKKK--!
...WHOSE TURN IS IT...?
I'LL GO.
WAAAAAAAAAAAA!
KLIK
Uhhhh...
WAAAAAAAAAAAA!
Shhh... BETTY-BABY... MAMA LOVES YOU...Shhh...

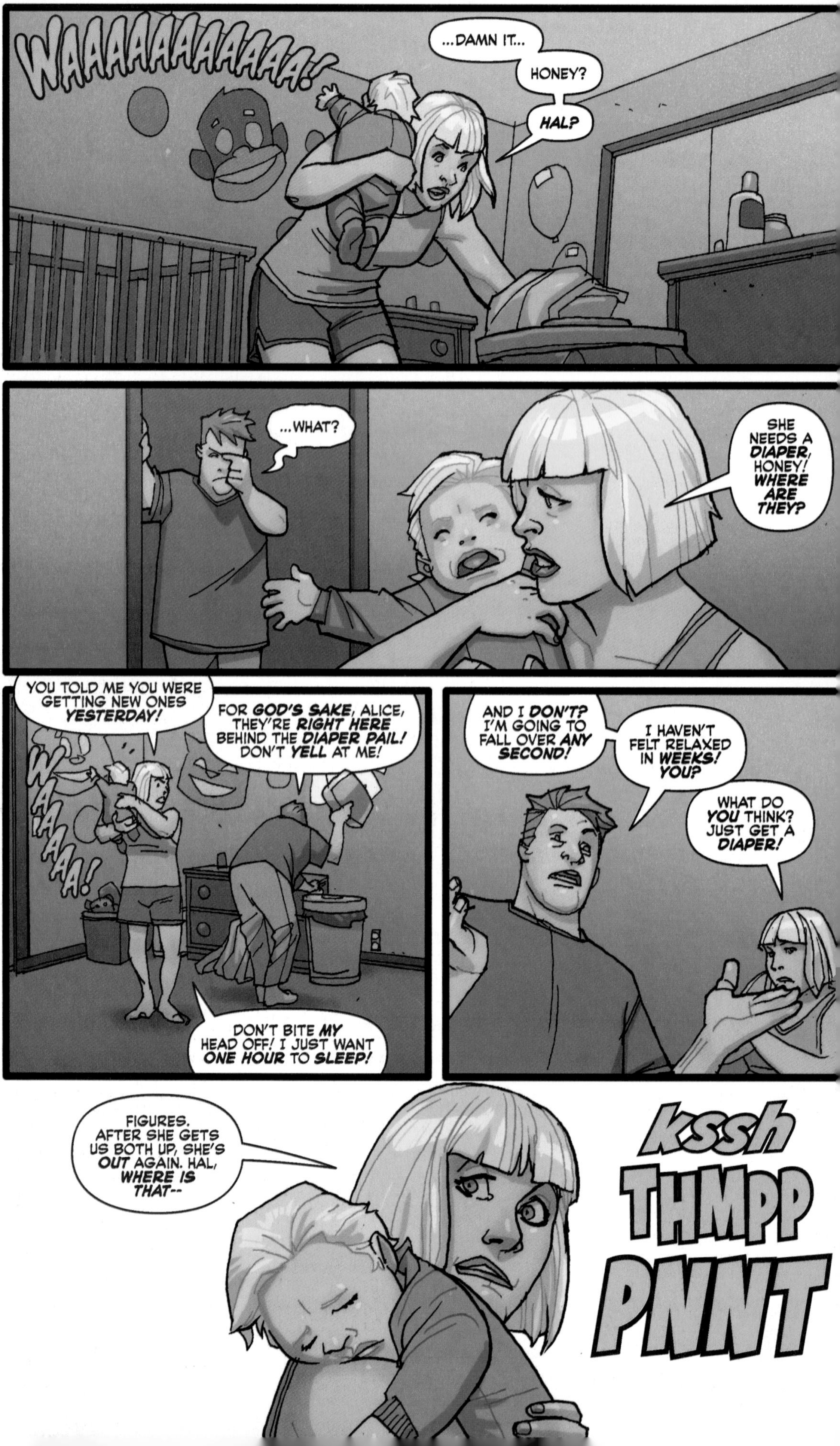
WAAAAAAAAAAA!
...DAMN IT...
HONEY?
HAL?
...WHAT?
SHE NEEDS A DIAPER, HONEY! WHERE ARE THEY?
YOU TOLD ME YOU WERE GETTING NEW ONES YESTERDAY!
FOR GOD'S SAKE, ALICE, THEY'RE RIGHT HERE BEHIND THE DIAPER PAIL! DON'T YELL AT ME!
WAAAAAA!
DON'T BITE MY HEAD OFF! I JUST WANT ONE HOUR TO SLEEP!
AND I DON'T? I'M GOING TO FALL OVER ANY SECOND!
I HAVEN'T FELT RELAXED IN WEEKS! YOU?
WHAT DO YOU THINK? JUST GET A DIAPER!
FIGURES. AFTER SHE GETS US BOTH UP, SHE'S OUT AGAIN. HAL, WHERE IS THAT--
kssh
THMPP
PNNT

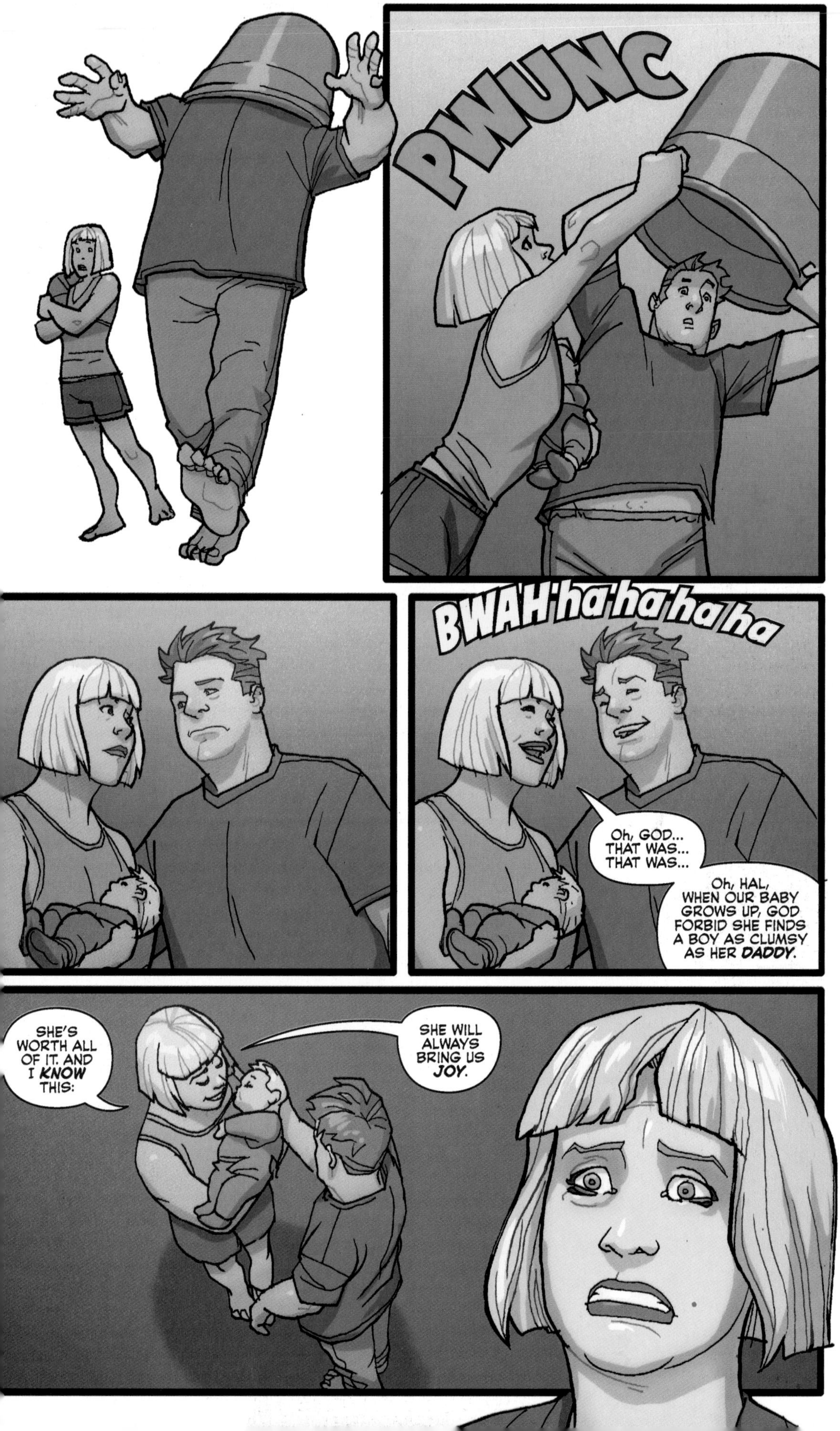
PWUNC
BWAH-ha-ha-ha-ha
Oh, GOD... THAT WAS... THAT WAS...
Oh, HAL, WHEN OUR BABY GROWS UP, GOD FORBID SHE FINDS A BOY AS CLUMSY AS HER *DADDY*.
SHE'S WORTH ALL OF IT. AND I *KNOW* THIS:
SHE WILL ALWAYS BRING US *JOY*.

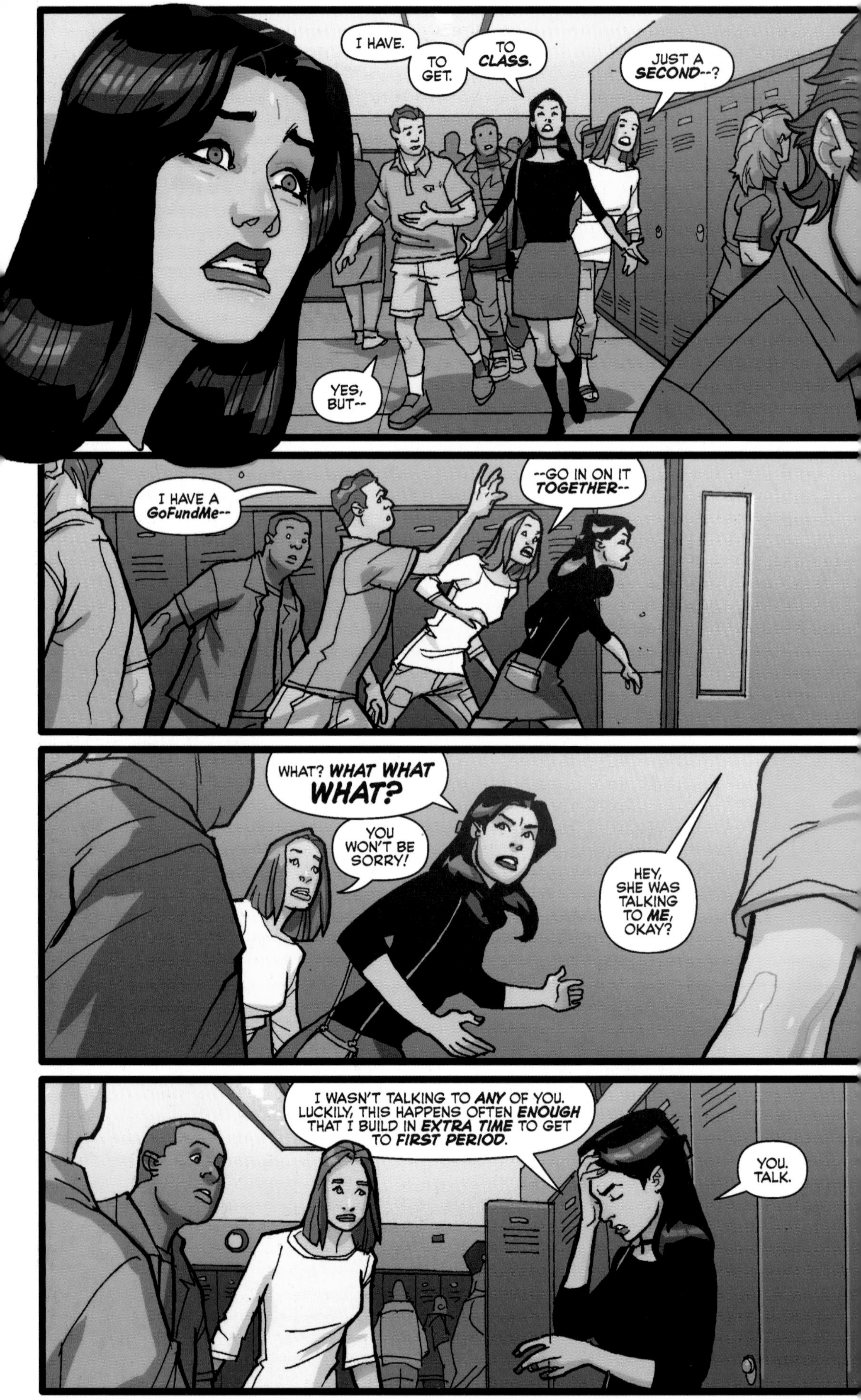
I HAVE.
TO GET.
TO CLASS.
JUST A SECOND--?
YES, BUT--
I HAVE A GoFundMe--
--GO IN ON IT TOGETHER--
WHAT? WHAT WHAT WHAT?
YOU WON'T BE SORRY!
HEY, SHE WAS TALKING TO ME, OKAY?
I WASN'T TALKING TO ANY OF YOU. LUCKILY, THIS HAPPENS OFTEN ENOUGH THAT I BUILD IN EXTRA TIME TO GET TO FIRST PERIOD.
YOU. TALK.

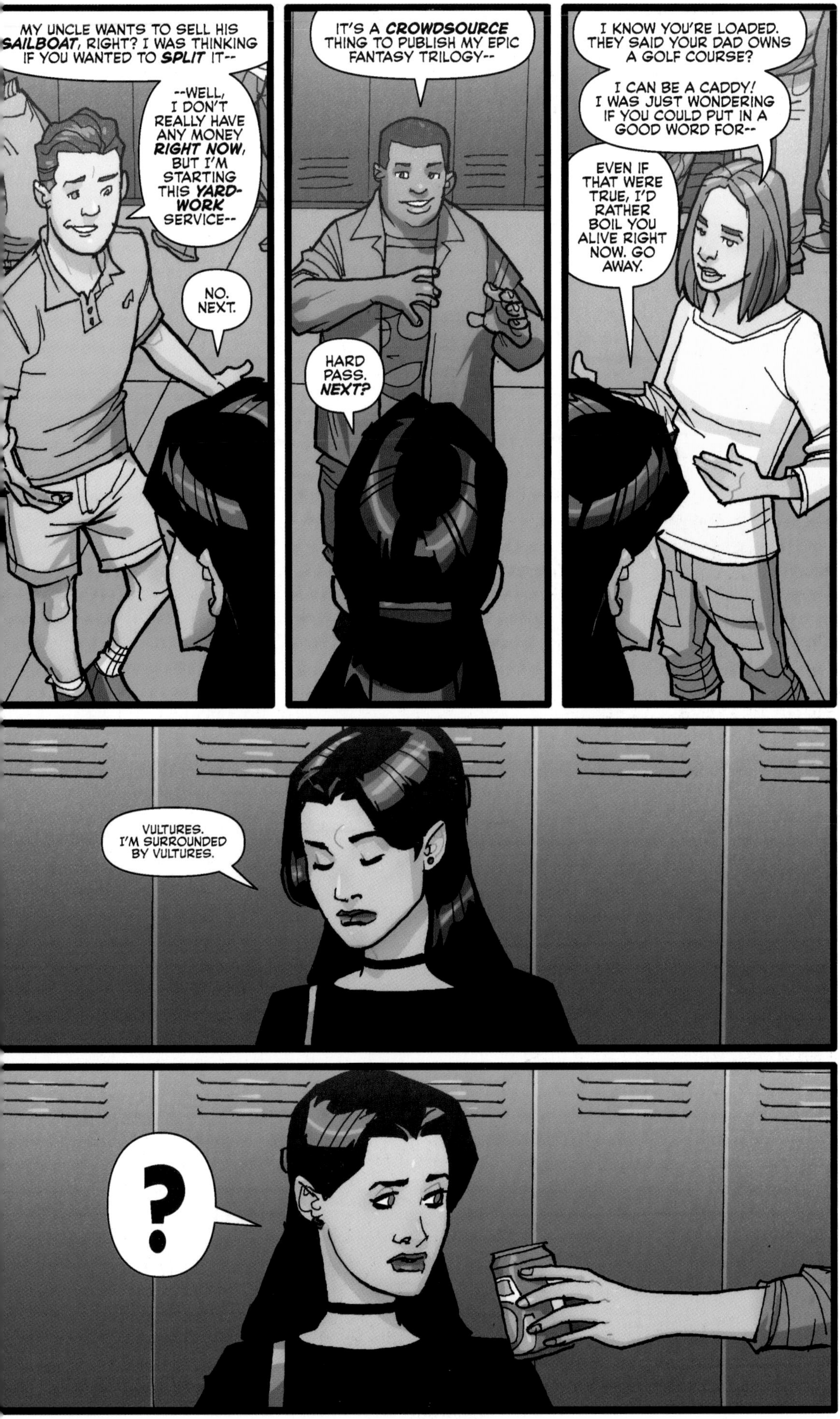
MY UNCLE WANTS TO SELL HIS SAILBOAT, RIGHT? I WAS THINKING IF YOU WANTED TO SPLIT IT--
--WELL, I DON'T REALLY HAVE ANY MONEY RIGHT NOW, BUT I'M STARTING THIS YARD-WORK SERVICE--
NO. NEXT.
IT'S A CROWDSOURCE THING TO PUBLISH MY EPIC FANTASY TRILOGY--
HARD PASS. NEXT?
I KNOW YOU'RE LOADED. THEY SAID YOUR DAD OWNS A GOLF COURSE?
I CAN BE A CADDY! I WAS JUST WONDERING IF YOU COULD PUT IN A GOOD WORD FOR--
EVEN IF THAT WERE TRUE, I'D RATHER BOIL YOU ALIVE RIGHT NOW. GO AWAY.
VULTURES. I'M SURROUNDED BY VULTURES.
?

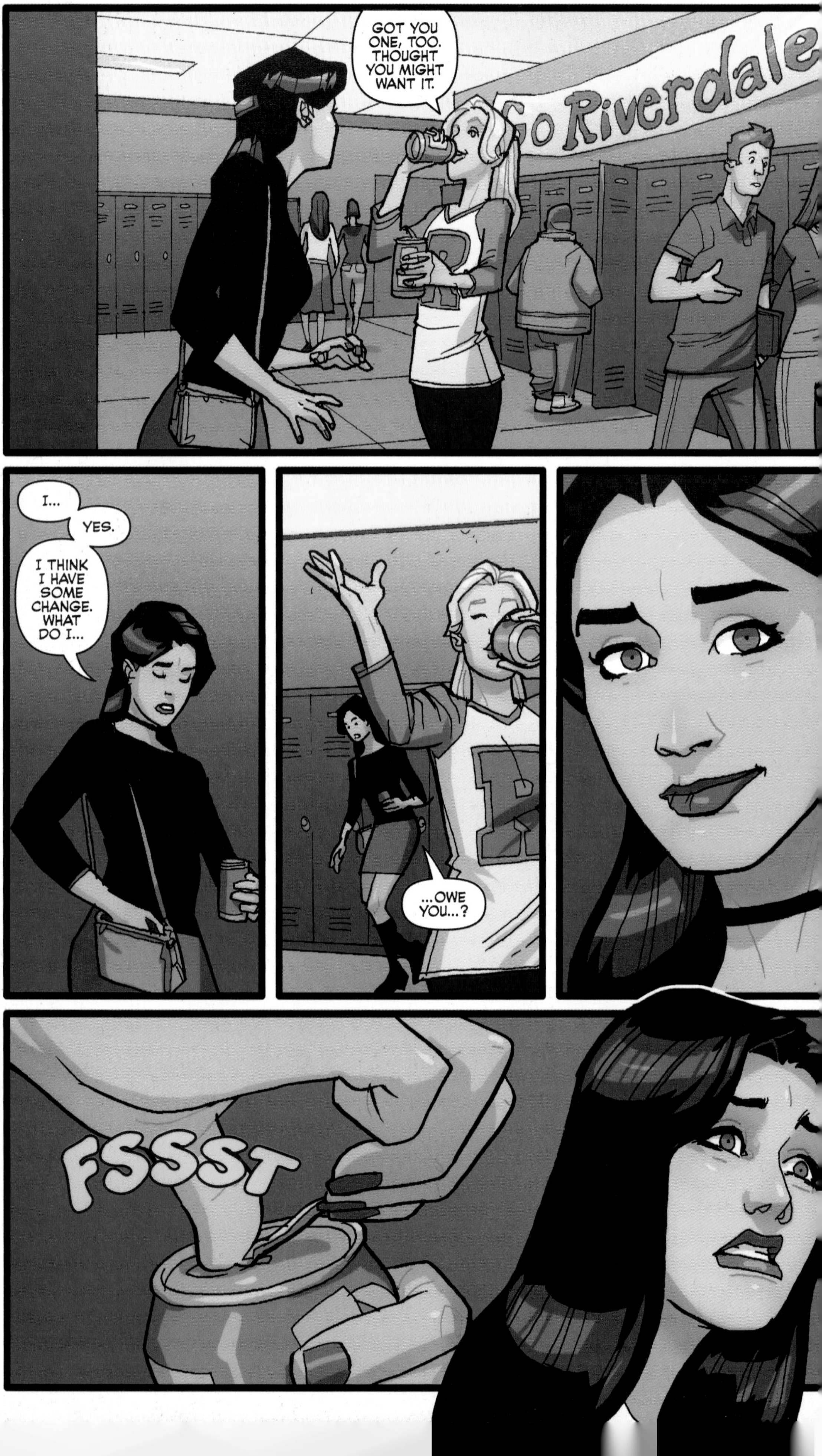
GOT YOU ONE, TOO. THOUGHT YOU MIGHT WANT IT.
Go Riverdale
I...
YES.
I THINK I HAVE SOME CHANGE. WHAT DO I...
...OWE YOU...?
FSSST

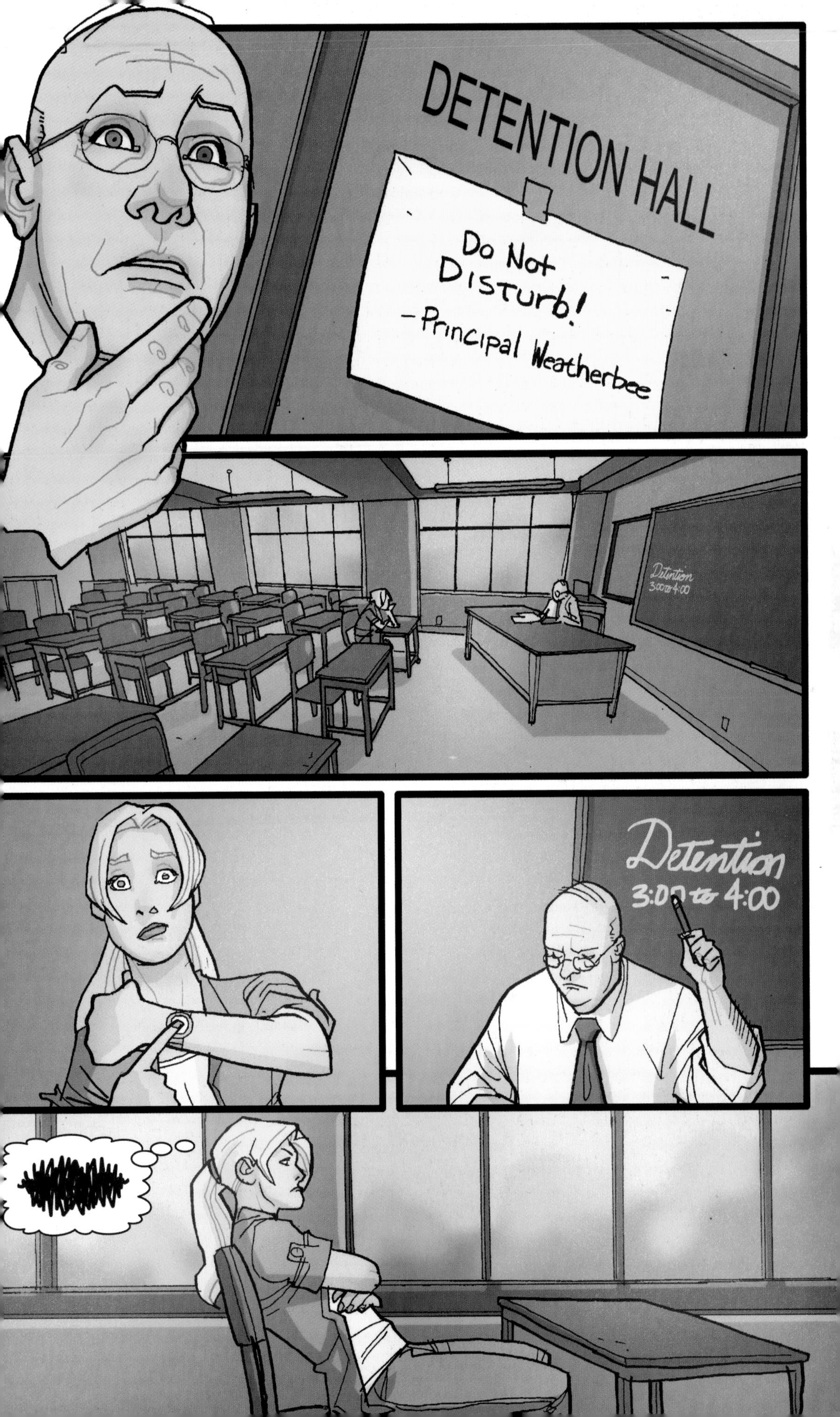
DETENTION HALL
Do Not Disturb!
-Principal Weatherbee
Detention 3:00 to 4:00
Detention 3:00 to 4:00

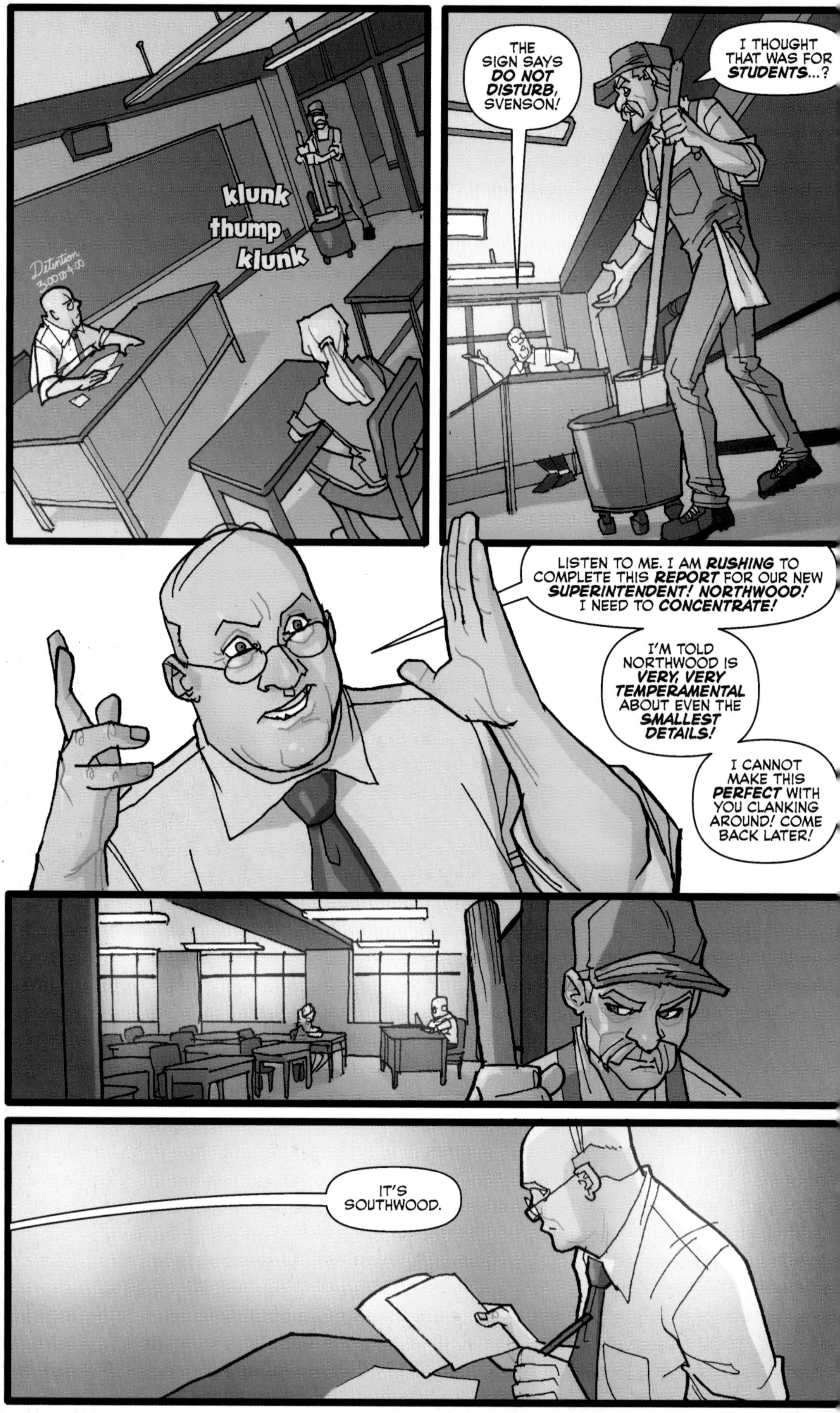
klunk
thump
klunk
Detention 3:00 to 4:00
THE SIGN SAYS DO NOT DISTURB, SVENSON!
I THOUGHT THAT WAS FOR STUDENTS...?
LISTEN TO ME. I AM RUSHING TO COMPLETE THIS REPORT FOR OUR NEW SUPERINTENDENT! NORTHWOOD! I NEED TO CONCENTRATE!
I'M TOLD NORTHWOOD IS VERY, VERY TEMPERAMENTAL ABOUT EVEN THE SMALLEST DETAILS!
I CANNOT MAKE THIS PERFECT WITH YOU CLANKING AROUND! COME BACK LATER!
IT'S SOUTHWOOD.

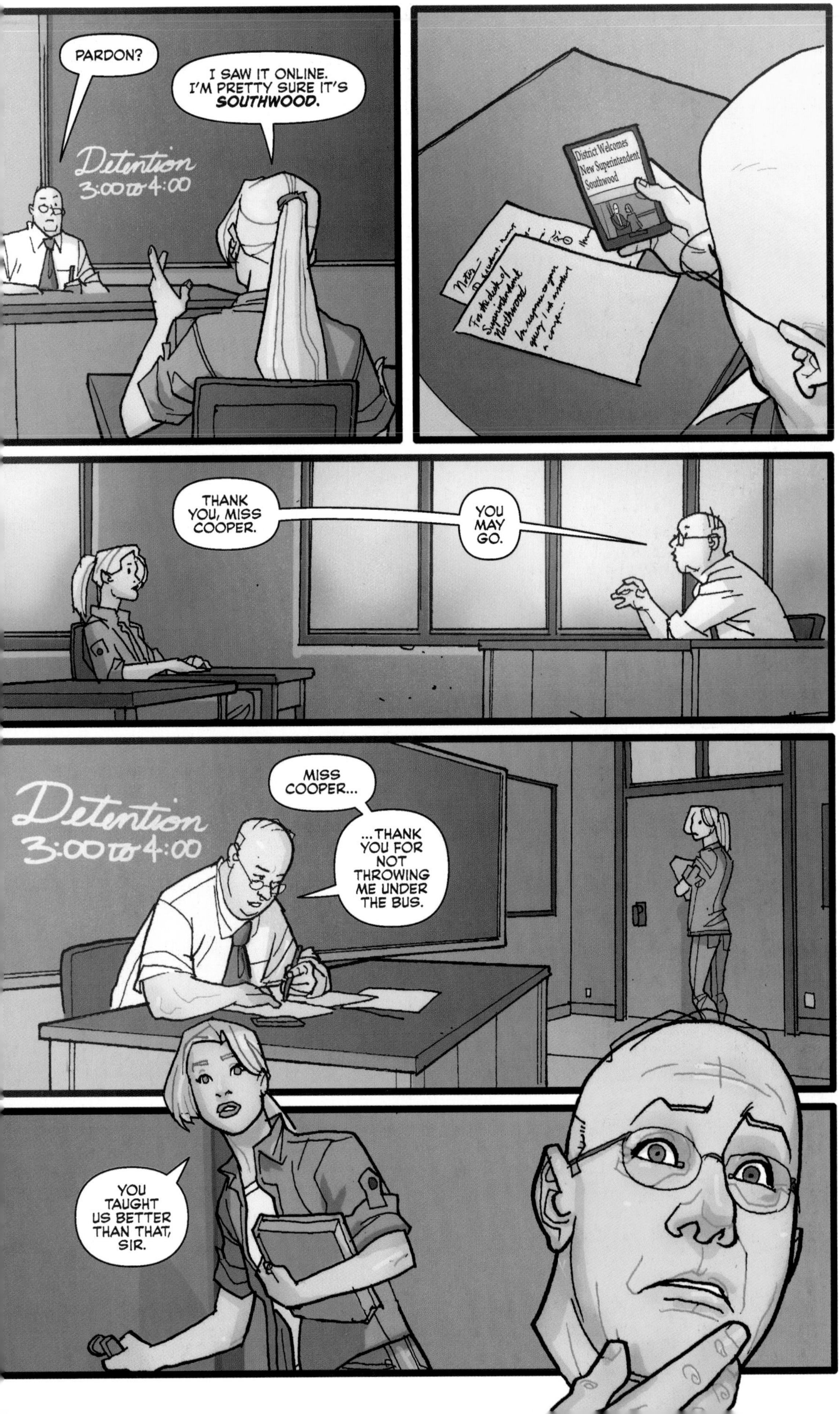

PARDON?
I SAW IT ONLINE. I'M PRETTY SURE IT'S *SOUTHWOOD.*
Detention 3:00 to 4:00
District Welcomes New Superintendent Southwood
THANK YOU, MISS COOPER.
YOU MAY GO.
Detention 3:00 to 4:00
MISS COOPER...
...THANK YOU FOR NOT THROWING ME UNDER THE BUS.
YOU TAUGHT US BETTER THAN THAT, SIR.

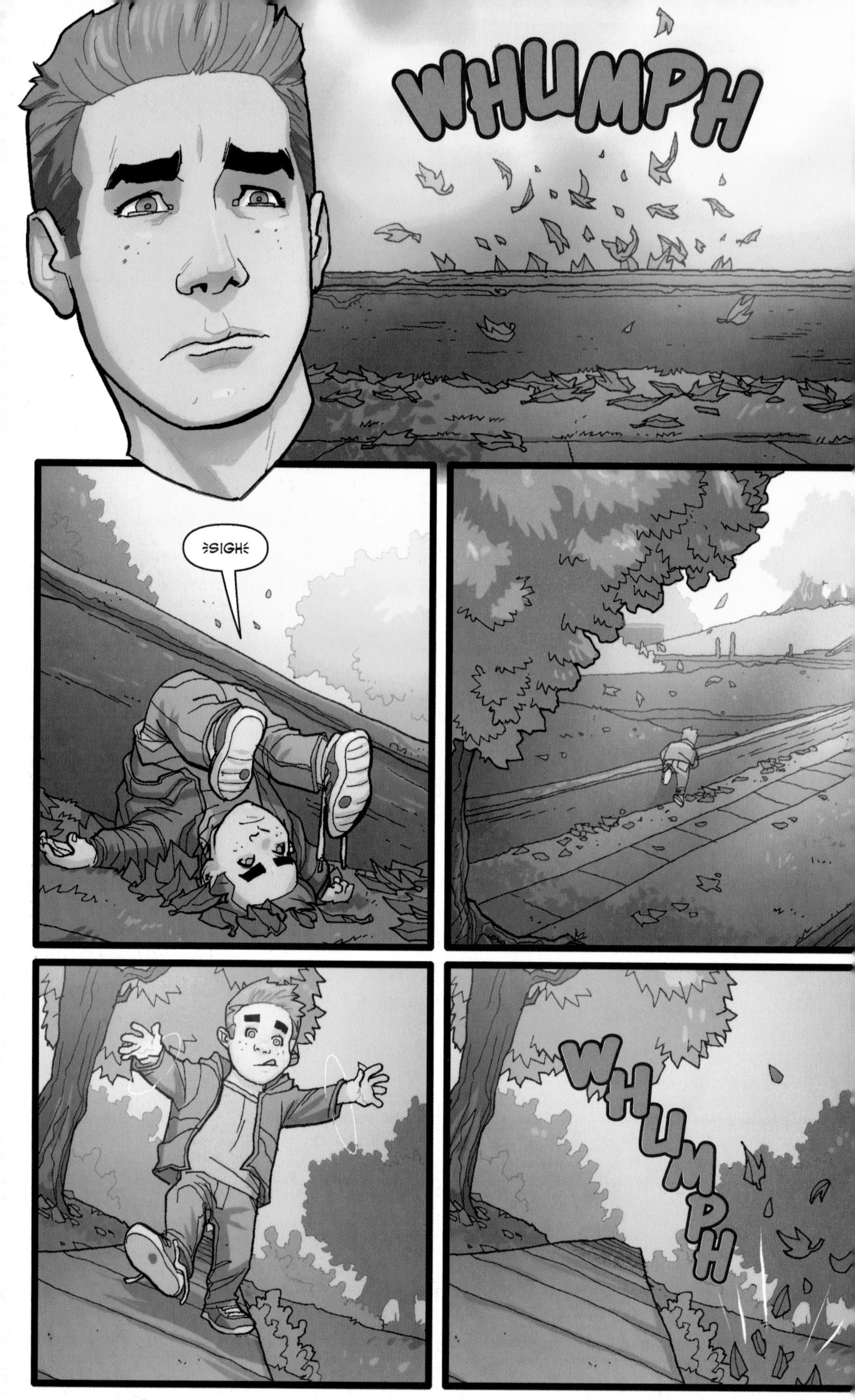
WHUMPH
SIGH
WHUMPH

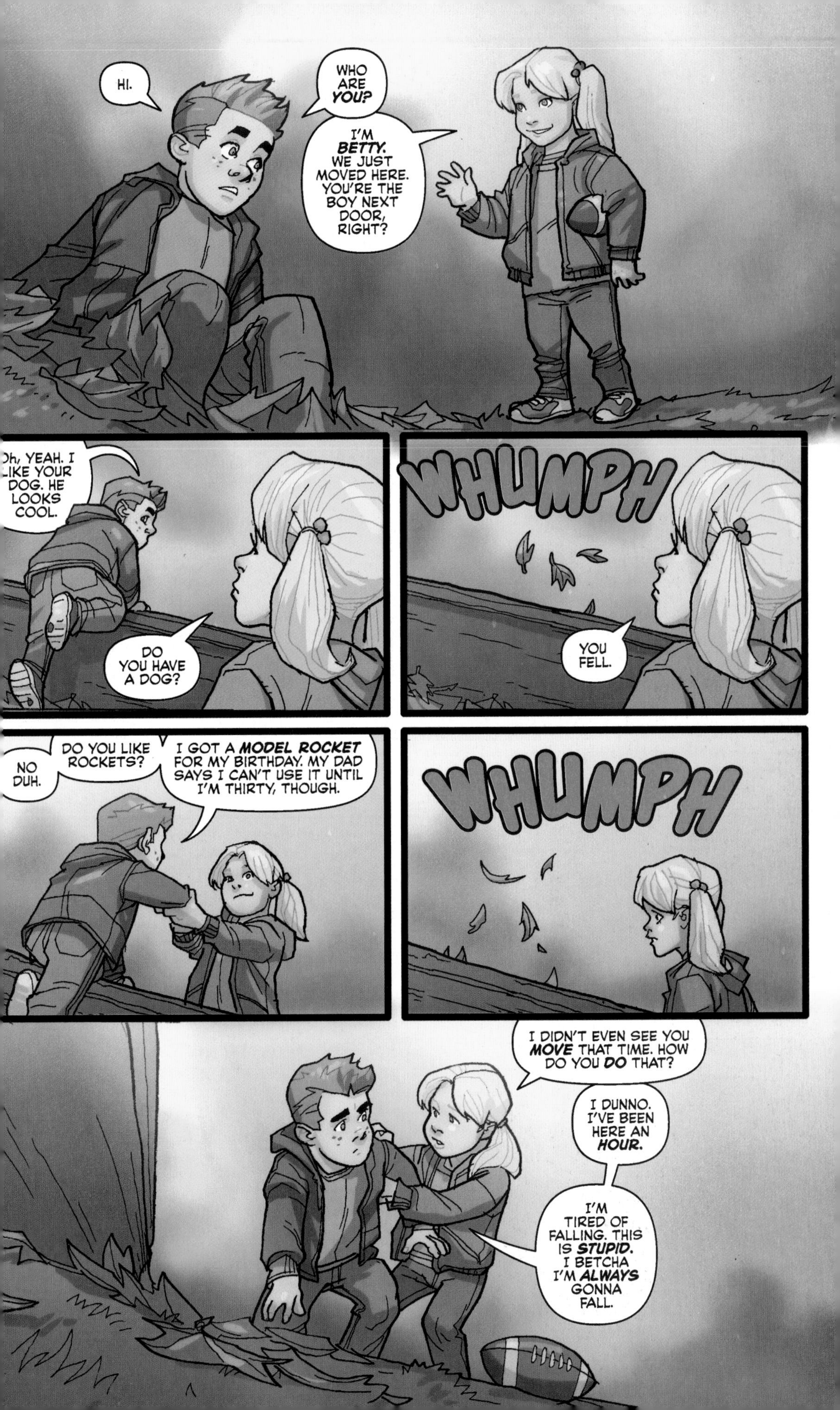
HI.
WHO ARE YOU?
I'M BETTY. WE JUST MOVED HERE. YOU'RE THE BOY NEXT DOOR, RIGHT?
Oh, YEAH. I LIKE YOUR DOG. HE LOOKS COOL.
DO YOU HAVE A DOG?
WHUMPH
YOU FELL.
NO DUH.
DO YOU LIKE ROCKETS?
I GOT A MODEL ROCKET FOR MY BIRTHDAY. MY DAD SAYS I CAN'T USE IT UNTIL I'M THIRTY, THOUGH.
WHUMPH
I DIDN'T EVEN SEE YOU MOVE THAT TIME. HOW DO YOU DO THAT?
I DUNNO. I'VE BEEN HERE AN HOUR.
I'M TIRED OF FALLING. THIS IS STUPID. I BETCHA I'M ALWAYS GONNA FALL.

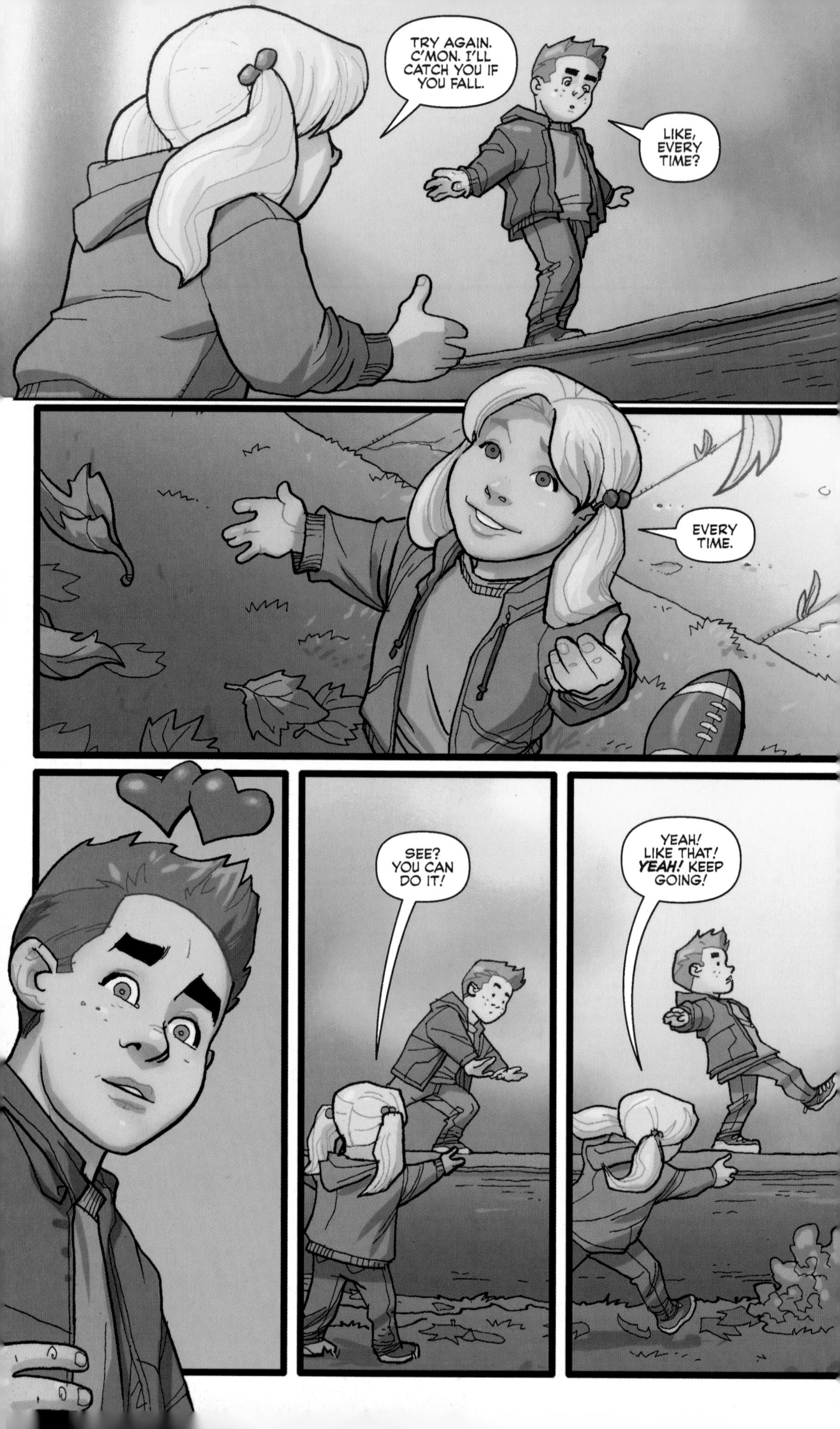
TRY AGAIN. C'MON. I'LL CATCH YOU IF YOU FALL.
LIKE, EVERY TIME?
EVERY TIME.
SEE? YOU CAN DO IT!
YEAH! LIKE THAT! *YEAH!* KEEP GOING!

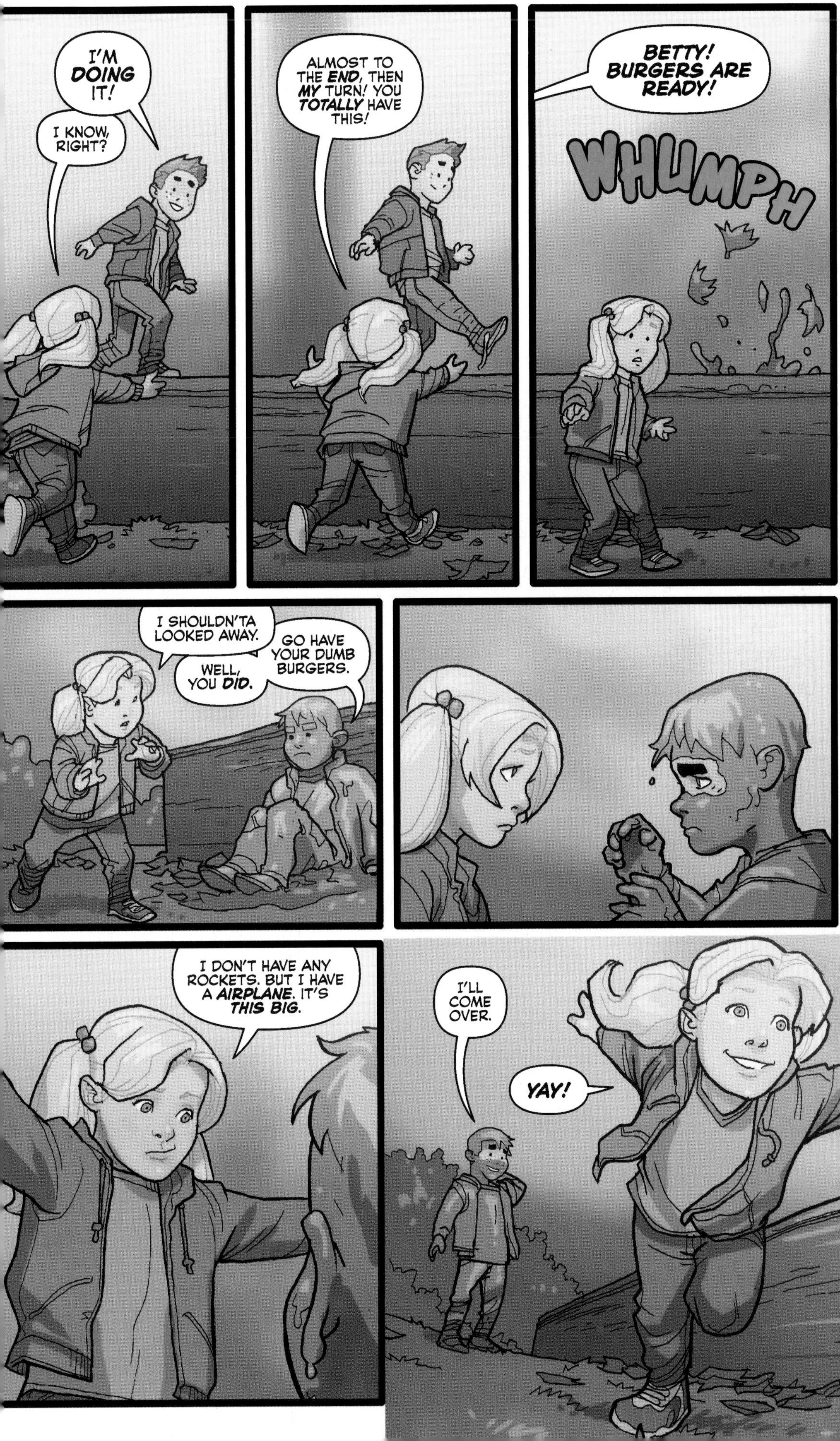
I'M DOING IT!
I KNOW, RIGHT?
ALMOST TO THE END, THEN MY TURN! YOU TOTALLY HAVE THIS!
BETTY! BURGERS ARE READY!
WHUMPH
I SHOULDN'TA LOOKED AWAY.
WELL, YOU DID.
GO HAVE YOUR DUMB BURGERS.
I DON'T HAVE ANY ROCKETS. BUT I HAVE A AIRPLANE. IT'S THIS BIG.
I'LL COME OVER.
YAY!

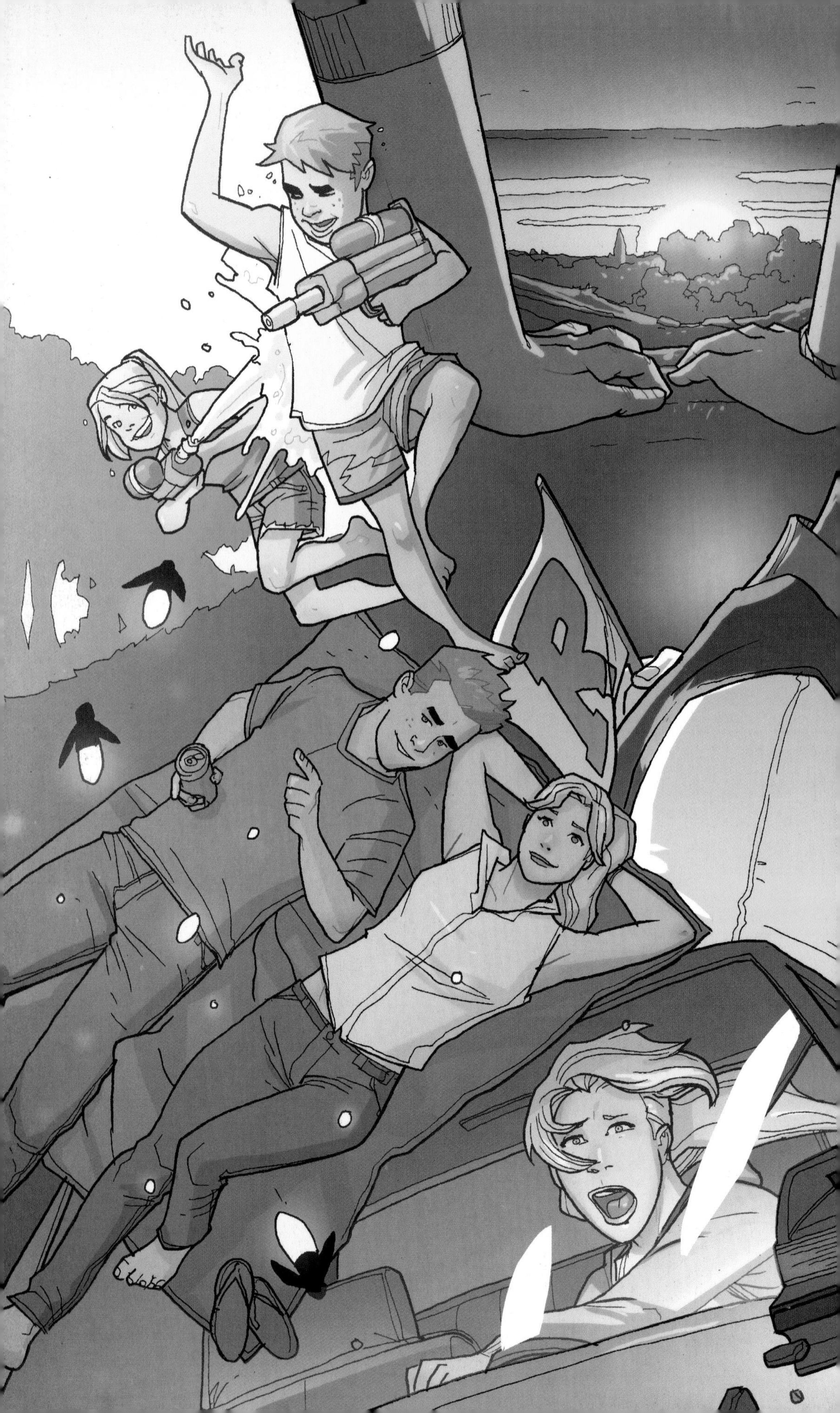

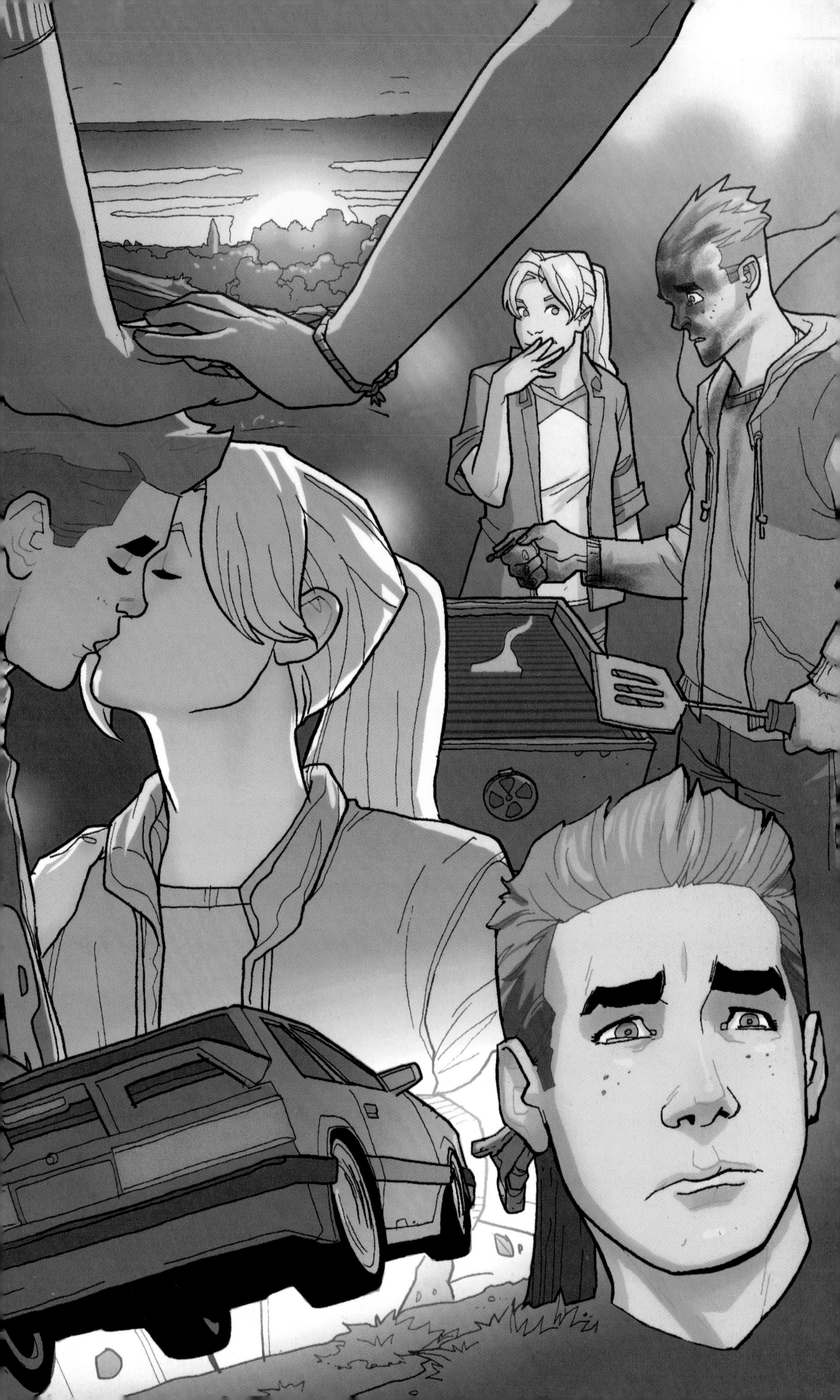

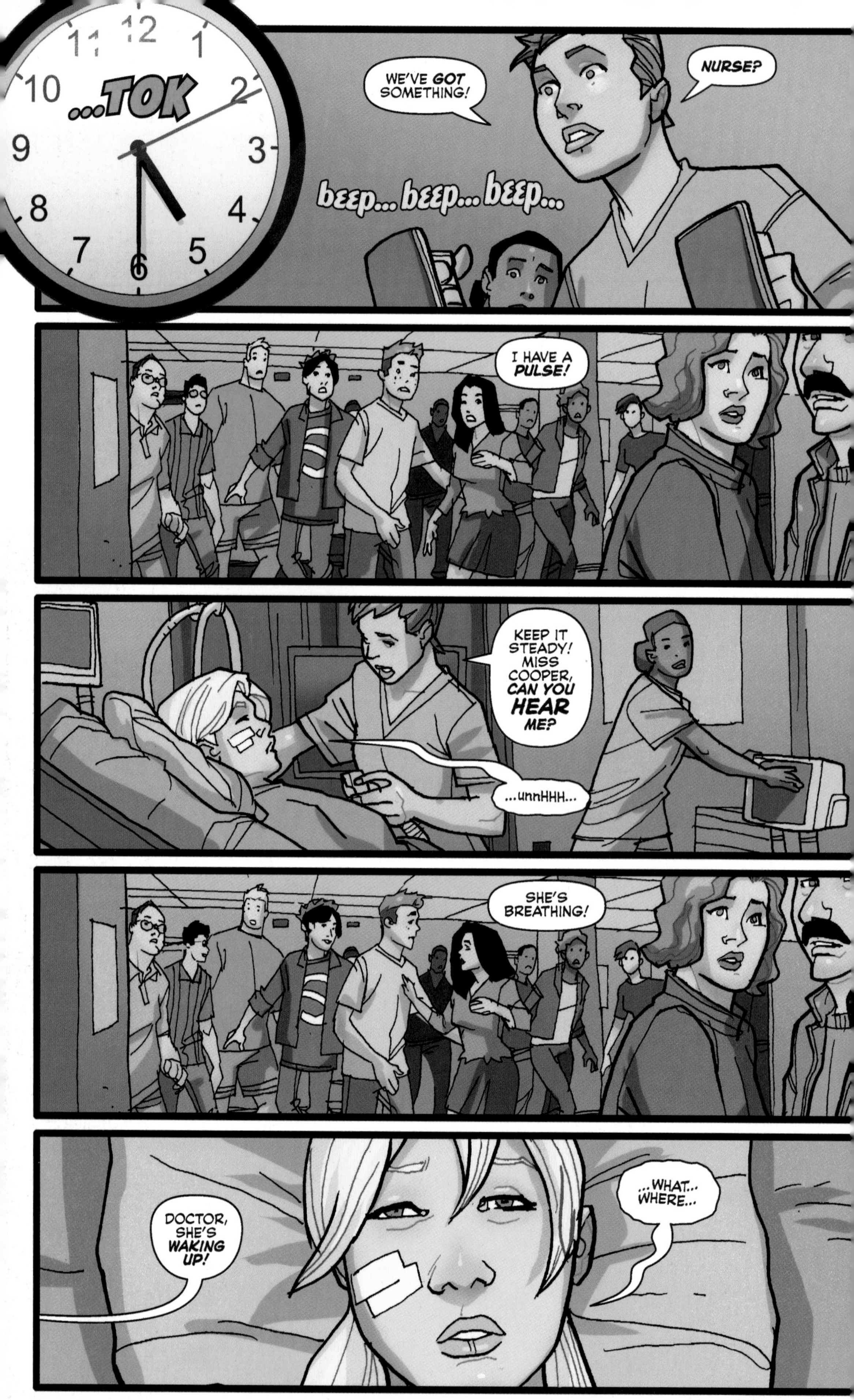
...TOK
WE'VE GOT SOMETHING!
NURSE?
beep... beep... beep...
I HAVE A PULSE!
KEEP IT STEADY! MISS COOPER, CAN YOU HEAR ME?
...unnHHH...
SHE'S BREATHING!
DOCTOR, SHE'S WAKING UP!
...WHAT... WHERE...

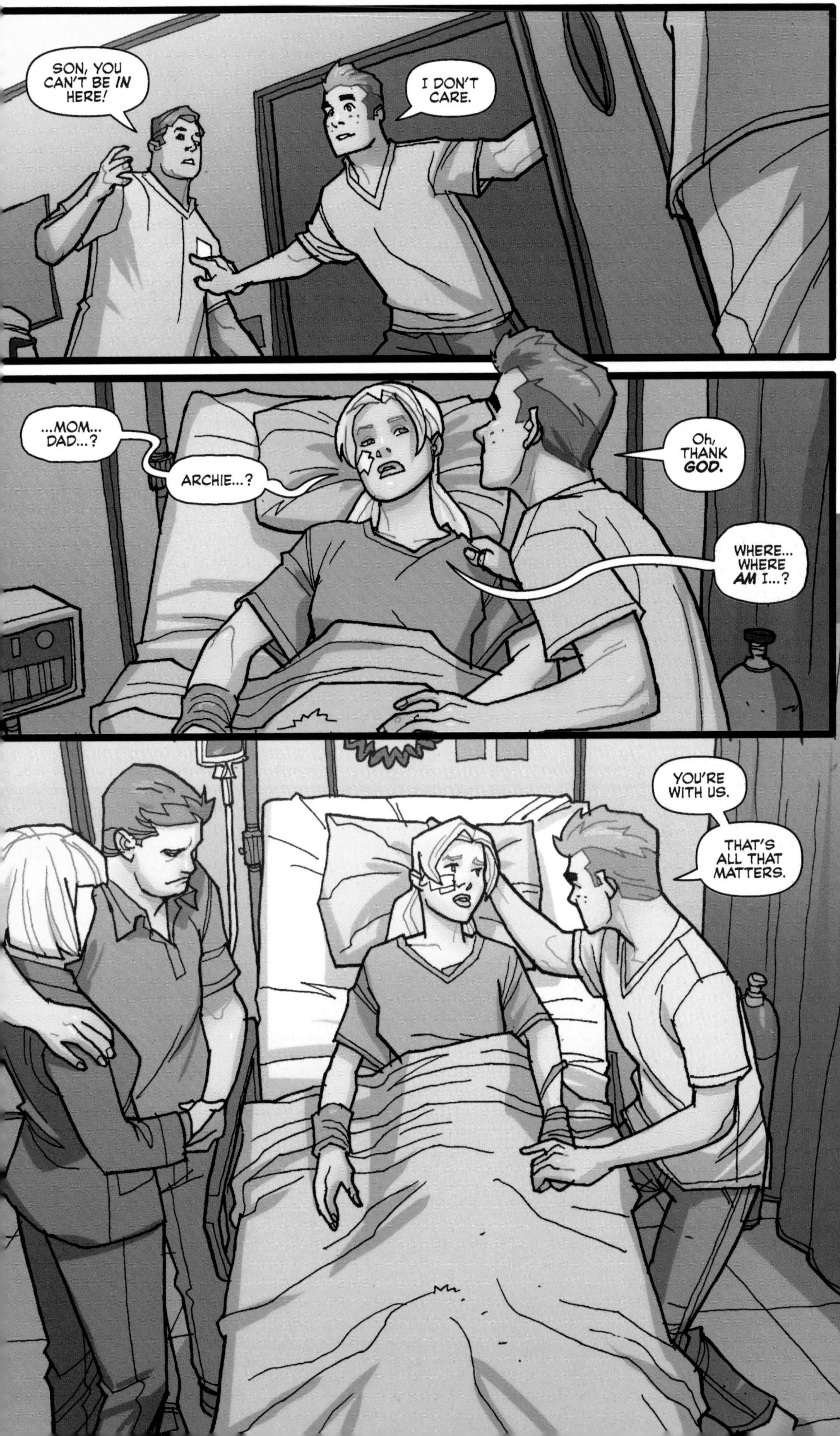
SON, YOU CAN'T BE *IN* HERE!
I DON'T CARE.
...MOM... DAD...?
ARCHIE...?
Oh, THANK *GOD*.
WHERE... WHERE *AM* I...?
YOU'RE WITH US.
THAT'S ALL THAT MATTERS.

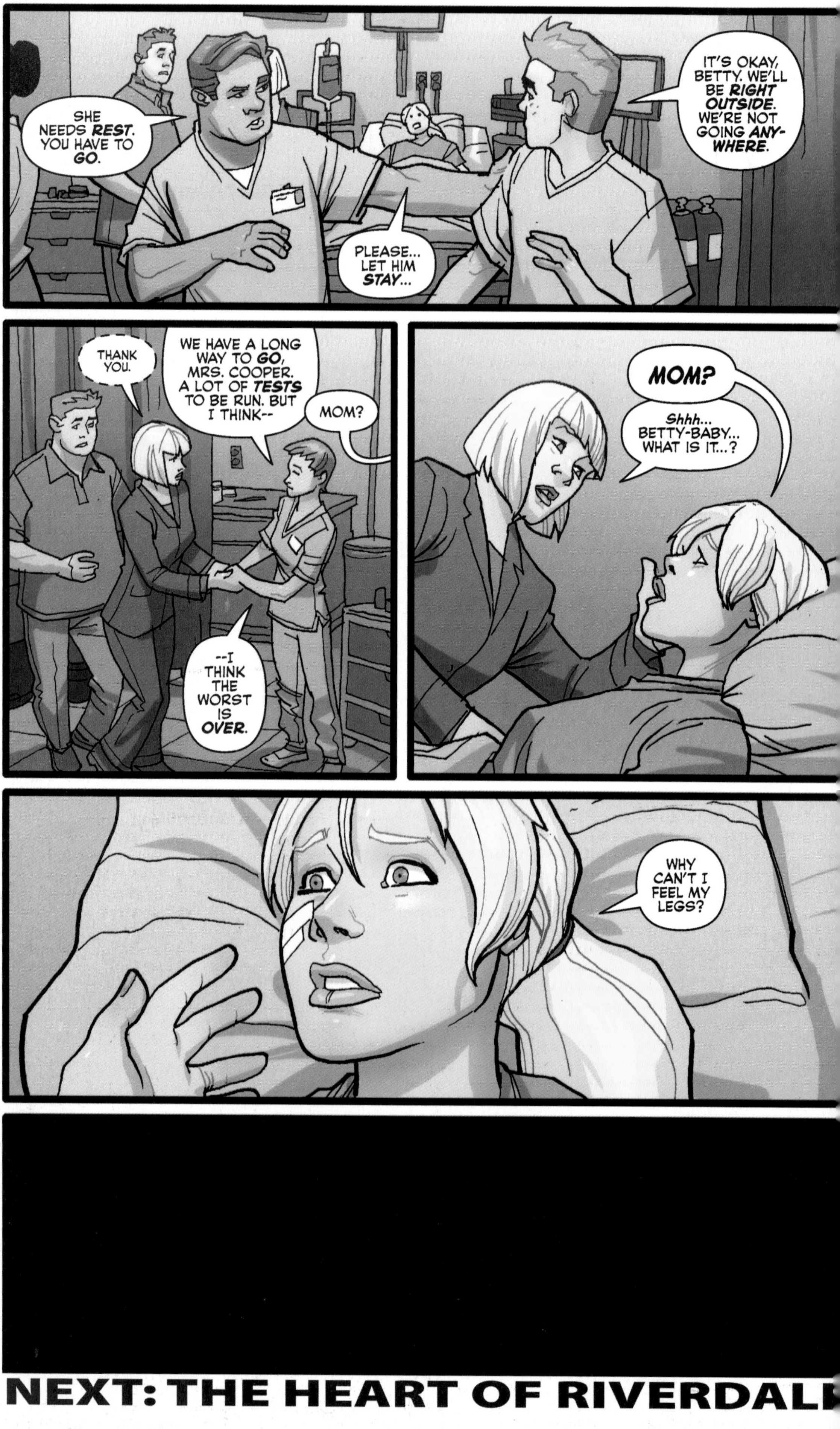
SHE NEEDS REST. YOU HAVE TO GO.
IT'S OKAY, BETTY. WE'LL BE RIGHT OUTSIDE. WE'RE NOT GOING ANYWHERE.
PLEASE... LET HIM STAY...
THANK YOU.
WE HAVE A LONG WAY TO GO, MRS. COOPER. A LOT OF TESTS TO BE RUN. BUT I THINK--
MOM?
--I THINK THE WORST IS OVER.
MOM?
Shhh... BETTY-BABY... WHAT IS IT...?
WHY CAN'T I FEEL MY LEGS?
NEXT: THE HEART OF RIVERDAL

ARCHIE®

SPECIAL FEATURES

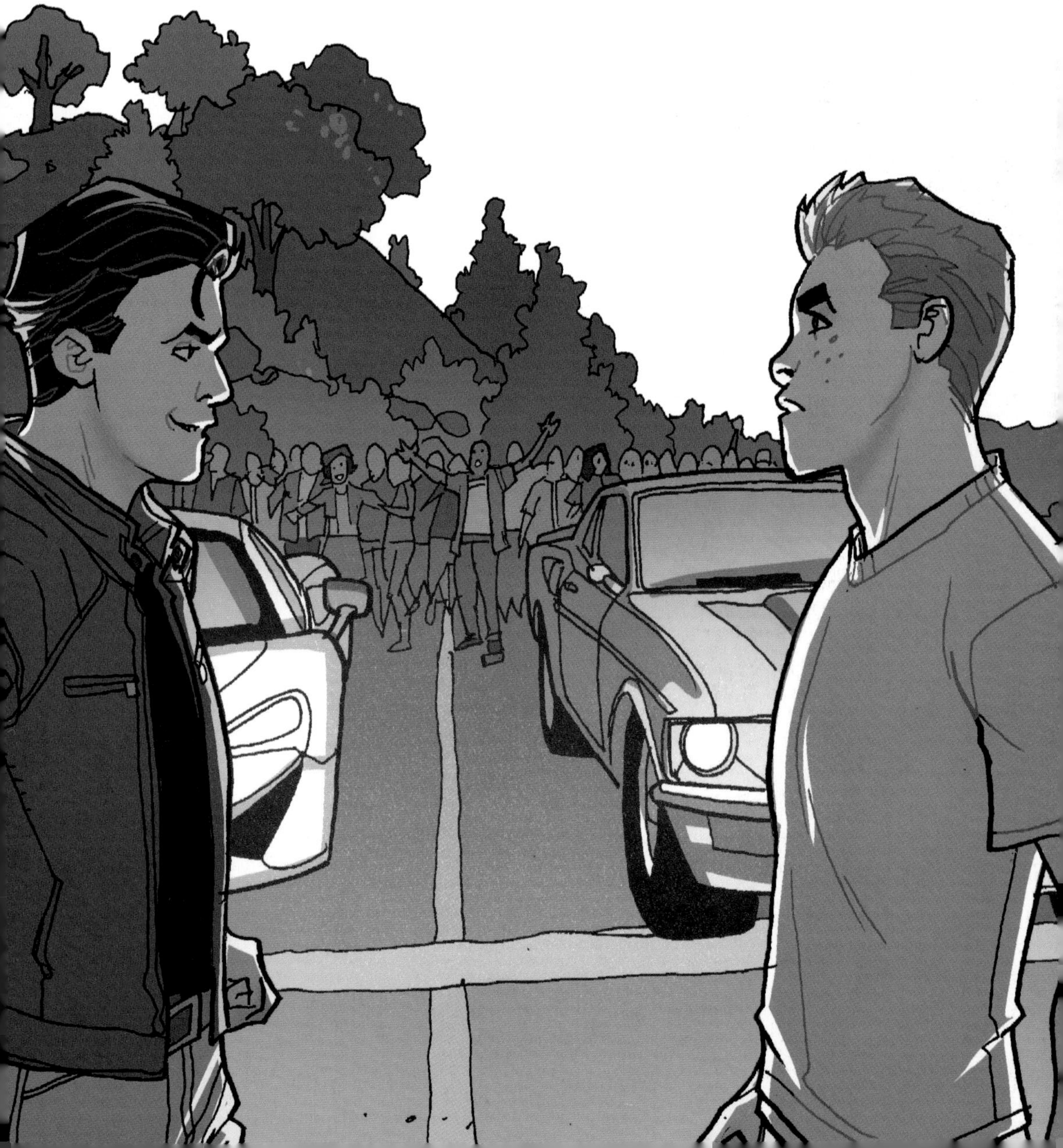

ARCHIE®

COVER GALLERY

In addition to the amazing main covers we have for each issue, we also receive gorgeous artwork from an array of talented artists for our direct market exclusive covers—and our artists really went the extra mile to craft some beautifully heartbreaking imagery for the headline-making "Over the Edge" story. Here are all of the main and variant covers for each of the five issues in Archie Volume Four.

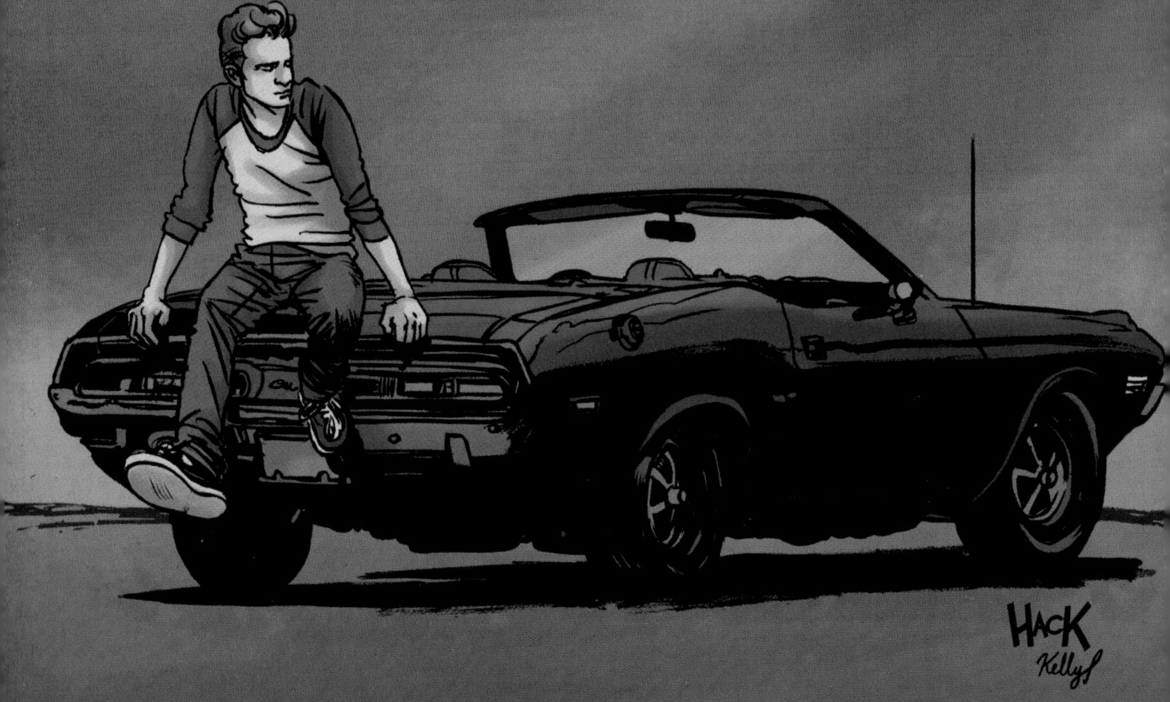
HACK
Kelly

ISSUE
EIGHTEEN

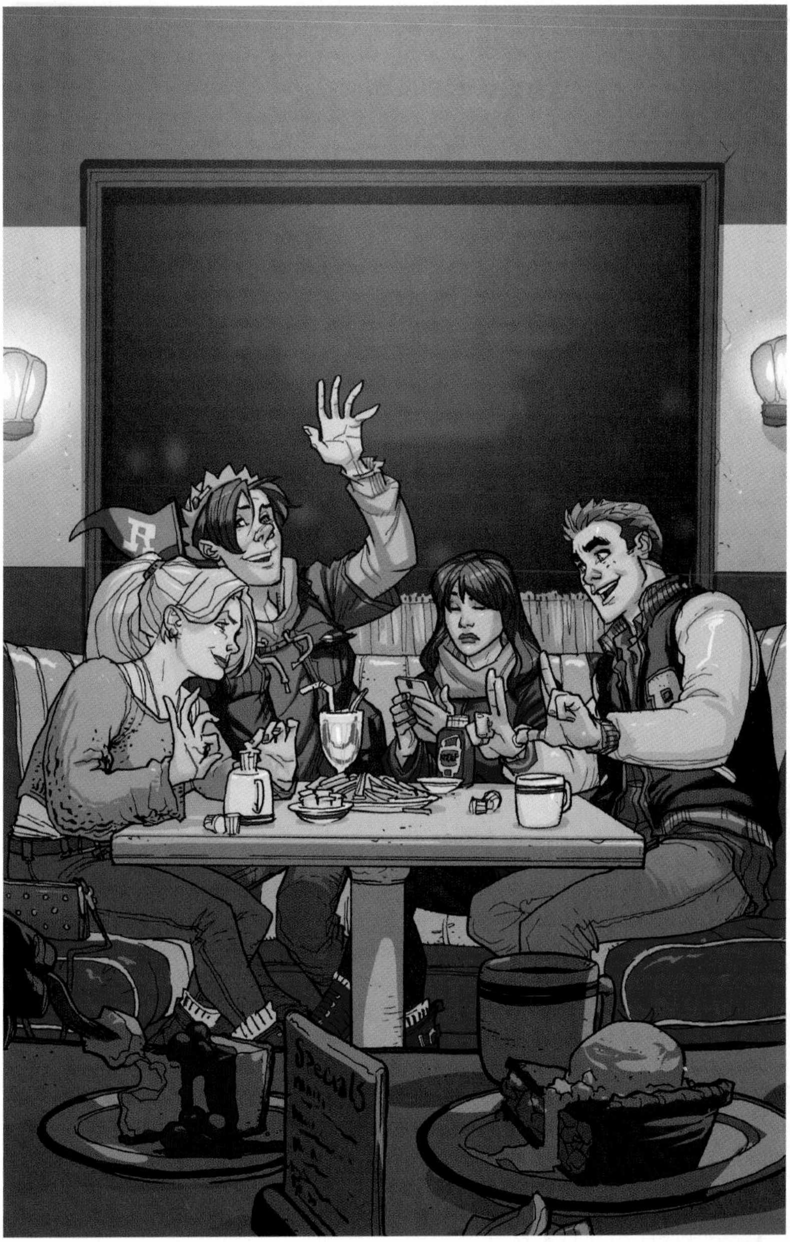

PETE
WOODS

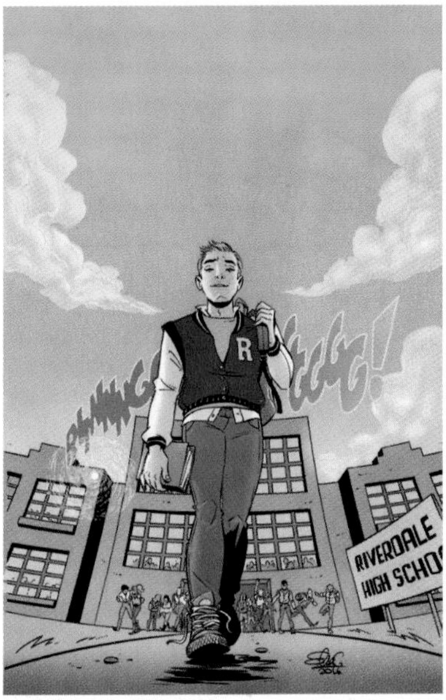
RIVERDALE
HIGH SCHO

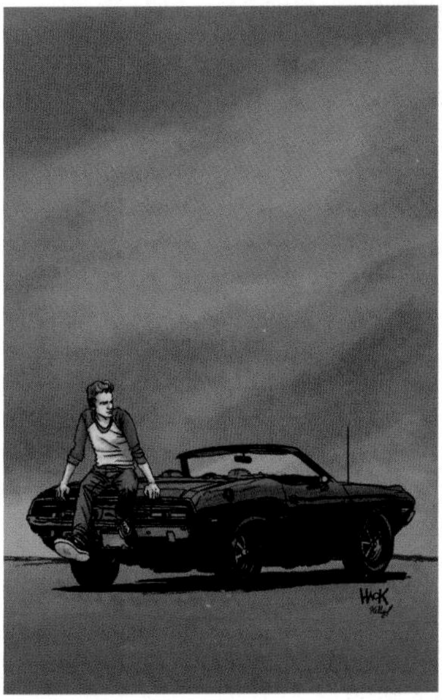

(L)
ELSA
CHARRETIER

(R)
ROBERT
HACK

ISSUE
NINETEEN

PETE
WOODS

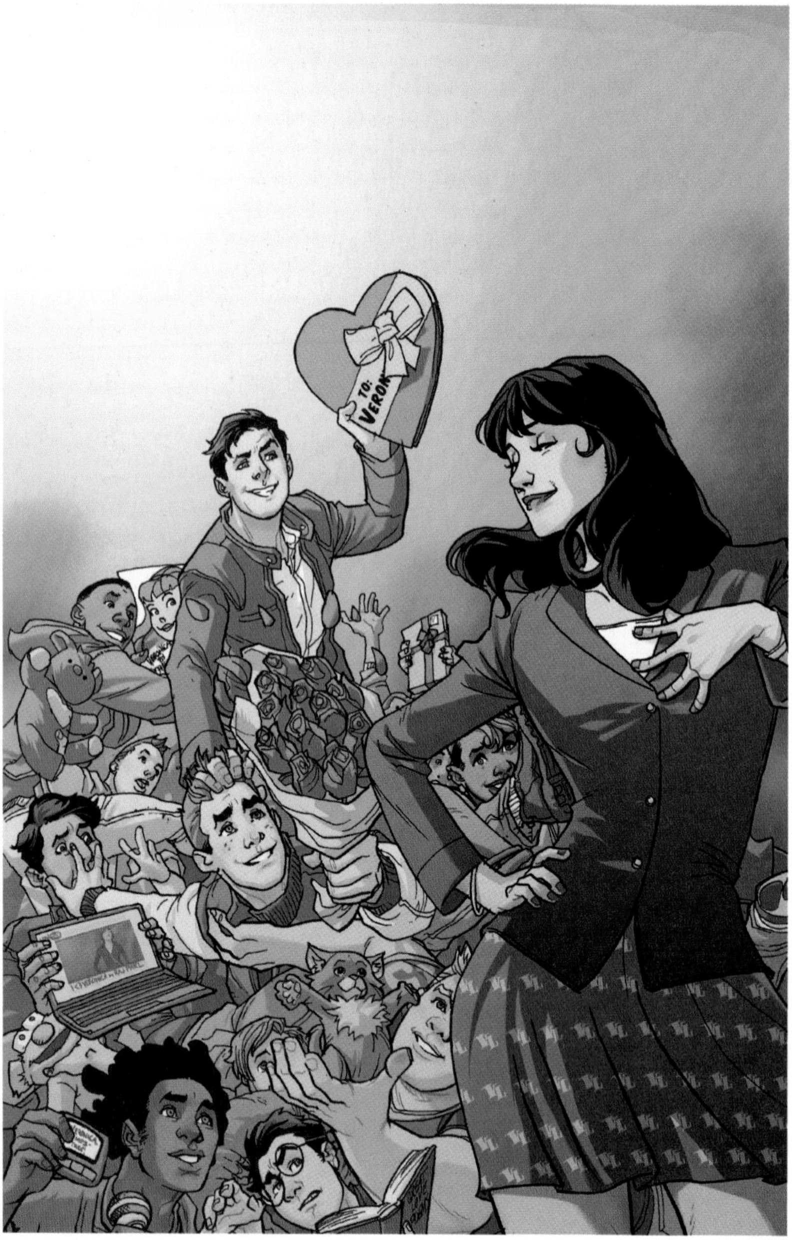

(L)
EMANUELA
LUPACCHINO

(R)
GREG
SMALLWOOD

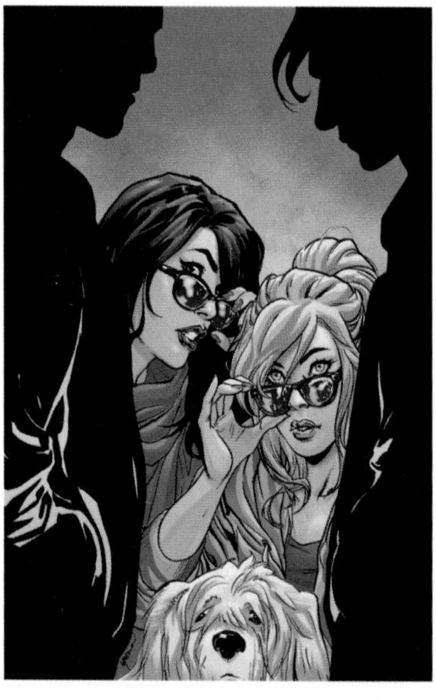

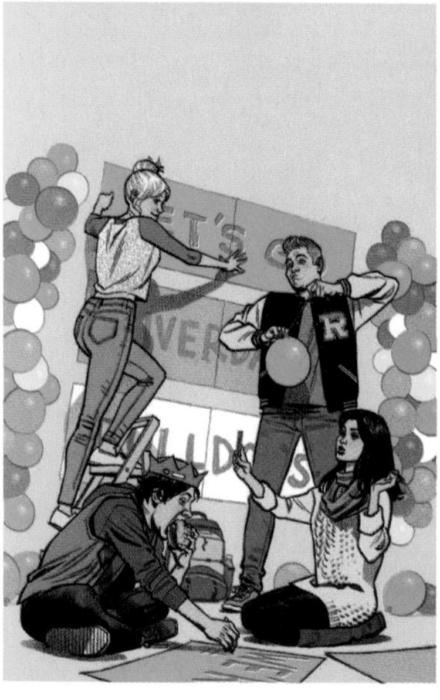

ISSUE TWENTY

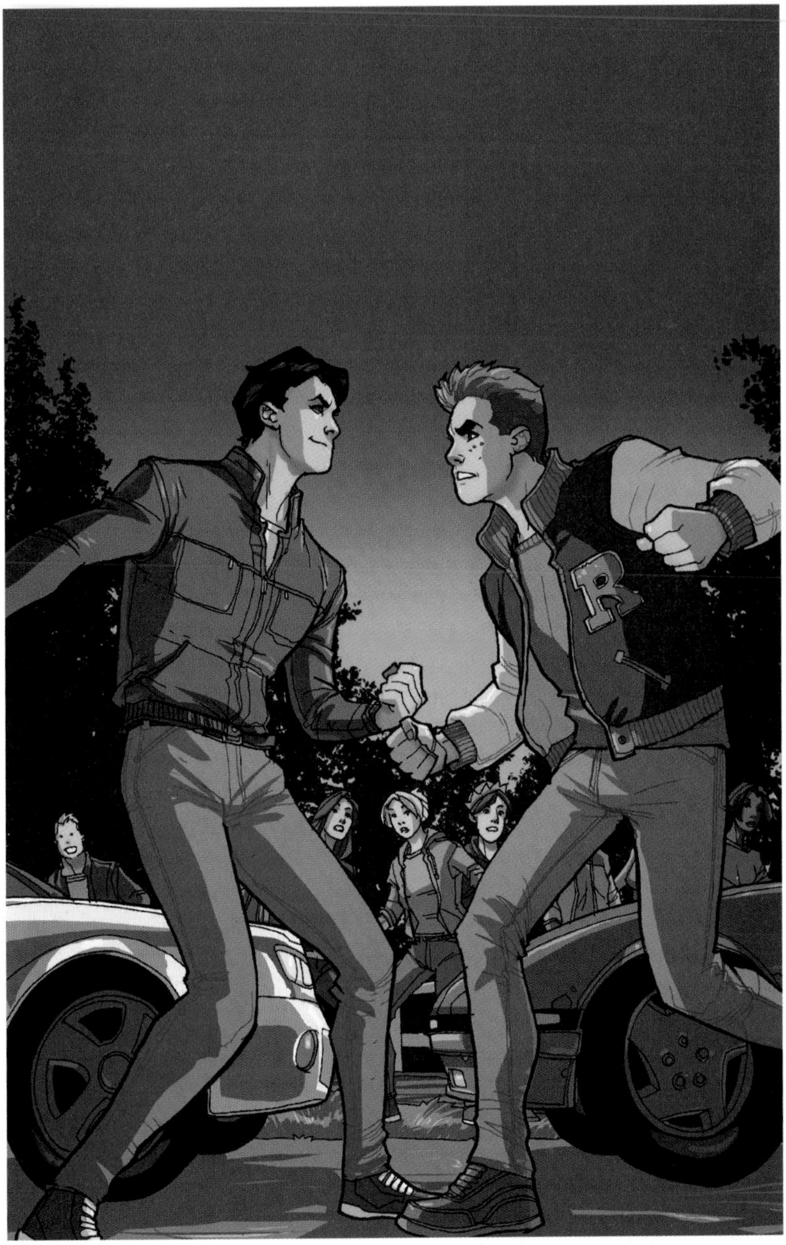

PETE WOODS

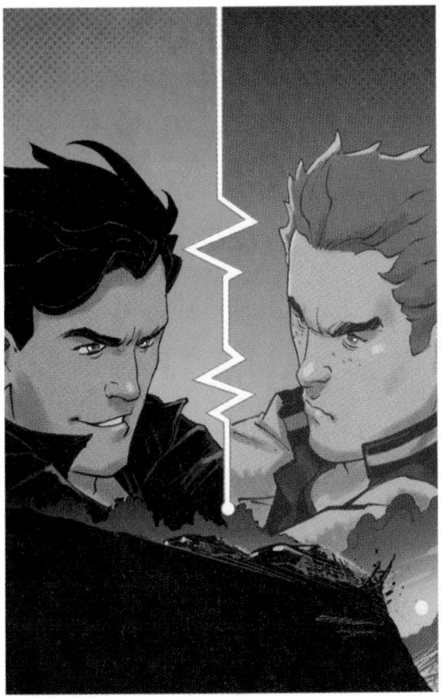

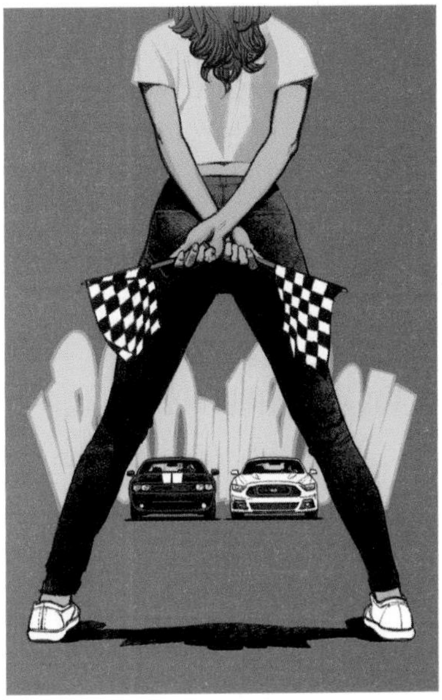

(L)
ELLIOT FERNANDEZ

(R)
GREG SMALLWOOD

ISSUE TWENTY ONE

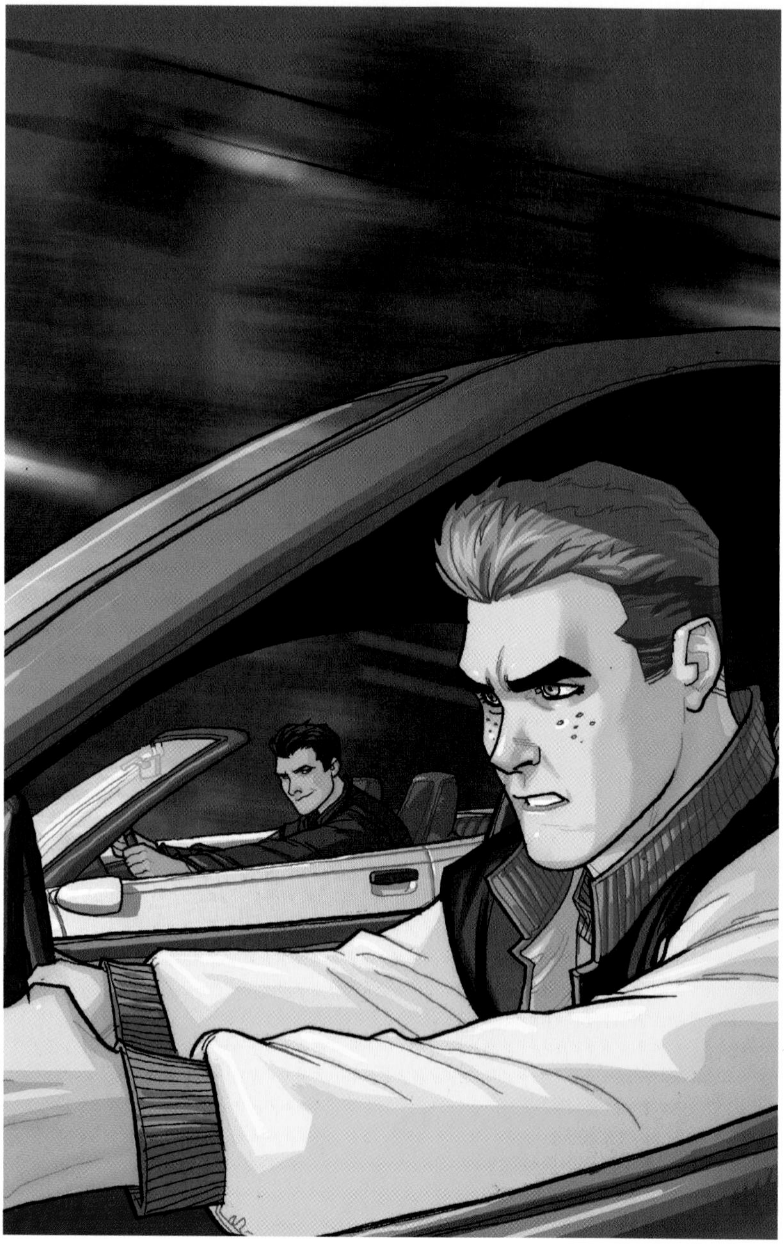

PETE WOODS

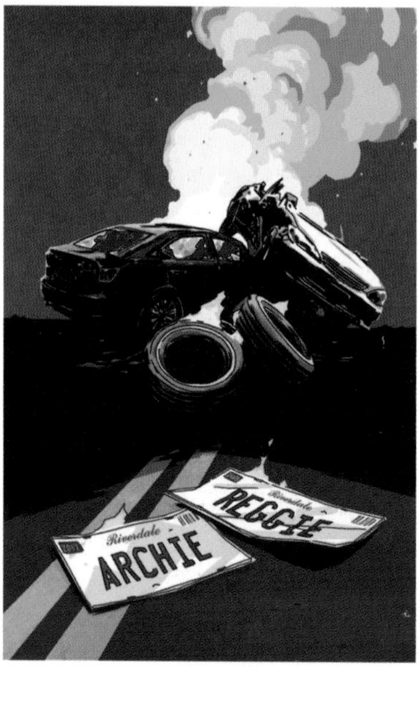
Riverdale
ARCHIE
Riverdale
REGGIE

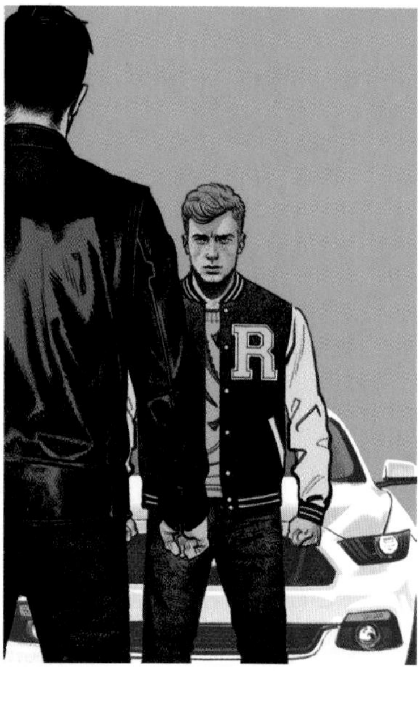

(L)
MATTHEW DOW SMITH

(R)
GREG SMALLWOOD

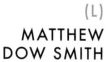

ISSUE
TWENTY
TWO

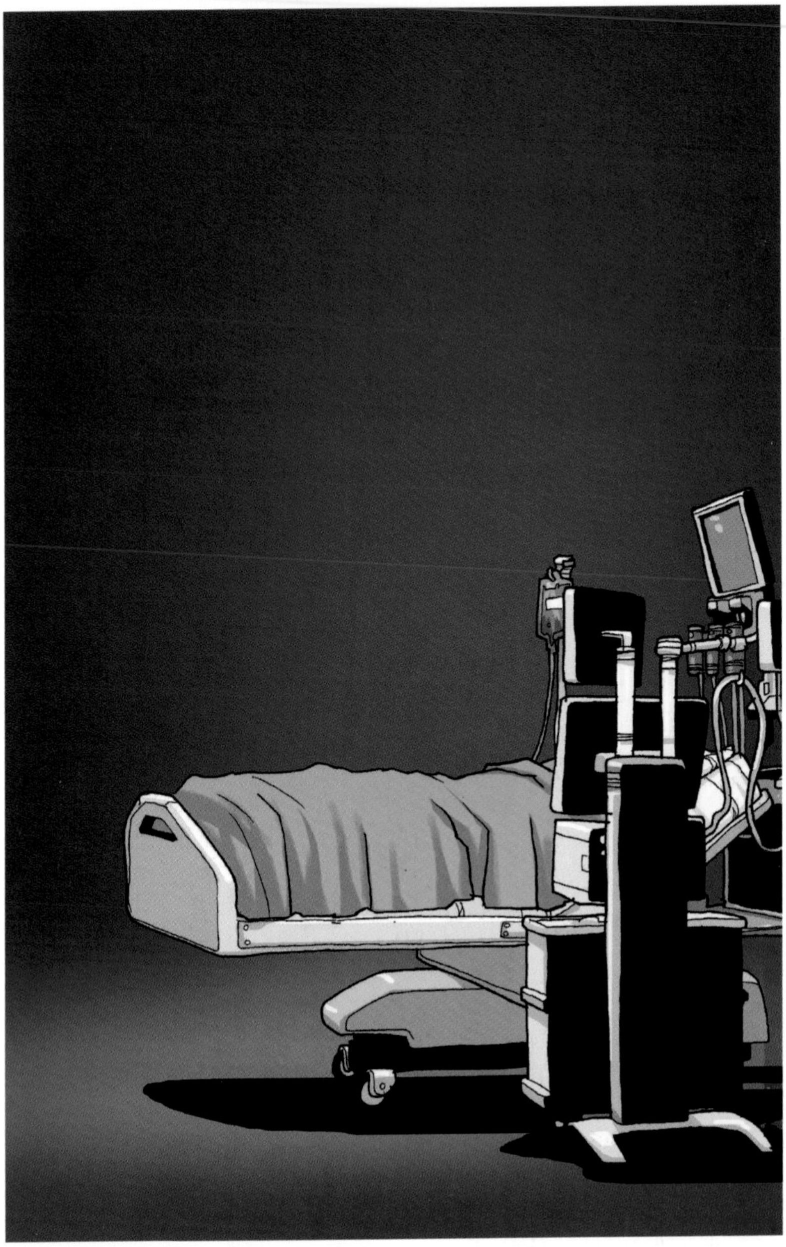

PETE
WOODS

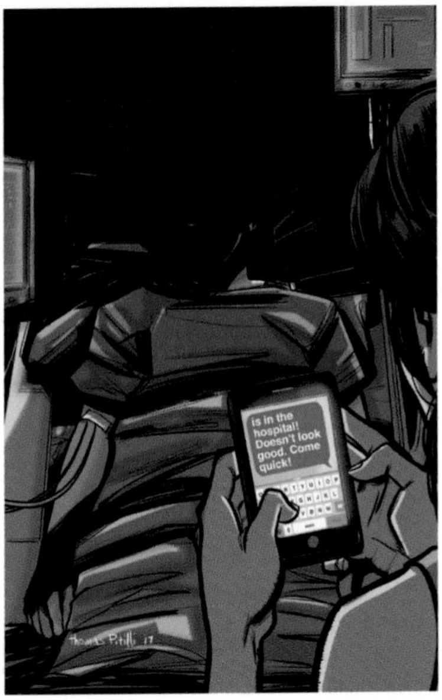
is in the hospital! Doesn't look good. Come quick!

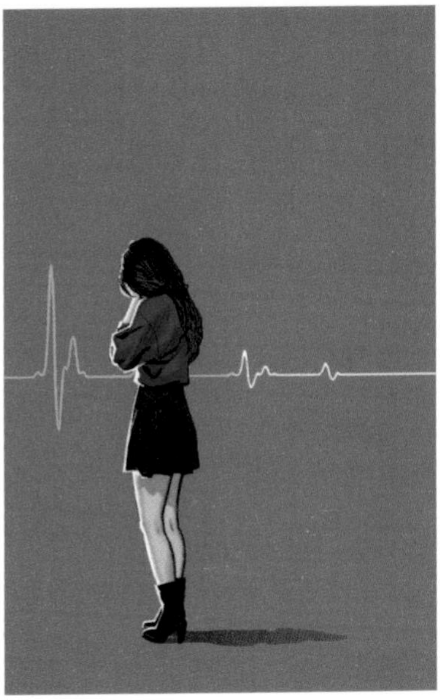

(L)
THOMAS
PITILLI

(R)
GREG
SMALLWOOD

SPECIAL PREVIEW

THE ARCHIES ONE SHOT

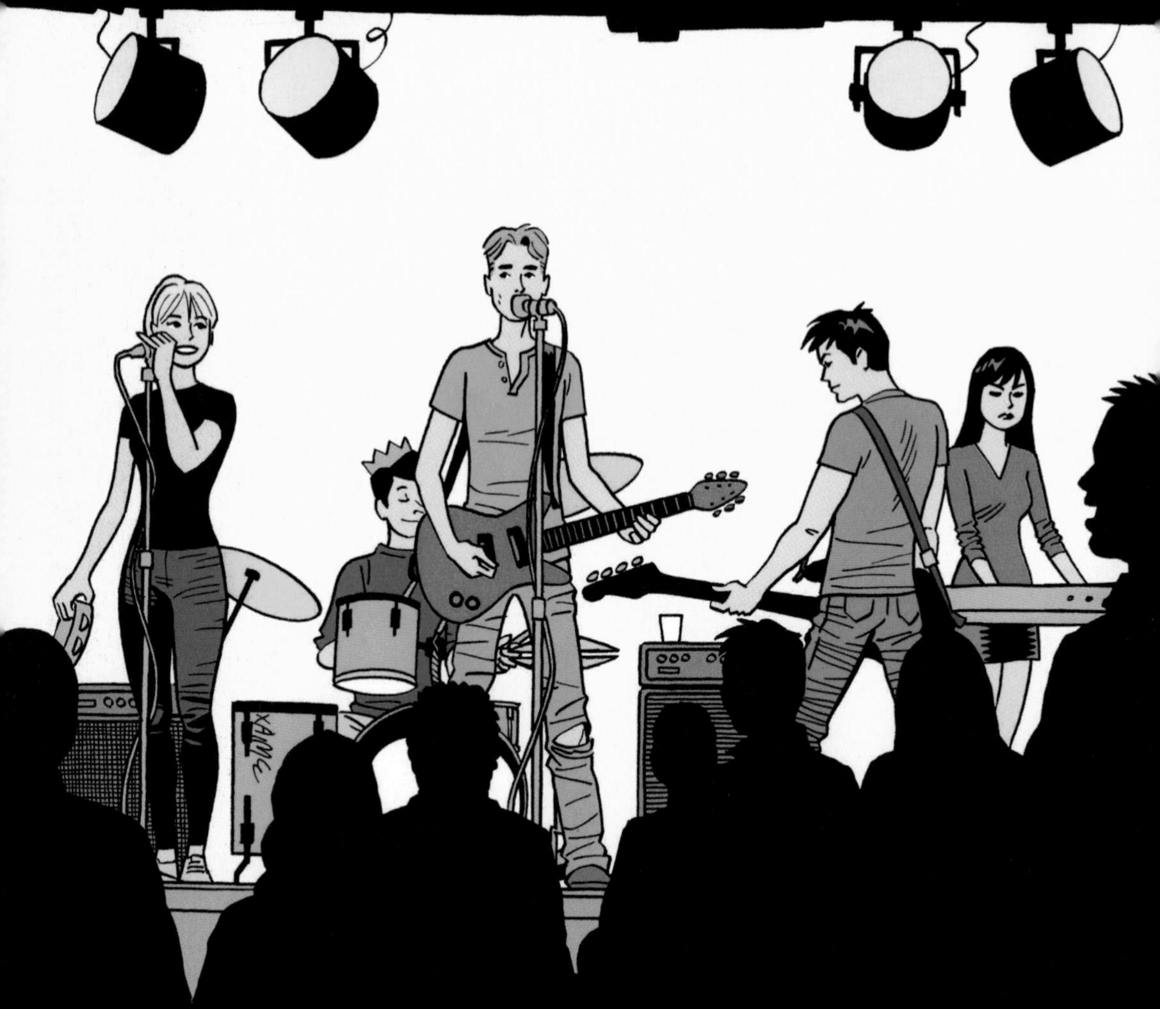

STORY BY
ALEX SEGURA AND MATTHEW ROSENBERG

ART BY
JOE EISMA

COLORING BY
MATT HERMS

LETTERING BY
JACK MORELLI

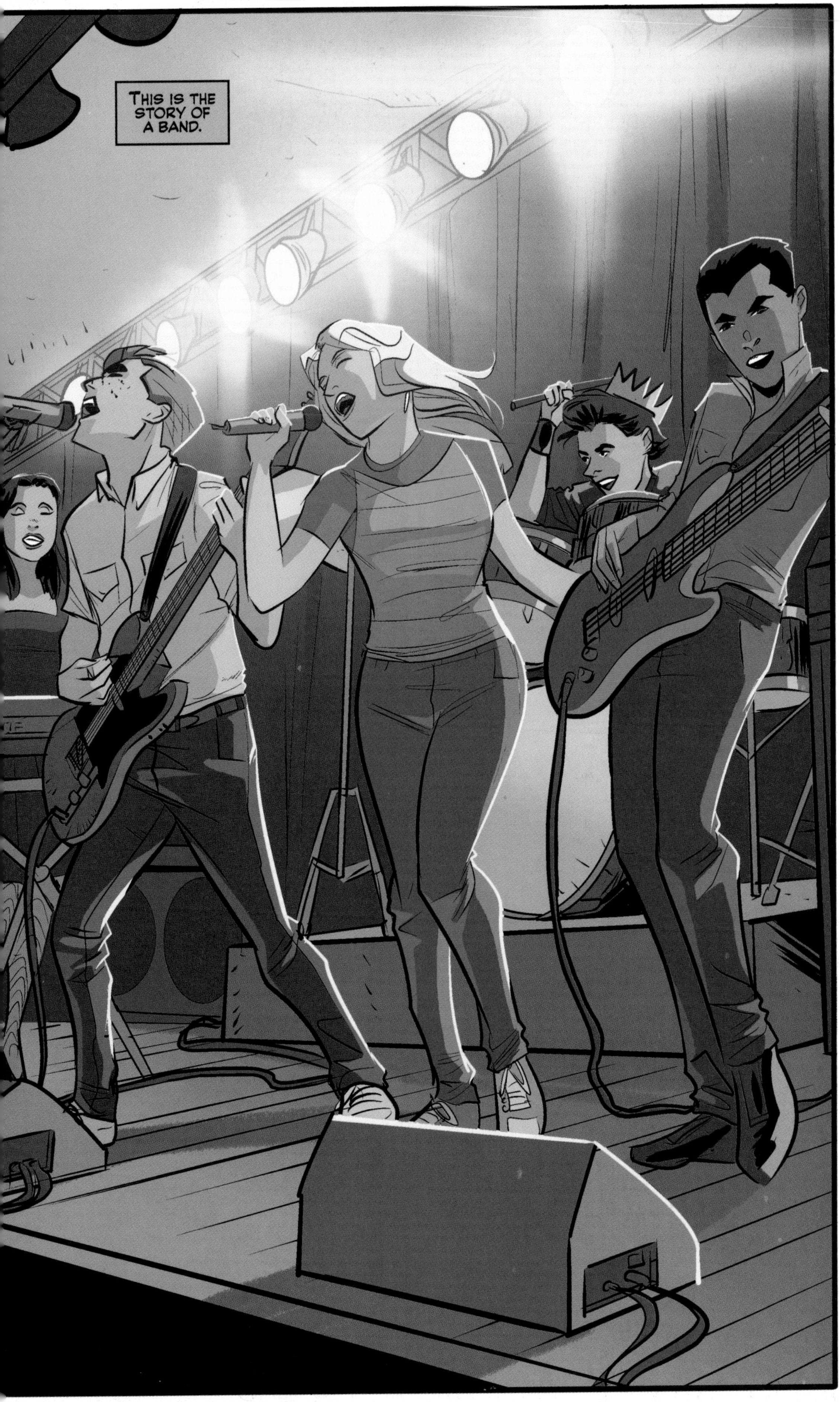
THIS IS THE STORY OF A BAND.

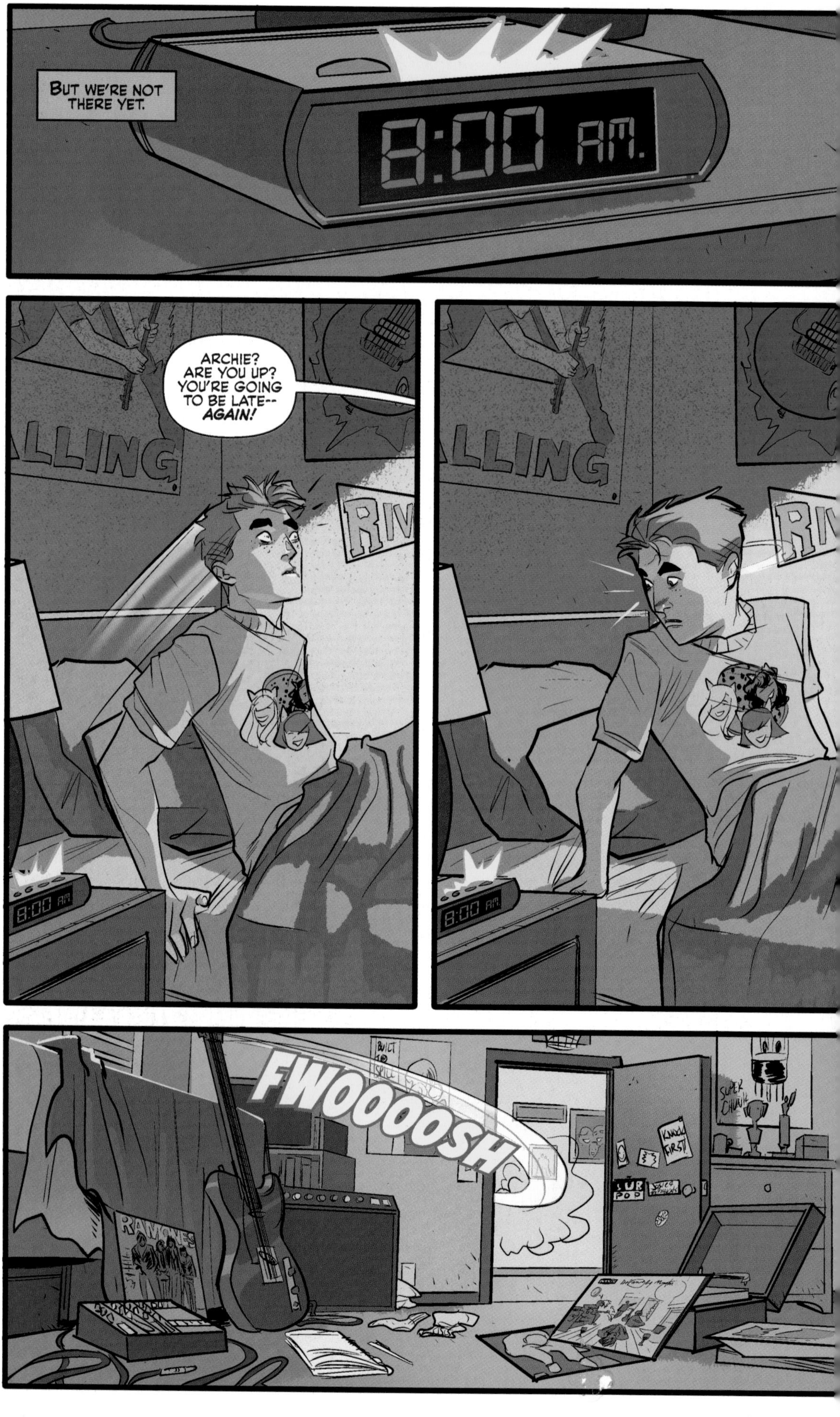

BUT WE'RE NOT THERE YET.
8:00 AM.
ARCHIE? ARE YOU UP? YOU'RE GOING TO BE LATE-- ***AGAIN!***
FWOOOOSH

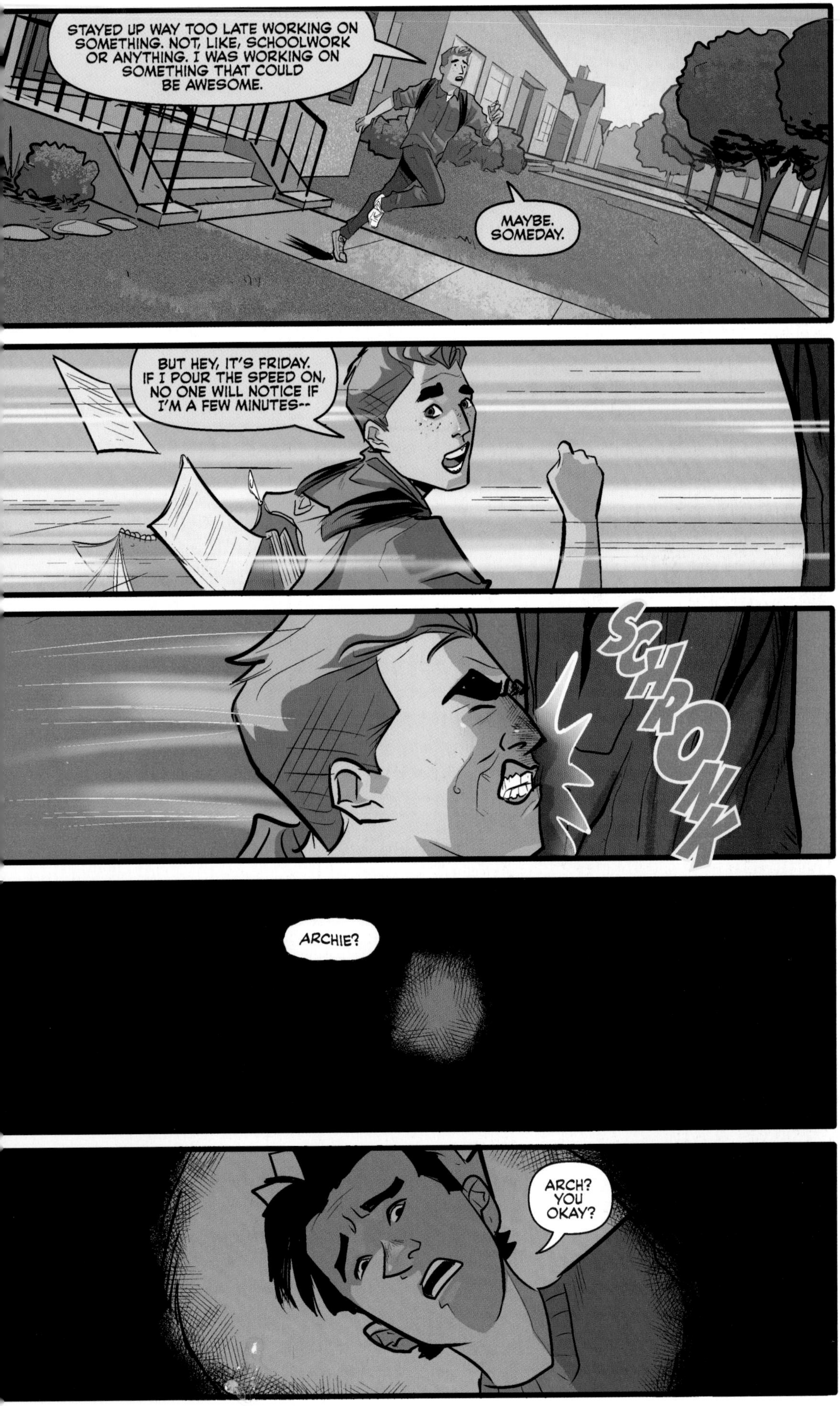
STAYED UP WAY TOO LATE WORKING ON SOMETHING. NOT, LIKE, SCHOOLWORK OR ANYTHING. I WAS WORKING ON SOMETHING THAT COULD BE AWESOME.
MAYBE. SOMEDAY.
BUT HEY, IT'S FRIDAY. IF I POUR THE SPEED ON, NO ONE WILL NOTICE IF I'M A FEW MINUTES--
SCHRONK
ARCHIE?
ARCH? YOU OKAY?

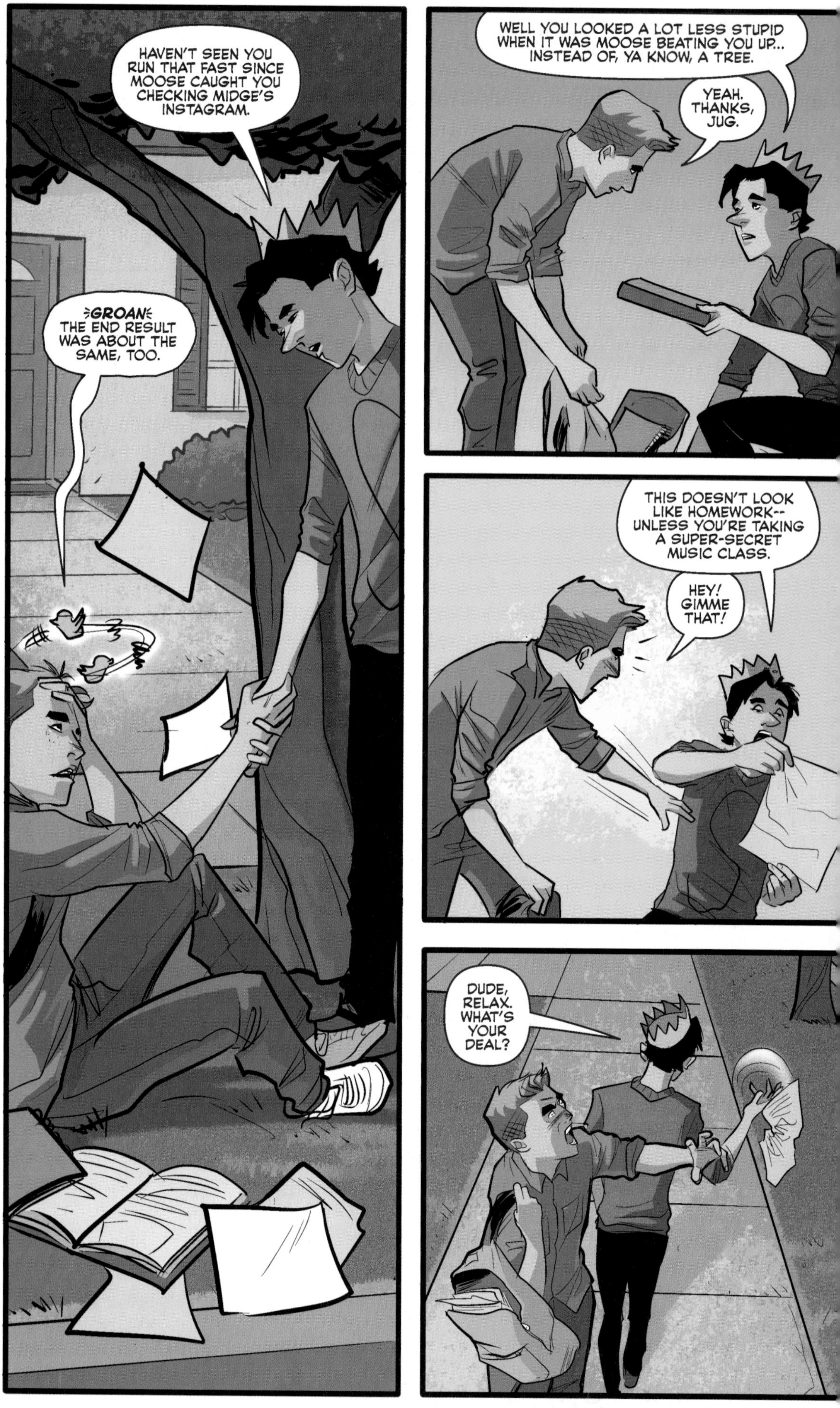
HAVEN'T SEEN YOU RUN THAT FAST SINCE MOOSE CAUGHT YOU CHECKING MIDGE'S INSTAGRAM.
GROAN
THE END RESULT WAS ABOUT THE SAME, TOO.
WELL YOU LOOKED A LOT LESS STUPID WHEN IT WAS MOOSE BEATING YOU UP... INSTEAD OF, YA KNOW, A TREE.
YEAH. THANKS, JUG.
THIS DOESN'T LOOK LIKE HOMEWORK-- UNLESS YOU'RE TAKING A SUPER-SECRET MUSIC CLASS.
HEY! GIMME THAT!
DUDE, RELAX. WHAT'S YOUR DEAL?

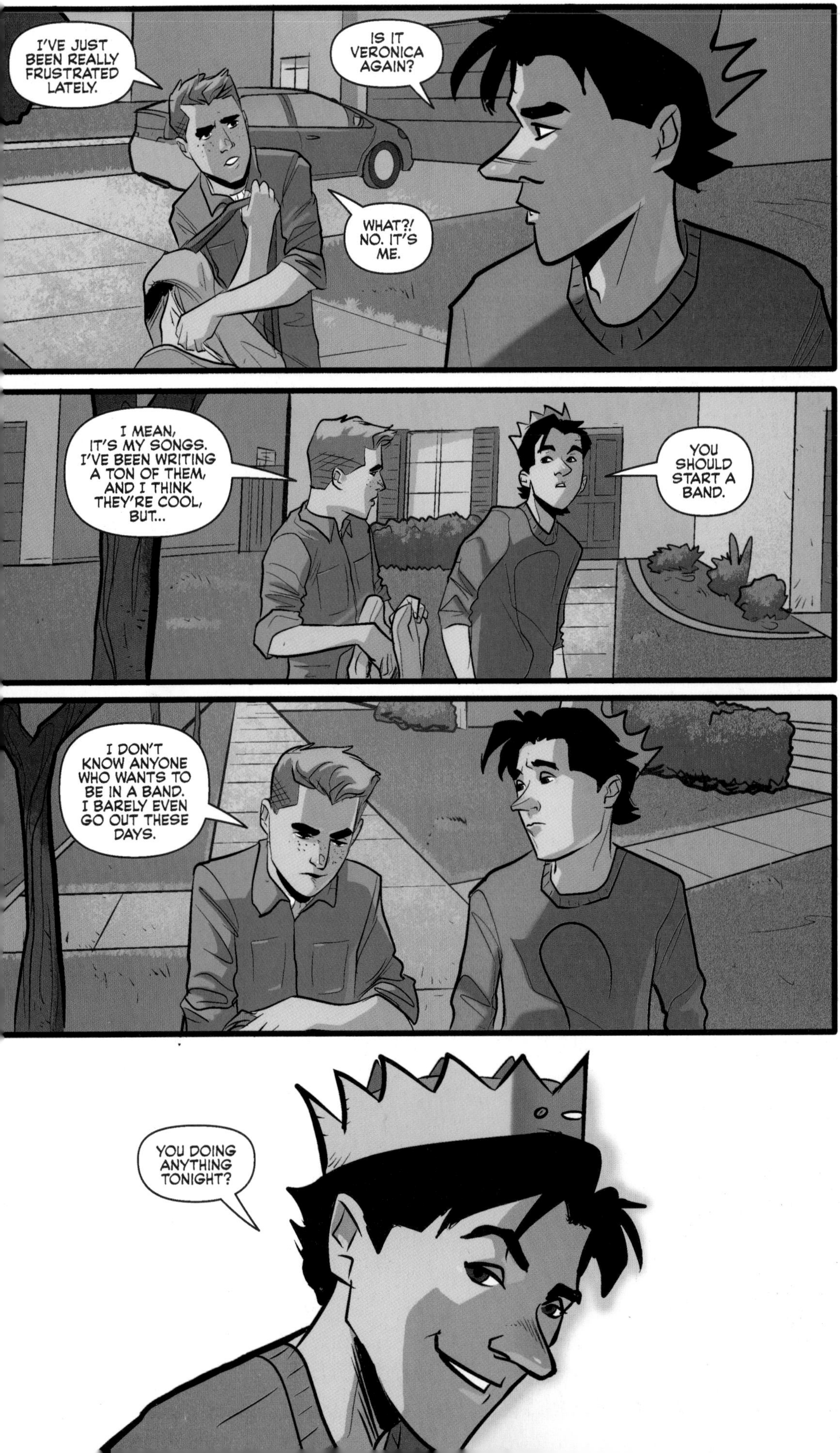
I'VE JUST BEEN REALLY FRUSTRATED LATELY.
IS IT VERONICA AGAIN?
WHAT?! NO. IT'S ME.
I MEAN, IT'S MY SONGS. I'VE BEEN WRITING A TON OF THEM, AND I THINK THEY'RE COOL, BUT...
YOU SHOULD START A BAND.
I DON'T KNOW ANYONE WHO WANTS TO BE IN A BAND. I BARELY EVEN GO OUT THESE DAYS.
YOU DOING ANYTHING TONIGHT?

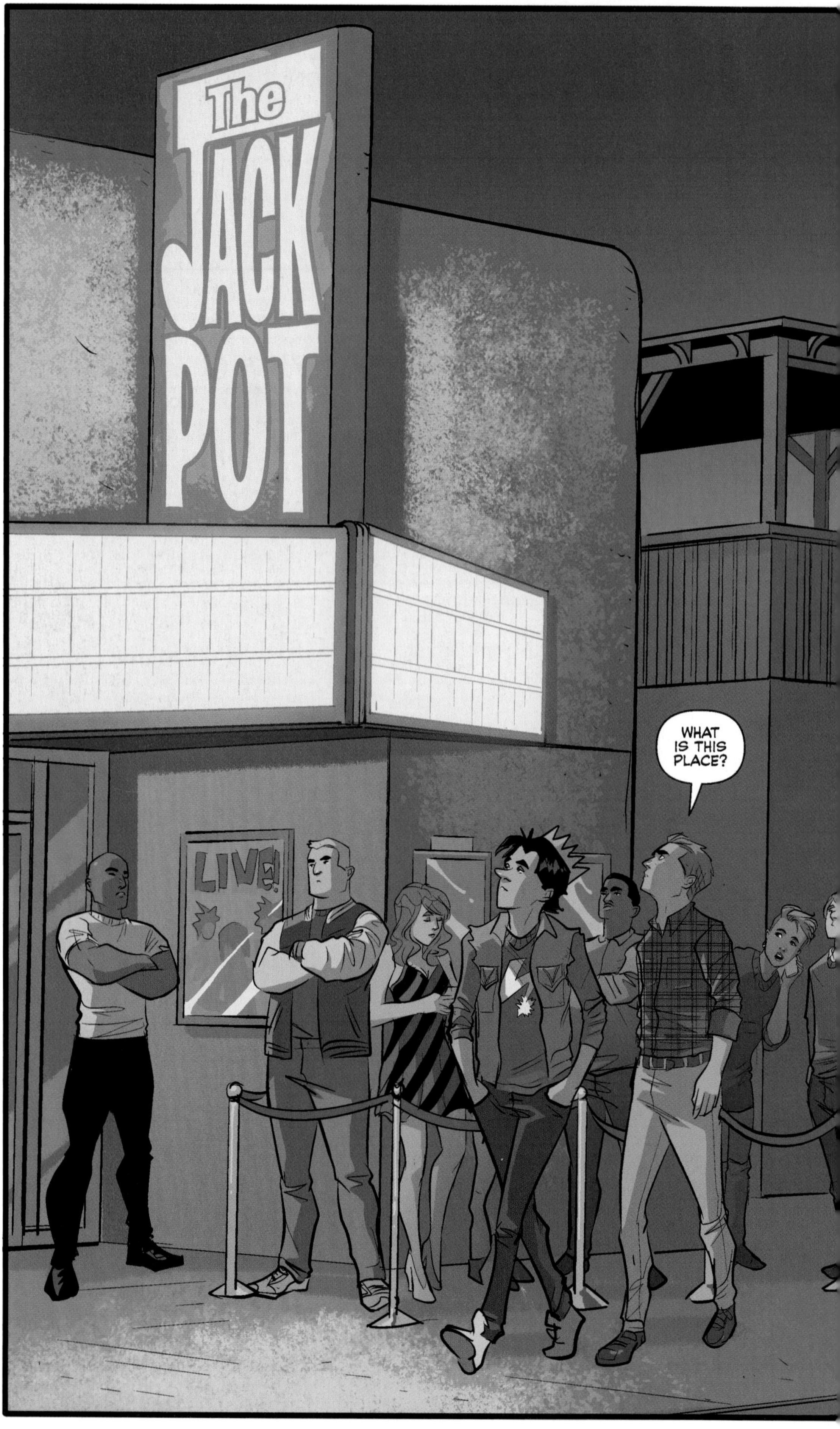
The JACK POT
LIVE!
WHAT IS THIS PLACE?

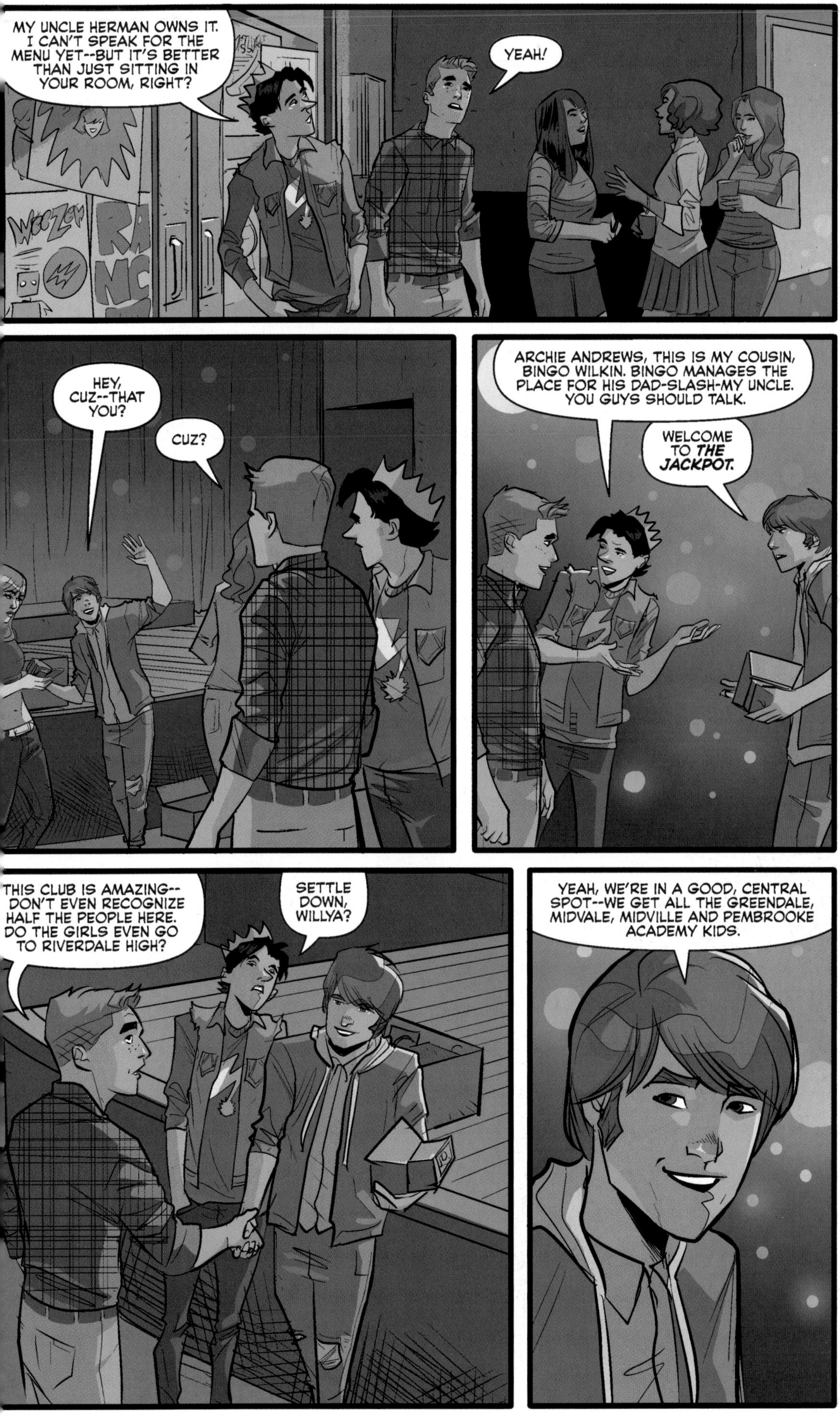
MY UNCLE HERMAN OWNS IT. I CAN'T SPEAK FOR THE MENU YET--BUT IT'S BETTER THAN JUST SITTING IN YOUR ROOM, RIGHT?
YEAH!
HEY, CUZ--THAT YOU?
CUZ?
ARCHIE ANDREWS, THIS IS MY COUSIN, BINGO WILKIN. BINGO MANAGES THE PLACE FOR HIS DAD-SLASH-MY UNCLE. YOU GUYS SHOULD TALK.
WELCOME TO *THE JACKPOT.*
THIS CLUB IS AMAZING-- DON'T EVEN RECOGNIZE HALF THE PEOPLE HERE. DO THE GIRLS EVEN GO TO RIVERDALE HIGH?
SETTLE DOWN, WILLYA?
YEAH, WE'RE IN A GOOD, CENTRAL SPOT--WE GET ALL THE GREENDALE, MIDVALE, MIDVILLE AND PEMBROOKE ACADEMY KIDS.

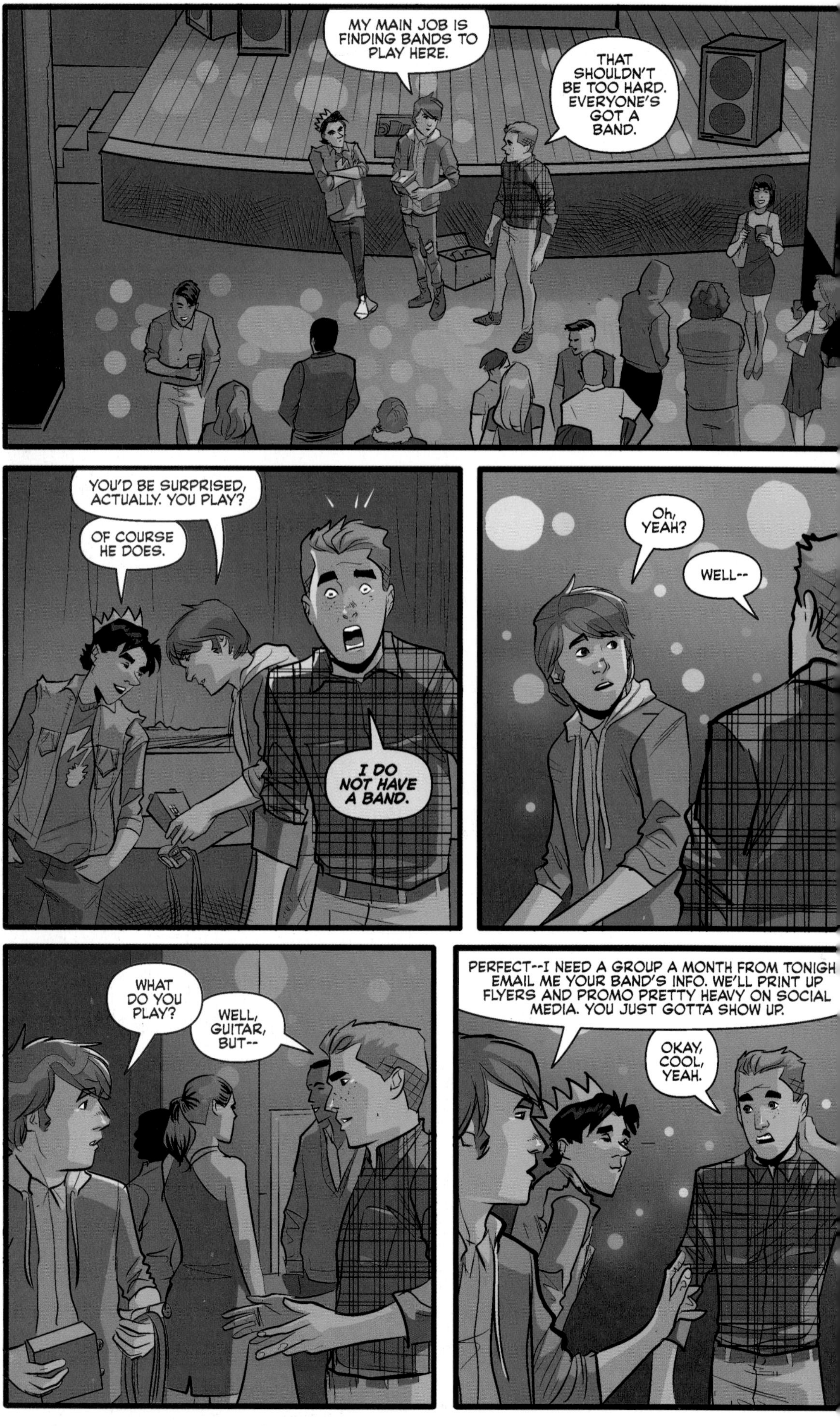
MY MAIN JOB IS FINDING BANDS TO PLAY HERE.
THAT SHOULDN'T BE TOO HARD. EVERYONE'S GOT A BAND.
YOU'D BE SURPRISED, ACTUALLY. YOU PLAY?
OF COURSE HE DOES.
I DO NOT HAVE A BAND.
Oh, YEAH?
WELL--
WHAT DO YOU PLAY?
WELL, GUITAR, BUT--
PERFECT--I NEED A GROUP A MONTH FROM TONIGH
EMAIL ME YOUR BAND'S INFO. WE'LL PRINT UP FLYERS AND PROMO PRETTY HEAVY ON SOCIAL MEDIA. YOU JUST GOTTA SHOW UP.
OKAY, COOL, YEAH.

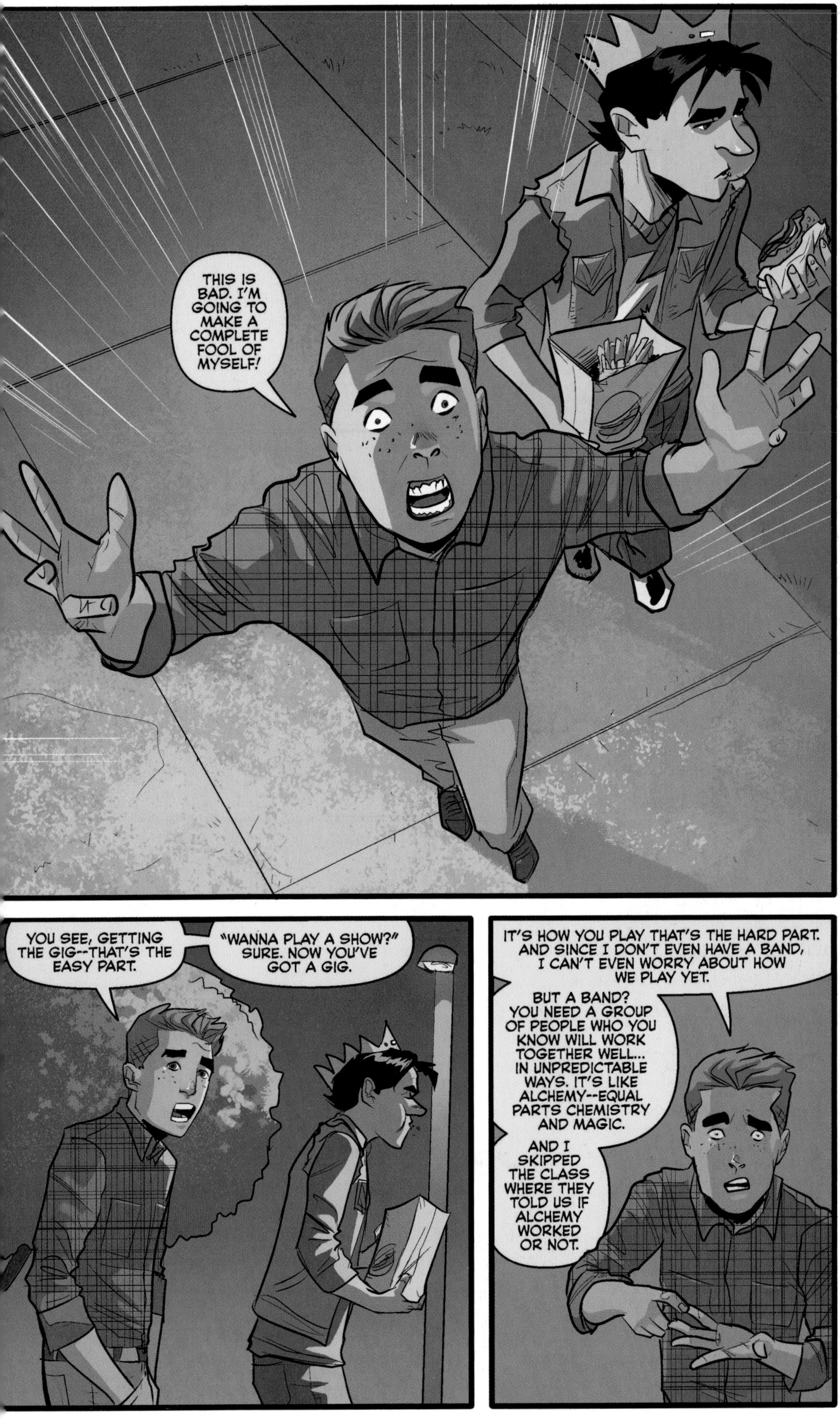
THIS IS BAD. I'M GOING TO MAKE A COMPLETE FOOL OF MYSELF!
YOU SEE, GETTING THE GIG--THAT'S THE EASY PART.
"WANNA PLAY A SHOW?" SURE. NOW YOU'VE GOT A GIG.
IT'S HOW YOU PLAY THAT'S THE HARD PART. AND SINCE I DON'T EVEN HAVE A BAND, I CAN'T EVEN WORRY ABOUT HOW WE PLAY YET.
BUT A BAND? YOU NEED A GROUP OF PEOPLE WHO YOU KNOW WILL WORK TOGETHER WELL... IN UNPREDICTABLE WAYS. IT'S LIKE ALCHEMY--EQUAL PARTS CHEMISTRY AND MAGIC.
AND I SKIPPED THE CLASS WHERE THEY TOLD US IF ALCHEMY WORKED OR NOT.

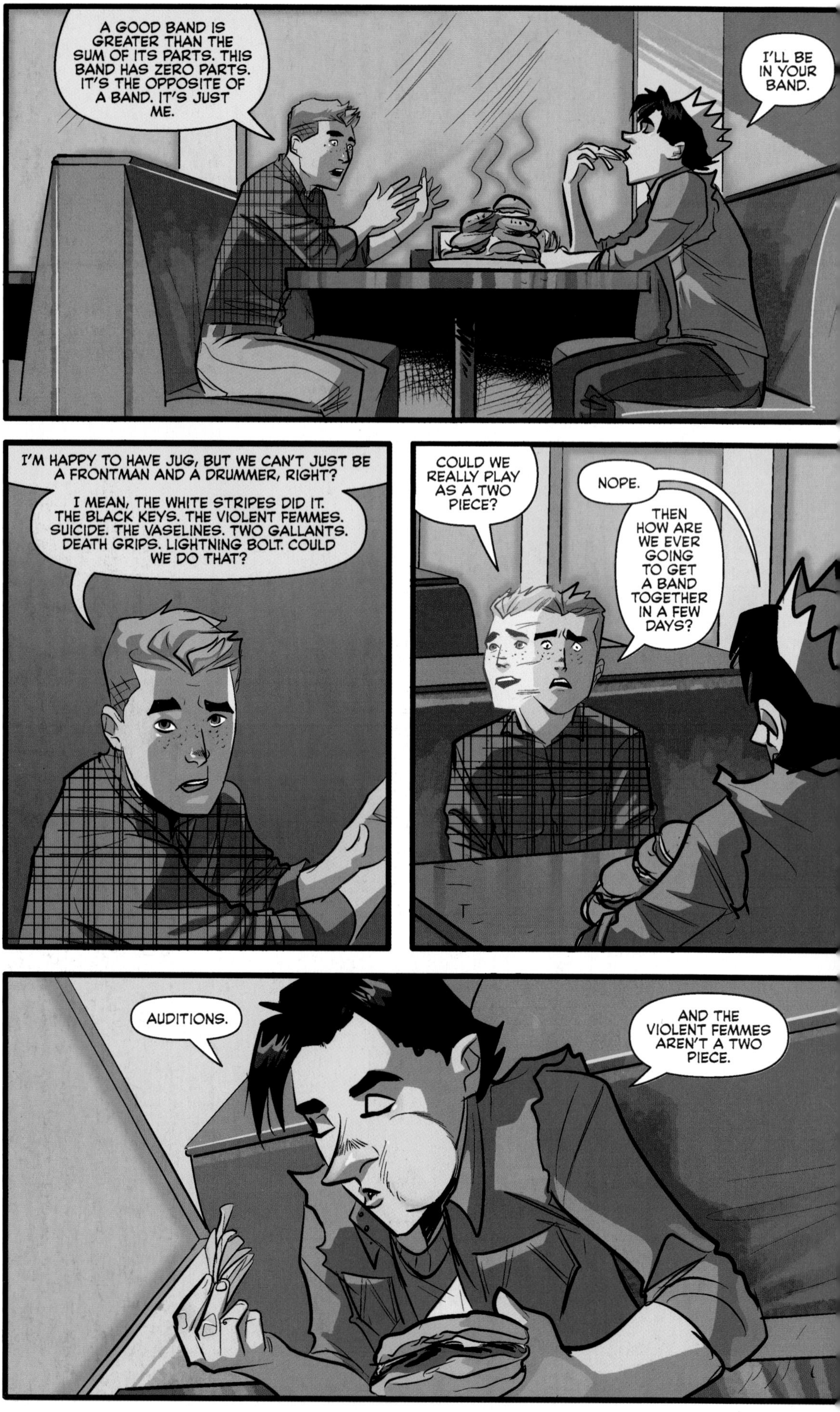
A GOOD BAND IS GREATER THAN THE SUM OF ITS PARTS. THIS BAND HAS ZERO PARTS. IT'S THE OPPOSITE OF A BAND. IT'S JUST ME.
I'LL BE IN YOUR BAND.
I'M HAPPY TO HAVE JUG, BUT WE CAN'T JUST BE A FRONTMAN AND A DRUMMER, RIGHT?
I MEAN, THE WHITE STRIPES DID IT. THE BLACK KEYS. THE VIOLENT FEMMES. SUICIDE. THE VASELINES. TWO GALLANTS. DEATH GRIPS. LIGHTNING BOLT. COULD WE DO THAT?
COULD WE REALLY PLAY AS A TWO PIECE?
NOPE.
THEN HOW ARE WE EVER GOING TO GET A BAND TOGETHER IN A FEW DAYS?
AUDITIONS.
AND THE VIOLENT FEMMES AREN'T A TWO PIECE.

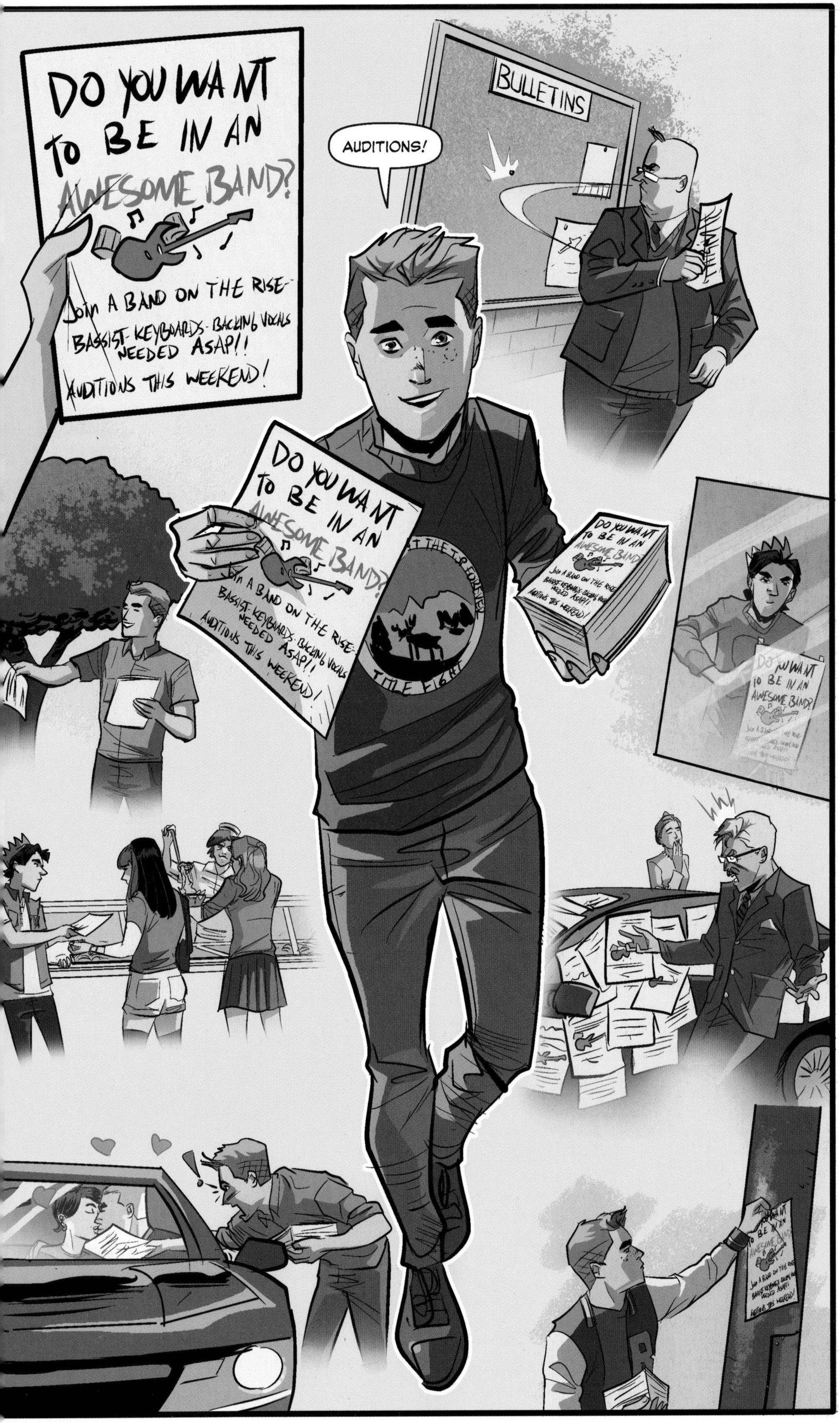
DO YOU WANT TO BE IN AN AWESOME BAND?
JOIN A BAND ON THE RISE-
BASSIST- KEYBOARDS- BACKING VOCALS NEEDED ASAP!!
AUDITIONS THIS WEEKEND!
BULLETINS
AUDITIONS!

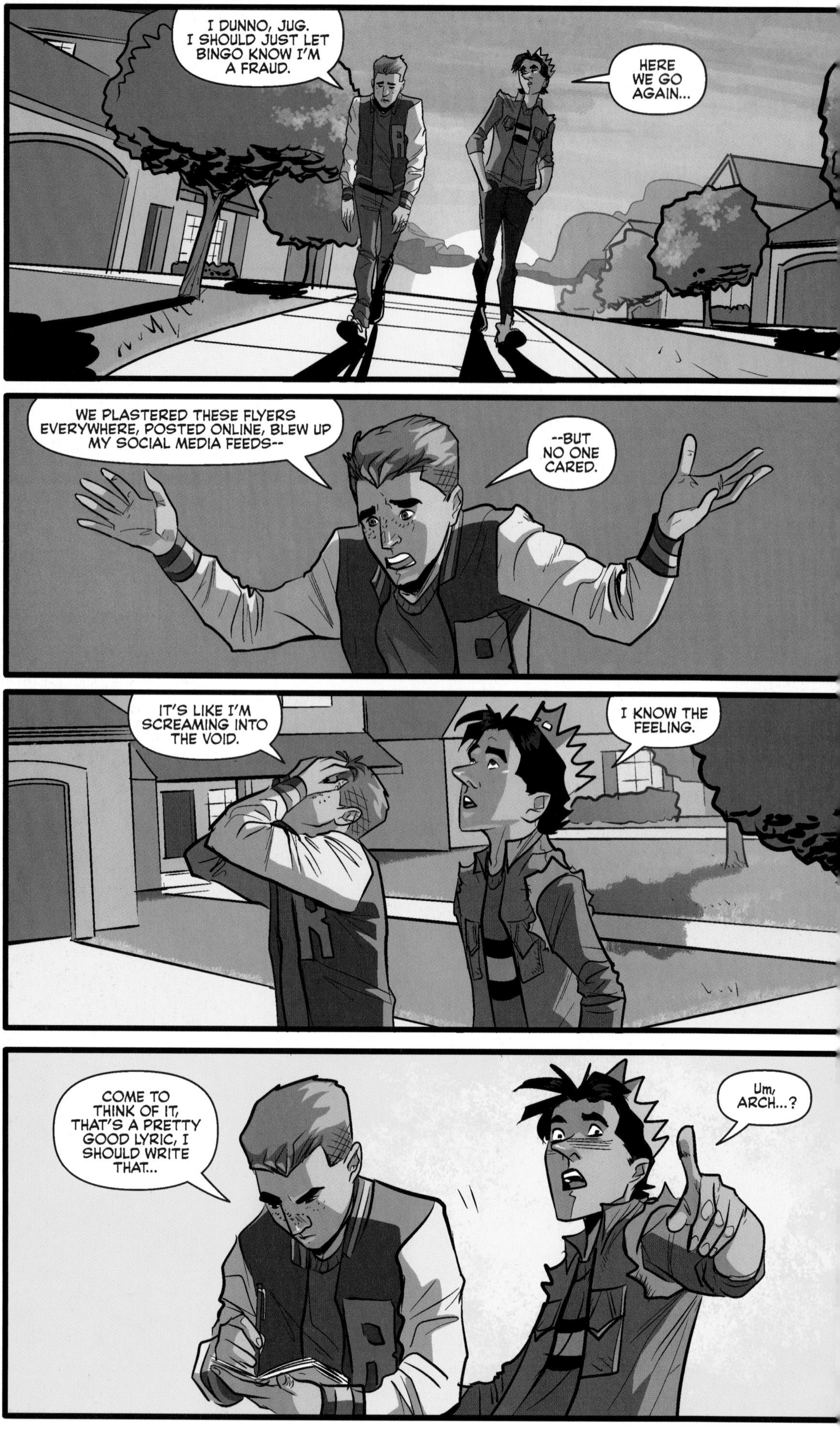
I DUNNO, JUG. I SHOULD JUST LET BINGO KNOW I'M A FRAUD.
HERE WE GO AGAIN...
WE PLASTERED THESE FLYERS EVERYWHERE, POSTED ONLINE, BLEW UP MY SOCIAL MEDIA FEEDS--
--BUT NO ONE CARED.
IT'S LIKE I'M SCREAMING INTO THE VOID.
I KNOW THE FEELING.
COME TO THINK OF IT, THAT'S A PRETTY GOOD LYRIC, I SHOULD WRITE THAT...
Um, ARCH...?

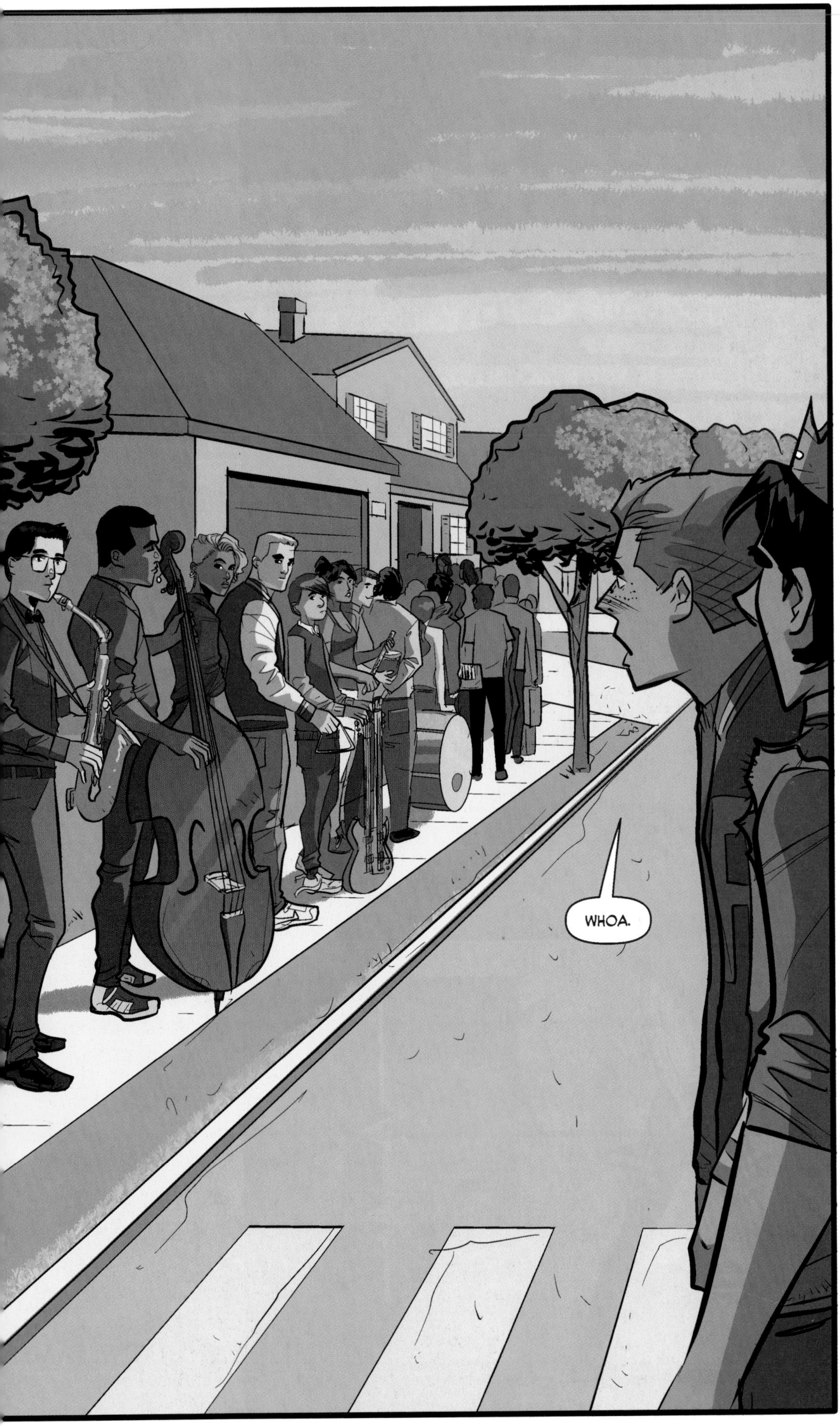
WHOA.

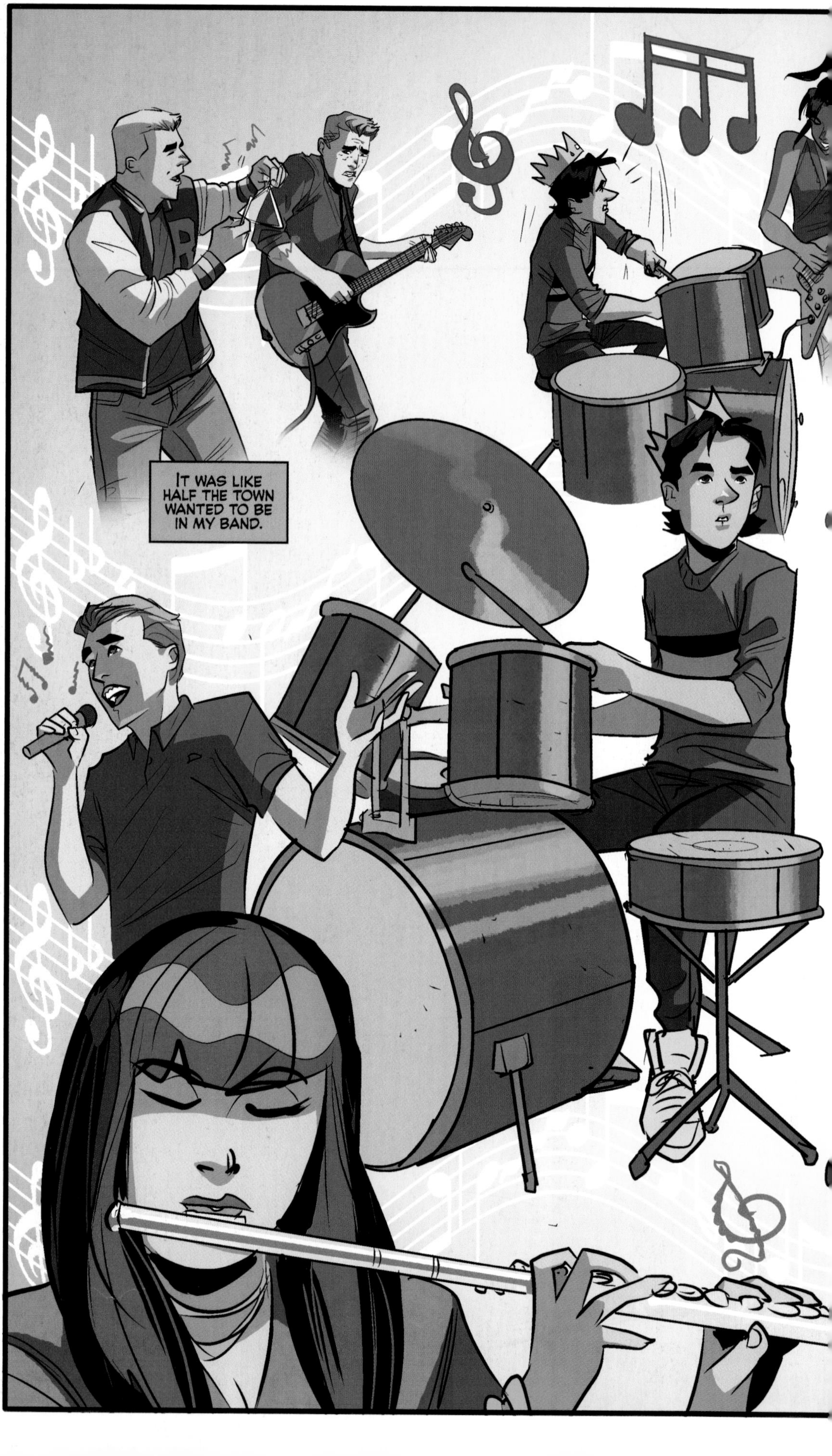
IT WAS LIKE HALF THE TOWN WANTED TO BE IN MY BAND.

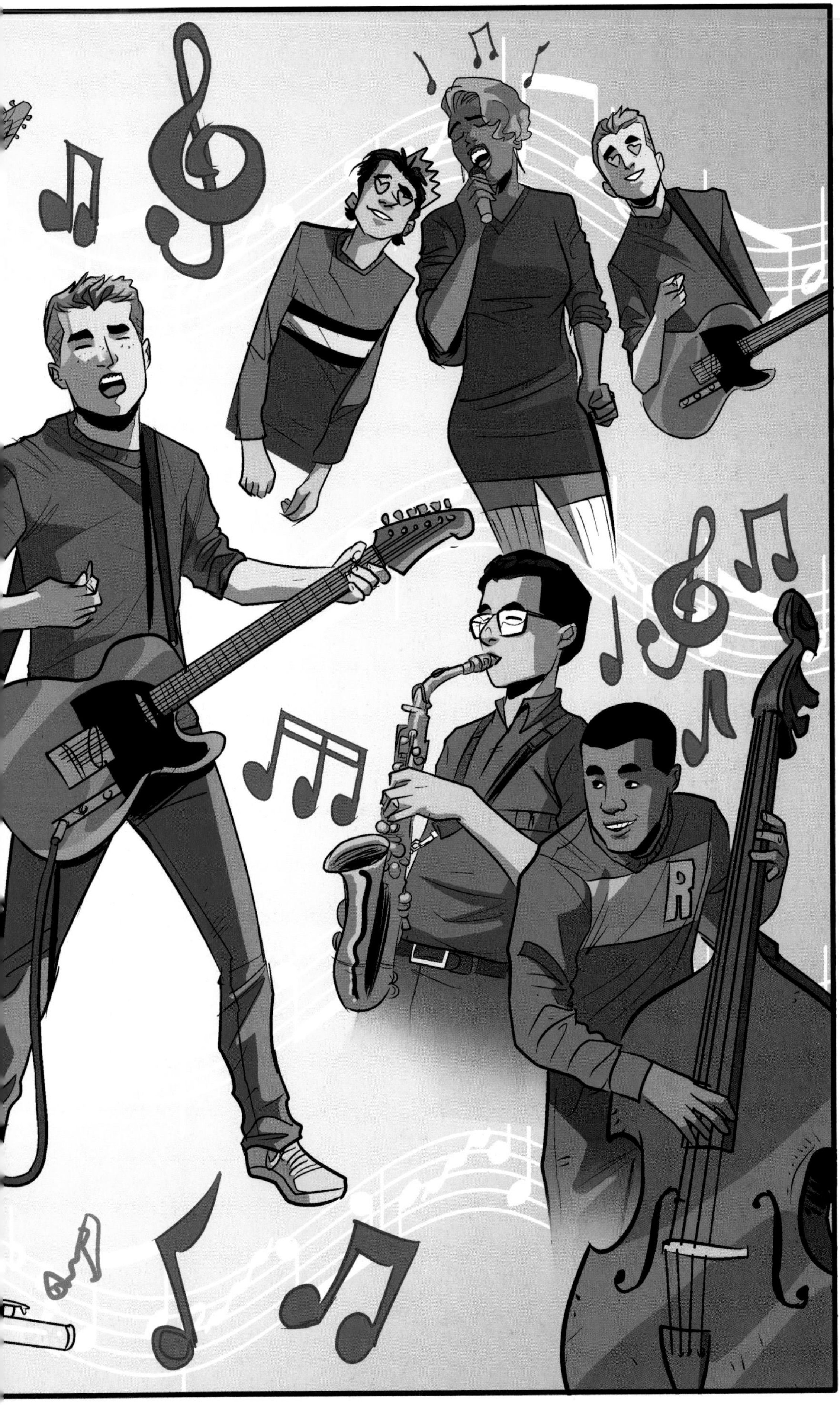

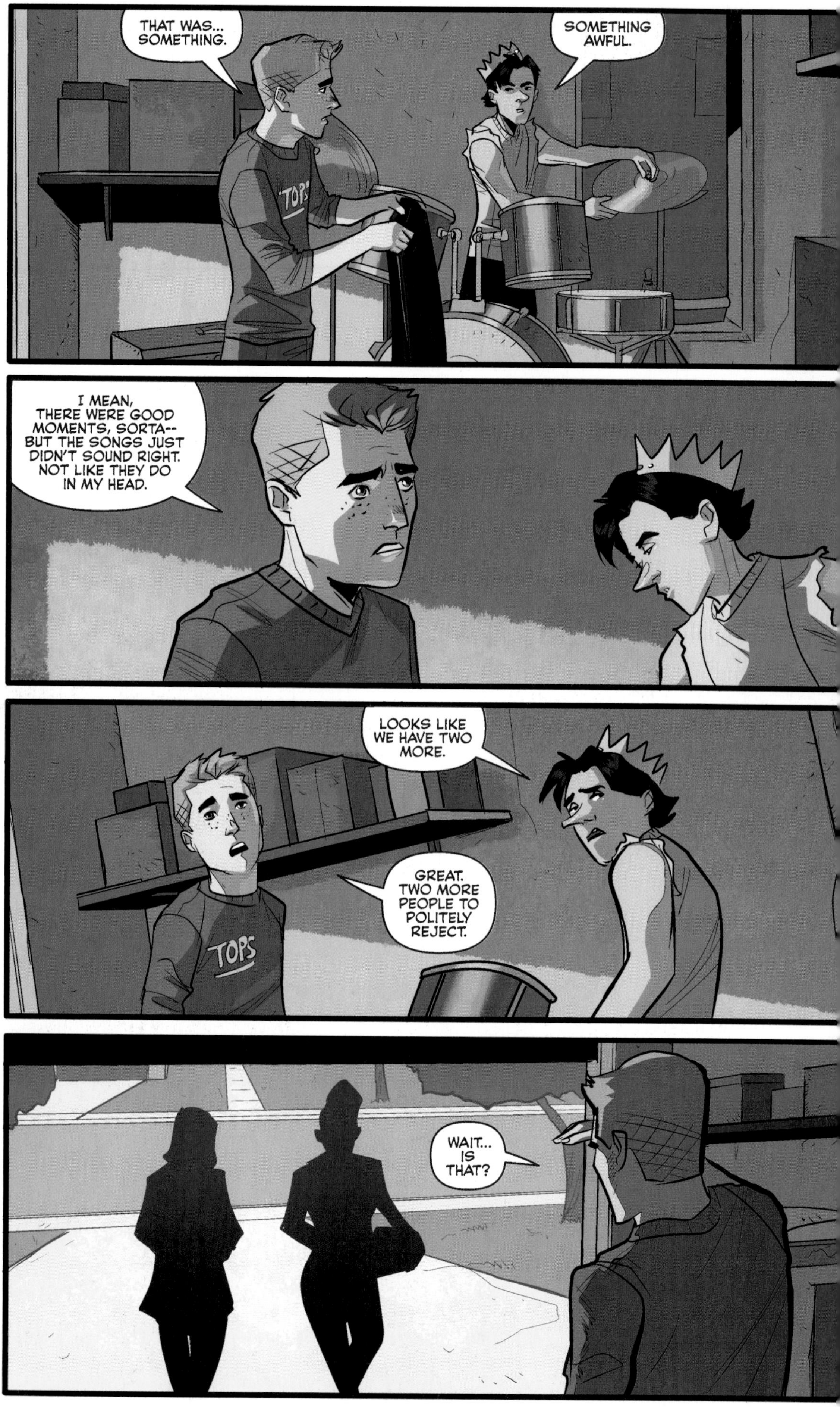
THAT WAS... SOMETHING.
SOMETHING AWFUL.
I MEAN, THERE WERE GOOD MOMENTS, SORTA-- BUT THE SONGS JUST DIDN'T SOUND RIGHT. NOT LIKE THEY DO IN MY HEAD.
LOOKS LIKE WE HAVE TWO MORE.
GREAT. TWO MORE PEOPLE TO POLITELY REJECT.
WAIT... IS THAT?

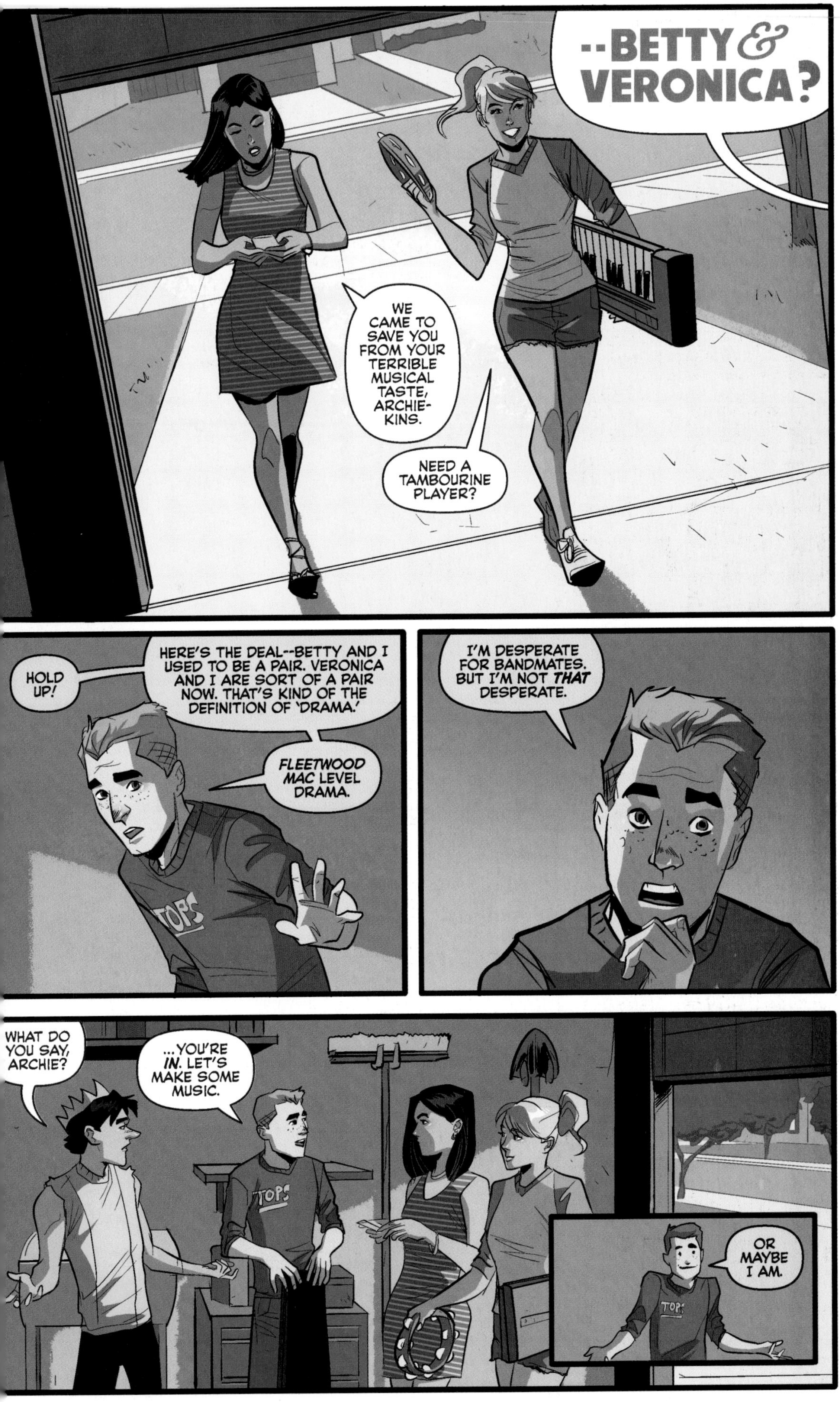
--BETTY & VERONICA?
WE CAME TO SAVE YOU FROM YOUR TERRIBLE MUSICAL TASTE, ARCHIE-KINS.
NEED A TAMBOURINE PLAYER?
HOLD UP!
HERE'S THE DEAL--BETTY AND I USED TO BE A PAIR. VERONICA AND I ARE SORT OF A PAIR NOW. THAT'S KIND OF THE DEFINITION OF 'DRAMA.'
FLEETWOOD MAC LEVEL DRAMA.
I'M DESPERATE FOR BANDMATES. BUT I'M NOT THAT DESPERATE.
WHAT DO YOU SAY, ARCHIE?
...YOU'RE IN. LET'S MAKE SOME MUSIC.
OR MAYBE I AM.

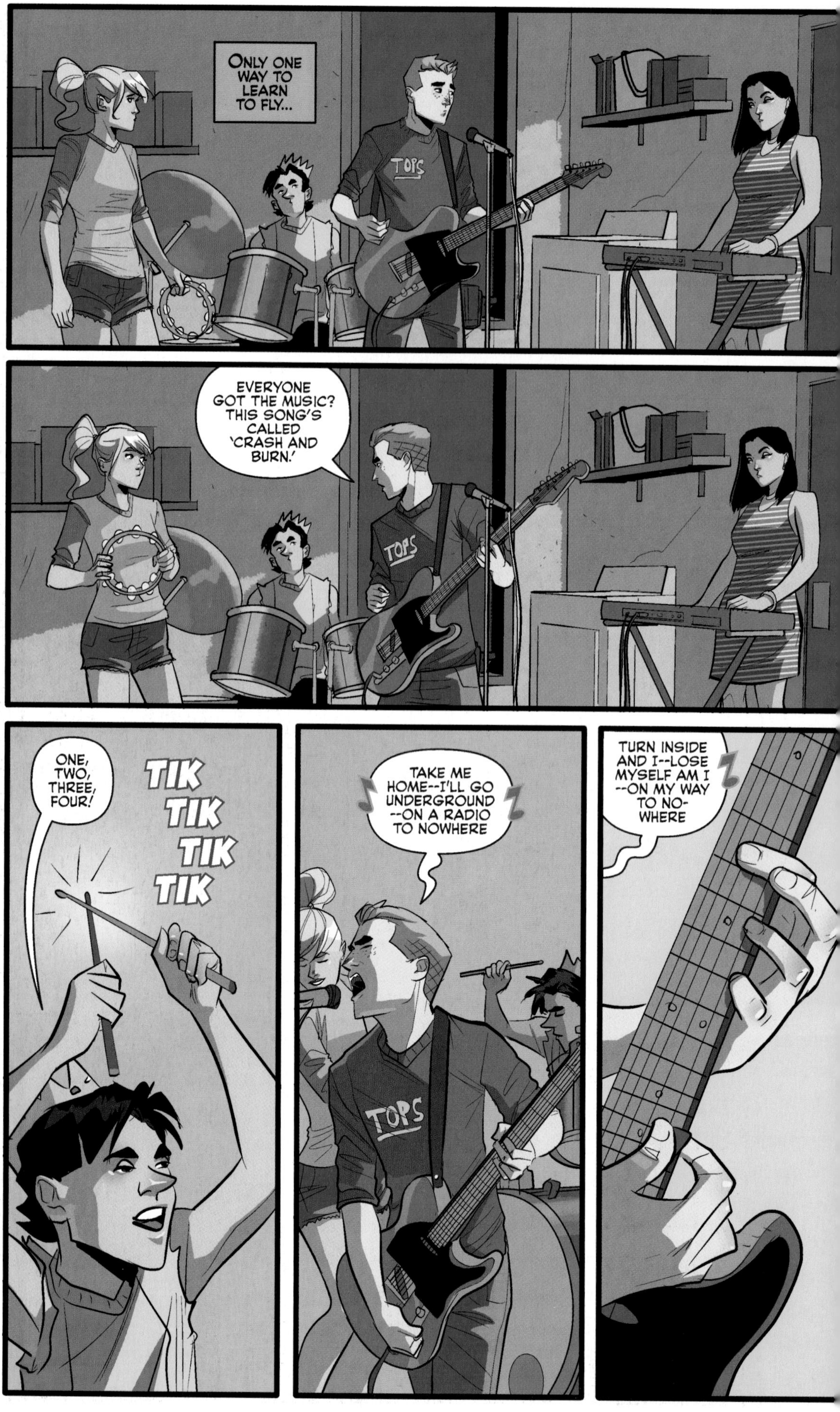
ONLY ONE WAY TO LEARN TO FLY...
TOPS
EVERYONE GOT THE MUSIC? THIS SONG'S CALLED 'CRASH AND BURN.'
TOPS
ONE, TWO, THREE, FOUR!
TIK TIK TIK TIK
TAKE ME HOME--I'LL GO UNDERGROUND --ON A RADIO TO NOWHERE
TOPS
TURN INSIDE AND I--LOSE MYSELF AM I --ON MY WAY TO NO-WHERE

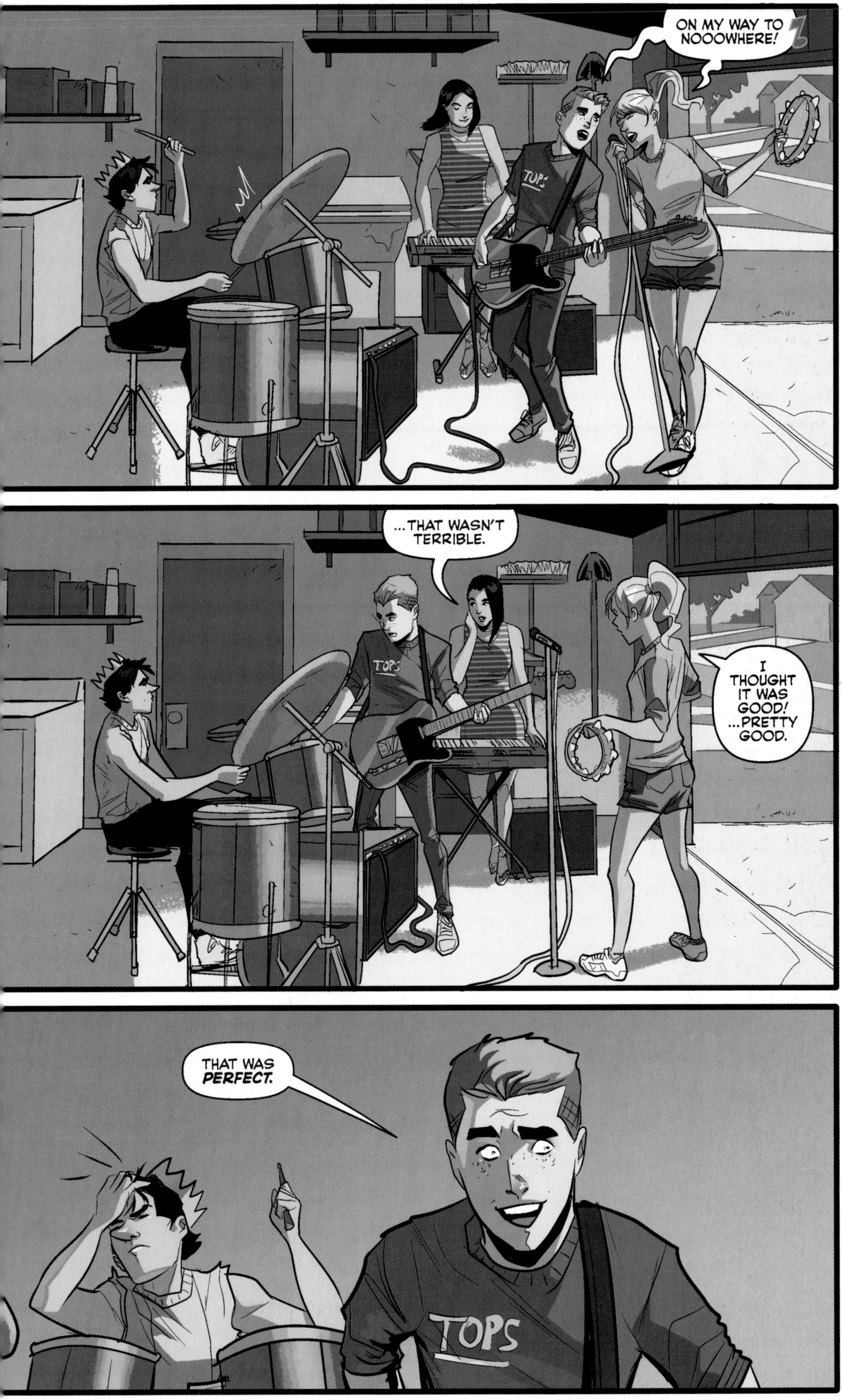
ON MY WAY TO NOOOWHERE!
...THAT WASN'T TERRIBLE.
I THOUGHT IT WAS GOOD! ...PRETTY GOOD.
THAT WAS *PERFECT.*

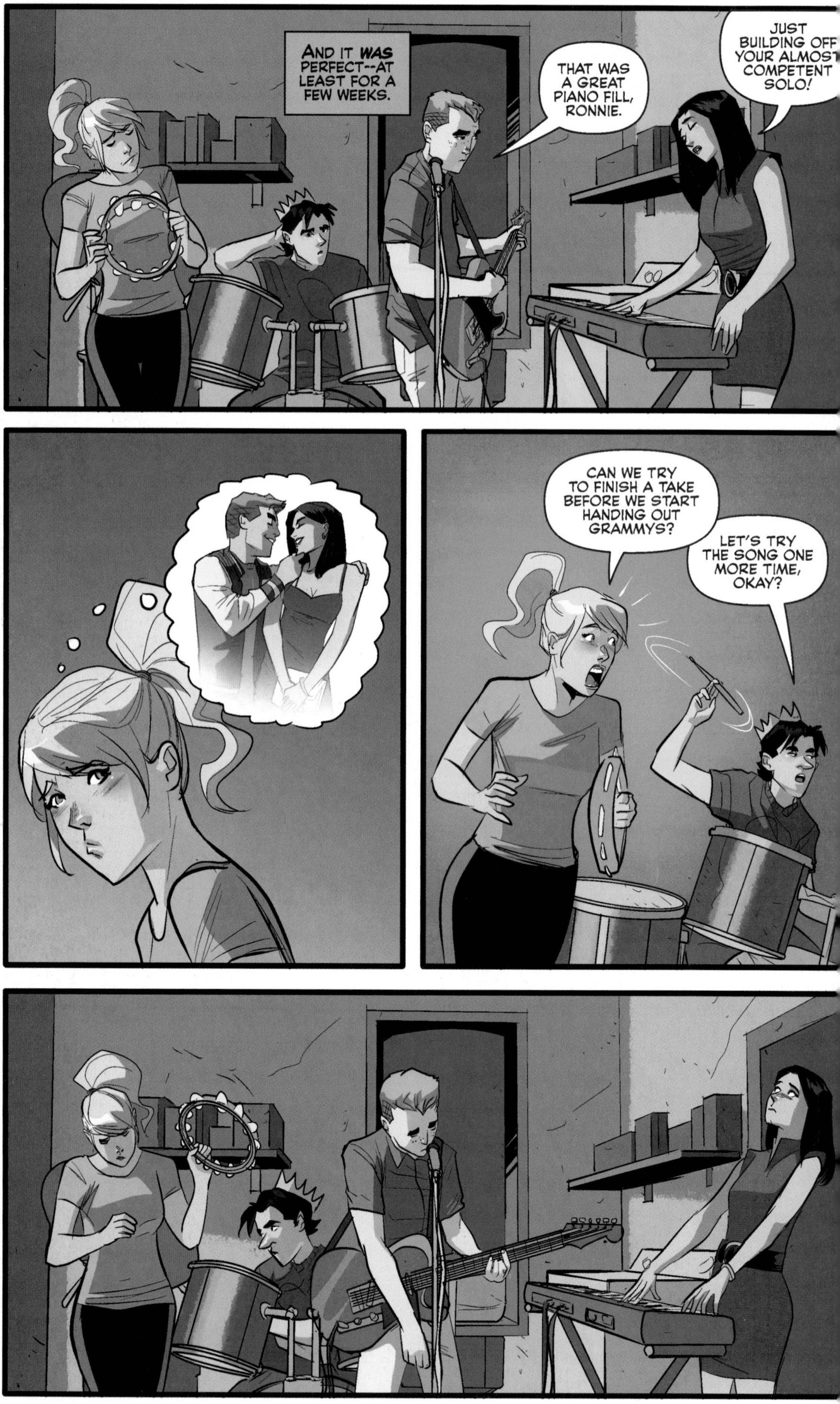
AND IT WAS PERFECT--AT LEAST FOR A FEW WEEKS.
THAT WAS A GREAT PIANO FILL, RONNIE.
JUST BUILDING OFF YOUR ALMOST COMPETENT SOLO!
CAN WE TRY TO FINISH A TAKE BEFORE WE START HANDING OUT GRAMMYS?
LET'S TRY THE SONG ONE MORE TIME, OKAY?

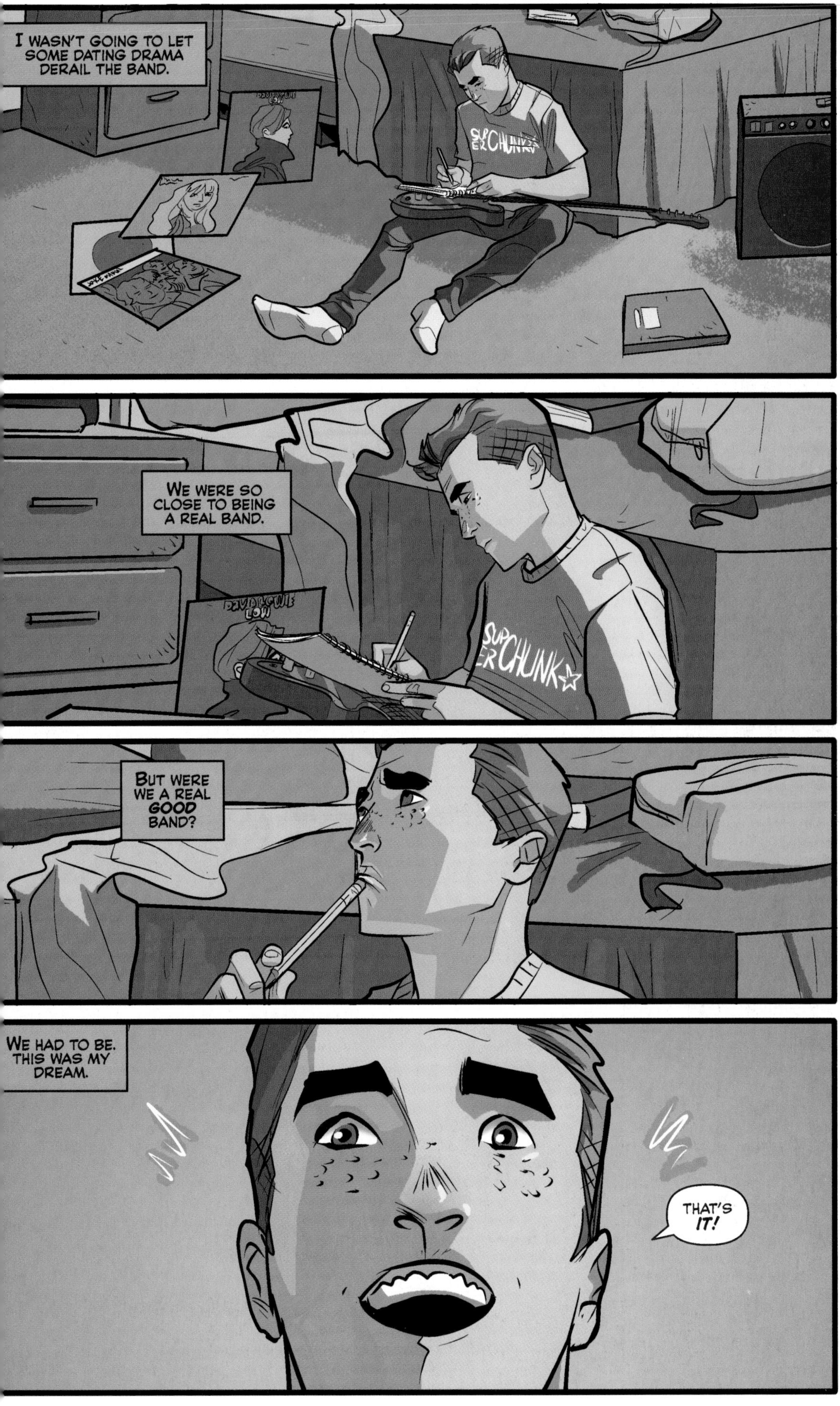

I WASN'T GOING TO LET SOME DATING DRAMA DERAIL THE BAND.
WE WERE SO CLOSE TO BEING A REAL BAND.
BUT WERE WE A REAL **GOOD** BAND?
WE HAD TO BE. THIS WAS MY DREAM.
THAT'S ***IT!***

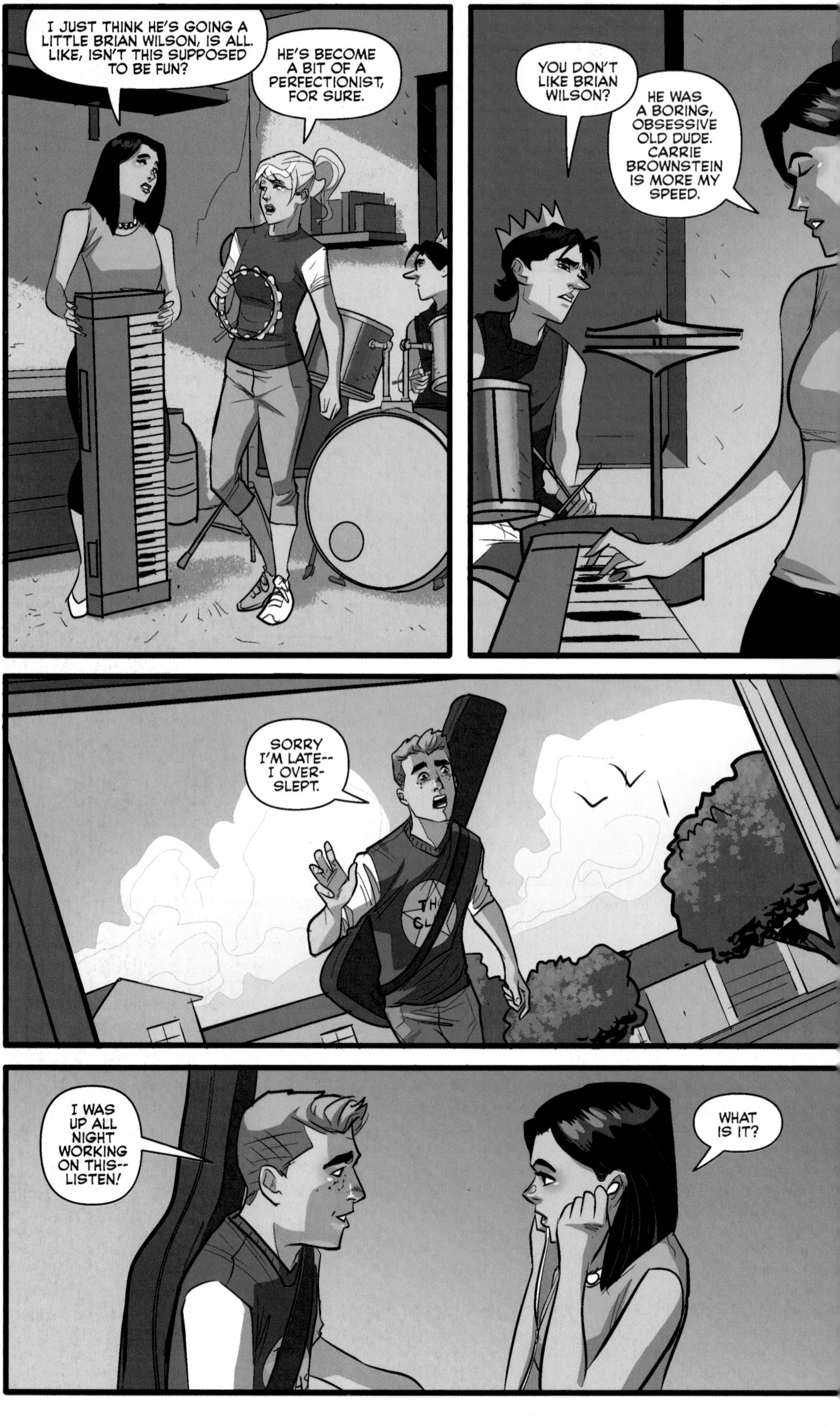
I JUST THINK HE'S GOING A LITTLE BRIAN WILSON, IS ALL. LIKE, ISN'T THIS SUPPOSED TO BE FUN?
HE'S BECOME A BIT OF A PERFECTIONIST, FOR SURE.
YOU DON'T LIKE BRIAN WILSON?
HE WAS A BORING, OBSESSIVE OLD DUDE. CARRIE BROWNSTEIN IS MORE MY SPEED.
SORRY I'M LATE-- I OVER-SLEPT.
I WAS UP ALL NIGHT WORKING ON THIS-- LISTEN!
WHAT IS IT?

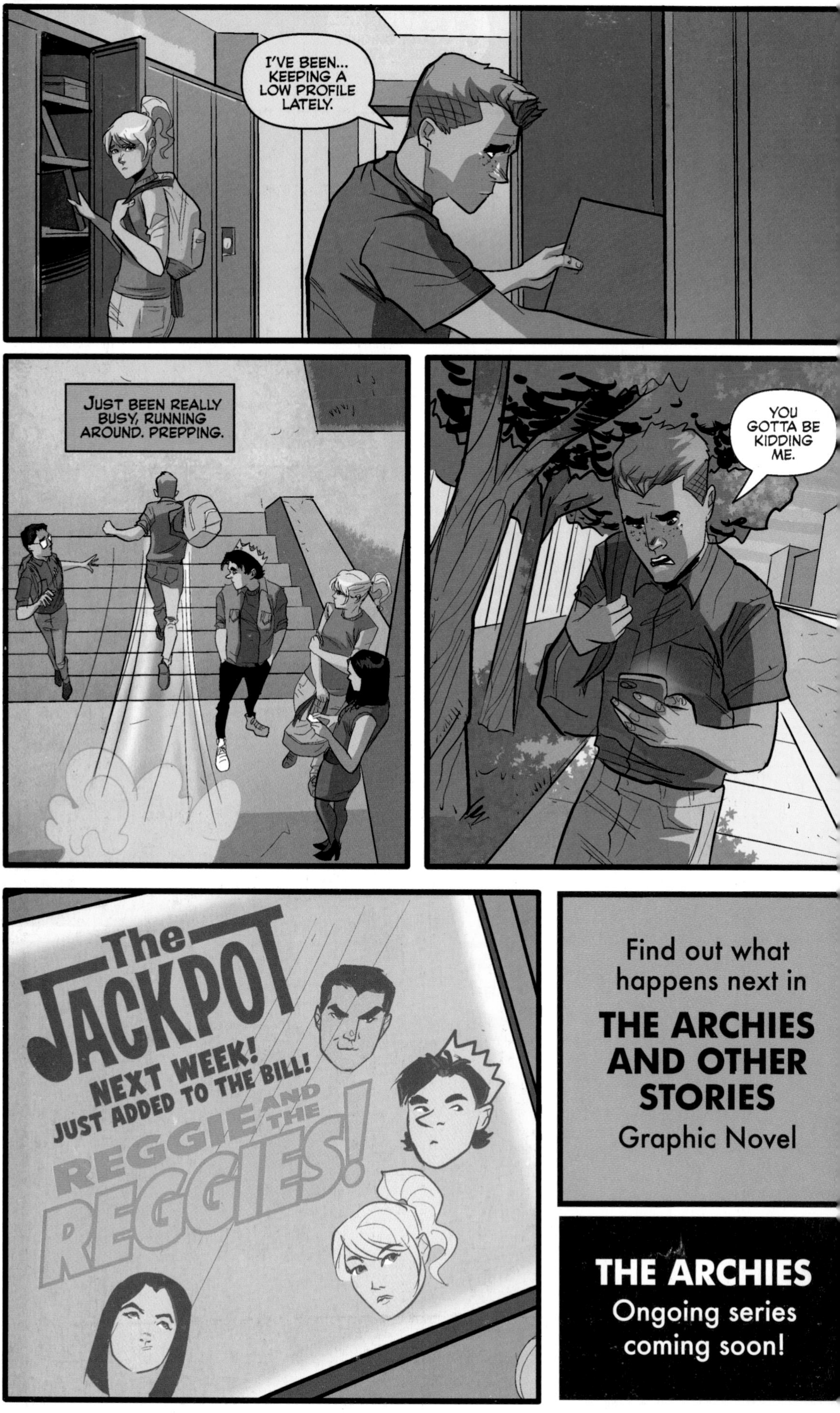
I'VE BEEN... KEEPING A LOW PROFILE LATELY.
JUST BEEN REALLY BUSY, RUNNING AROUND. PREPPING.
YOU GOTTA BE KIDDING ME.
The JACKPOT
NEXT WEEK!
JUST ADDED TO THE BILL!
REGGIE AND THE REGGIES!
Find out what happens next in
THE ARCHIES AND OTHER STORIES
Graphic Novel
THE ARCHIES
Ongoing series coming soon!

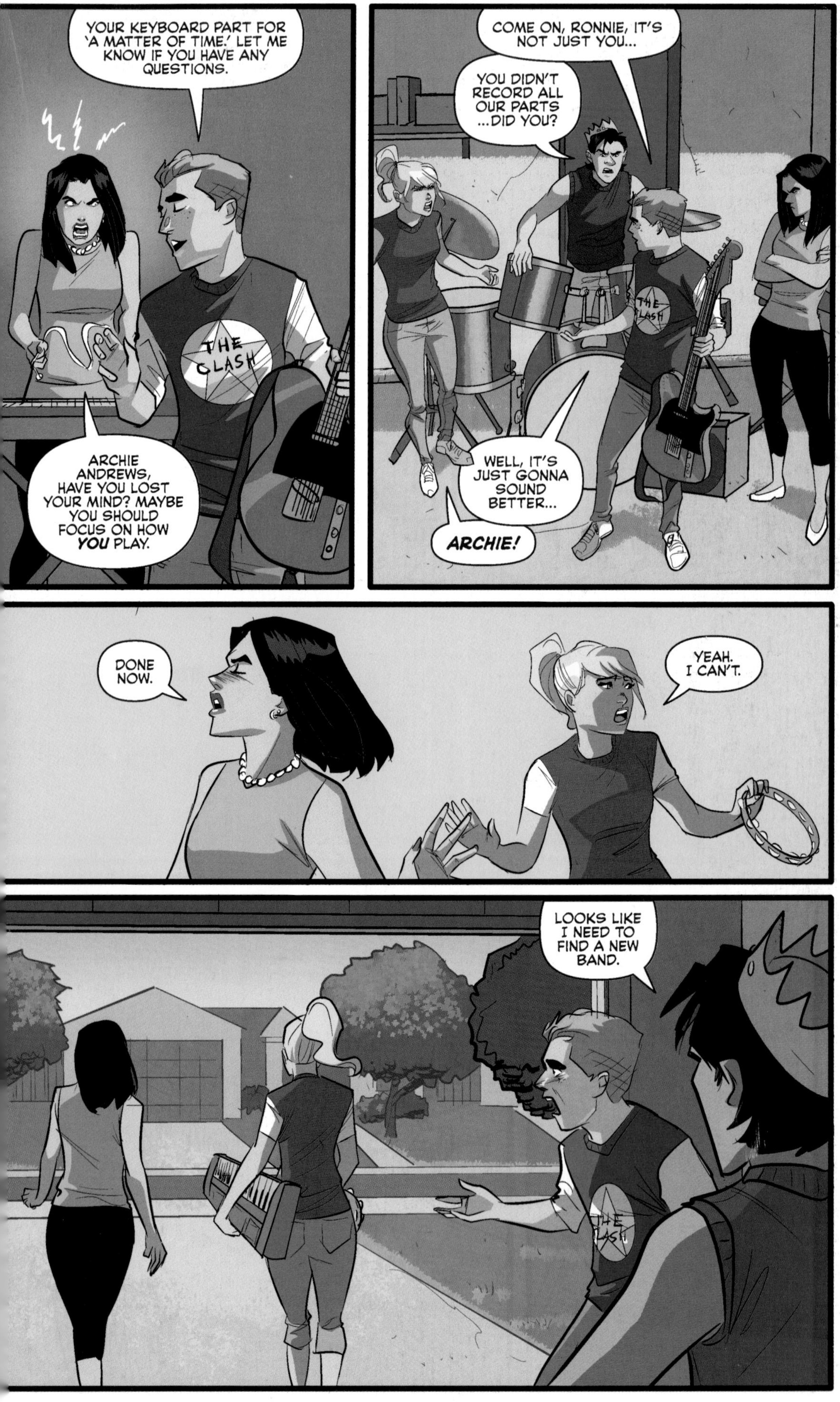
YOUR KEYBOARD PART FOR 'A MATTER OF TIME.' LET ME KNOW IF YOU HAVE ANY QUESTIONS.
ARCHIE ANDREWS, HAVE YOU LOST YOUR MIND? MAYBE YOU SHOULD FOCUS ON HOW *YOU* PLAY.
THE CLASH
COME ON, RONNIE, IT'S NOT JUST YOU...
YOU DIDN'T RECORD ALL OUR PARTS ...DID YOU?
WELL, IT'S JUST GONNA SOUND BETTER...
ARCHIE!
DONE NOW.
YEAH. I CAN'T.
LOOKS LIKE I NEED TO FIND A NEW BAND.